NEW AGE: A GUIDE

NEW AGE

A GUIDE

*Alternative Spiritualities from
Aquarian Conspiracy to Next Age*

DAREN KEMP

EDINBURGH UNIVERSITY PRESS

Granqvist, Pehr and Berit Hagekull (2001), *Journal for the
Scientific Study of Religion*, 40.3: 541–2 reprinted by permission
of the Society for the Scientific Study of Religion.

Ivakhiv, Adrian J. (2001), *Claiming Sacred Ground: Pilgrims and
Politics at Glastonbury and Sedona*, Indiana University Press
p. 40, reprinted by permission of Indiana University Press.

Kemp, Daren (2000), 'A Platonic delusion: the identification of
psychosis and mysticism', *Mental Health, Religion and Culture*,
3.2: 162, reprinted by permission of Taylor and Francis,
www.tandf.co.uk.

Lynch, Frederick (1977), *American Behavioral Scientist* 20.6: 895,
copyright © Sage Publications, Inc, reprinted by permission of
Sage Publications, Inc.

© Daren Kemp, 2004

Edinburgh University Press Ltd
22 George Square, Edinburgh

Typeset in Goudy Old Style by
&L Composition, Filey, North Yorkshire, and
printed and bound in Great Britain by
Antony Rowe Ltd, Chippenham

A CIP record for this book is available from the British Library

ISBN 0 7486 1531 8 (hardback)
ISBN 0 7486 1532 6 (paperback)

Contents

Analytical Table of Contents

Acknowledgements

This book began its life in 1992 as a therapeutic project during a prolonged period of convalescence which absented me from my undergraduate studies in religion and the history of ideas at the University of Wales, Cardiff. Little remains of these first scribblings, although at least one section of the current work is lifted from a booklet I attempted (unsuccessfully) to market on my return to health and university. Most of the fieldwork and serious academic research for this book was undertaken during doctoral research at King's College London into the sociology of New Age Christians, or Christaquarians as I call them, which I have now published (Kemp 2003a). This research was part-funded by the King's College Theological Trust, the St Olave's and St Saviour's Grammar School Foundation, the estate of George Henry Kent and my parents – to all of whom I am most grateful.

I also have a number of individuals to thank for seeing the book to term. Starting with the lady who gave me a copy of Louise Hay's *You Can Heal Your Life* (1984) to inspire recovery in a grim hospital ward, I am grateful to family, friends and health-care professionals who never gave up hope for me. This is especially the case with Ewa, now my wife, who saw me through a second period of ill health during my doctoral studies.

Fieldwork is not possible without the co-operation of participants, who must usually unfortunately remain anonymous, so far as acknowledgements are concerned. I must thank my supervisor at King's College London, Professor Peter B. Clarke. Mathew Guest and Paul Heelas generously provided helpful comments on a late draft of the whole manuscript, as did D. Patrick Miller, Rosemarie LoSasso and Ruth Bradby on the case study chapter. A large number of other scholars have also contributed to sections of the text, and I am also grateful to those who kindly sent me pre-publication versions of forthcoming works. Thanks go also to the anonymous external reviewer and my editor at Edinburgh University Press, Nicola Carr, for their redactive suggestions, spelling corrections and above all, their patience.

The book is dedicated to my first daughter, Jasmina, born in the year of the New Millennium, who makes it all worthwhile.

Daren Kemp
London, February 2003
ADMG

To Jasmina

CHAPTER 1

Overview and Starting Definition

What is New Age? Crystals, meditation and astrology. T'ai Chi, Reiki and Feng Shui. Reflexology, aromatherapy and past-life regression. *Conversations with God* (Walsch 1995), *The Celestine Prophecy* (Redfield [1993] 1994) and *Out on a Limb* (MacLaine 1983). The channelled entity Lazaris, the channelled text *A Course in Miracles* (1985) and many of the manifestations of channelled healing. Wicca, Druids and non-aligned Pagans. Esalen, the Findhorn Community and Damanhur. Marianne Williamson, Deepak Chopra and David Spangler.

Some of these examples of New Age are instantly recognisable; others will become clearer later in this text. But a list of examples of New Age like this could be endless. Conversely, we could also cut many of these examples: Spangler has qualified his acceptance of New Age; many Pagans distance themselves from New Age; and the Findhorn Community has described itself as an 'intentional community' rather than as New Age.

Again I ask, what is New Age? One of the few things on which all scholars are agreed concerning New Age is that it is difficult to define. Often, the definition actually given reflects the background of the scholar giving the definition. Thus, the New Ager views New Age as a revolutionary period of history dictated by the stars; the Christian apologist has often defined New Age as a cult; the historian of ideas understands it as a manifestation of the perennial tradition; the philosopher sees New Age as a monist or holistic worldview; the sociologist describes New Age as a new religious movement (NRM); while the psychologist describes it as a form of narcissism.

Early definitions of New Age now seem overdone. New Age was often described as 'the New Age movement' – sometimes abbreviated as NAM – or 'New Age spirituality' or even 'New Age religion'. 'The New Age', with the definite article emphasising its concreteness, has been deconstructed by a number of scholars (see Chapter 9), with the result that it is no longer appropriate to reify the phenomena in this way. Throughout this book, I use the simple term 'New Age' on its own, without an article or descriptive tag. In this way, New Age can be appreciated in its many aspects – which may be akin to movements, spiritualities, even religions, philosophies and worldviews – without making a prior definitional option for any one of those aspects.

Many definitions of New Age have been given. It might be helpful in this introductory chapter to review briefly some of these. They fall into three main groups: definitions by New Agers themselves, scholarly definitions, and definitions by Christians. After discussing the relative value of various definitions of New Age, I then suggest my own starting point for a definition of New Age, a synthesis of these and other definitions, using family resemblance theory.

– EMIC AND ETIC DEFINITIONS –

An important distinction must first be made between emic and etic definitions.[1] Definitions of New Age by New Agers themselves are examples of emic definitions: they are made by the participants or believers in their own terms. By contrast, scholarly and Christian definitions of New Age are examples of etic definitions: they are made by observers of the participants or believers. This distinction is analogous to that in historical studies between primary and secondary sources, where the former are first-hand witnesses to historical events and the latter are relating the history as it was told to them by primary sources or others.

The emic–etic distinction is central to any methodology in the study of social and religious phenomena. In this book, the main methodology employed is etic. That is to say, the chapters on the philosophy of New Age, the anthropology of New Age, the sociology of New Age and so on are primarily the understandings of observers of the phenomena, informed by the literature of the academic discipline concerned. New Age philosophy, New Age anthropology, New Age sociology and so on, that is disciplines of New Age thought as expounded by New Agers themselves, are to be distinguished from the philosophy of New Age etc. In the same way, there are distinct forms of Christian, Muslim and Buddhist thought – for example in cosmology – which are to be distinguished from etic understandings of, say, the psychology of Christians or the history of Buddhist ideas.

Emic understandings are of course a central informant of etic understandings. In many ways, only the subjects can know what they really believe. But etic understandings always contextualise and temper emic understandings with the insights of past scholarship.

– DEFINITIONS BY NEW AGERS –

As early as 1977, the late Sir George Trevelyan wrote *A Vision of the Aquarian Age*. This spiritual worldview was largely concerned with monism, higher selves, and salvation through wholeness, that is to say a New Age which is not yet fully distinguishable from Spiritualism. Yet even in this path-breaking work, commonly cited New Age roots play a large part including, among others, Pierre Teilhard de Chardin, Alice Bailey, David Spangler and Sri Aurobindo.

The Aquarian Conspiracy (Ferguson [1980] 1989), a more detailed tome, gave a definite form to this New Age. Marilyn Ferguson concentrates mainly on the practicalities of transformation from a technological viewpoint: how to transform the person and society. Although given mention, occult, Eastern and new religions do not figure strongly in this pseudo-scientific instruction manual. It takes concentrated reading to absorb the detailed scientific presentation, but millions were prepared to invest in the work.

Spangler has written:

> At its best, the New Age offers a vision of sacredness that does not separate the individual from the world or from everyday life. It explores a sense of holiness and wholeness that is life-affirming and world-affirming, intimate with nature and seeking out the spirit of God in the incarnate cosmos. It is this incarnational and ecological aspect that may make New Age spirituality seem 'new' to many folk, but in fact this aspect is also present in the best of our historical spiritual paths, particularly in the mystical traditions of our great religions. In fact, the whole idea of a 'new' spirituality emerging – a specifically 'New Age' spirituality – can be overdrawn and overemphasised, creating a division with past traditions where none really exists.
>
> Where a primary difference may lie between 'old age' and New Age spirituality is not in the destination but in the manner of the journey. One of the characteristics of the New Age is not in the destination but in the manner of the journey. One of the characteristics of the New Age fair is that it embodies a global spirit. The journey is not confined within a specific body of teachings but is conducted with openness to all the great faith traditions, including those that have special affinity with the spirituality of the land, such as the shamanistic traditions of many indigenous cultures. This eclectic openness can lead to diffusion and confusion and obviously carries risks: bits and pieces of traditions can be cobbled together in a way that seems pleasing to the celebrant but which

destroys the awakening and disciplining power of those traditions. A false synthesis or homogenization can lead us nowhere.

On the other hand, by exploring the boundaries where faith traditions touch and begin to commune with one another, one can begin to discern the primal voice of the Mystery from which all these traditions ultimately emerge, the God of the ecology as well as the God of the cathedral. (Spangler 1993: 101–2)

Shirley MacLaine, the actress, described New Age for the *Los Angeles Times*:

People involved in the spiritually awakening New Age movement are investigating the heights of the super-conscious . . . This is not a new religion. It is a new way of thinking that allows a connection with the 'kingdom of heaven within,' and each person makes his or her connection in a different way. It is what I call soul physics, because when the connection is made, there is a palpable reaction in the mind and physical body . . . Who are we really? Where did we come from? Where are we going? Dare we understand that we can make a difference? Dare we believe that we have access to wise and divine spiritual knowledge?

New Age consciousness doesn't believe these things. It knows them. And that knowledge is setting people free. Free from fear, rage, anxiety, anger, frustration, helplessness, futility and wilful destruction. (MacLaine 1987a)

– DEFINITIONS BY SCHOLARS –

The entry on New Age in the *Encyclopedia of New Religious Movements* reads:

The New Age Movement taken as a whole is more a vision than a coherent system of beliefs and practices. As a movement it is an acephalous movement though . . . the opinions of a number of its exponents, among them those of Baba Ram Dass (Richard Alpert), are widely respected and have acquired a form of scriptural authority – and a highly decentralised movement. It is also a decentralised movement though there are New Age communities with their own clearly defined beliefs and practices built. What more than anything else gives a degree of unity to the New Age Movement is the goal aspired to by all participants, transformation of consciousness. (Clarke ed., forthcoming)

Wouter Hanegraaff is unusual among scholars of New Age in that he gives an explicit and concise definition of New Age:

The New Age movement is the cultic milieu having become conscious of itself, in the later 1970s, as constituting a more or less unified 'movement'. All manifestations of this movement are characterized by a popular western culture criticism expressed in terms of a secularized esotericism. (Hanegraaff 1996: 522; original emphasis removed)

Paul Heelas has defined New Age thus:

The New Age is a highly optimistic, celebratory, utopian and spiritual form of humanism, many versions . . . also emphasizing the spirituality of the natural order as a whole. Ultimacy – God, the Goddess, the Higher Self – lies within, serving as the source of vitality, creativity, love, tranquillity, wisdom, responsibility, power and all those other qualities which are held to comprise the perfect inner life and which, when applied in daily practice (supposedly) ensure that all is utopian . . . New Agers universally suppose that it is crucial to 'work' on what it is to be a person. A new consciousness, and all that it brings with it, is essential . . .

And more analytically, as an internalized form of religiosity, the New Age is (albeit to varying degrees) detraditionalized. That is to say, autonomy and freedom are highly valued; and authority lies with the experience of the Self or, more broadly, the natural realm. This means that New Agers attach great importance to the Self-ethic, which includes emphasis on the exercise of Self-responsibility and which, more generally, serves as a 'meta-"narrative"' operating at the experiential level. Detraditionalization is also associated with the Movement's perennialized outlook, namely that the same wisdom can be found at the heart of all religious traditions. (Heelas 1996a: 28–9; original emphasis removed)

Michael York defines New Age by listing its roots in the occult, the East, American Transcendentalism, Esalen, and by presenting sketches of spokespersons such as Ram Dass and Shirley MacLaine. His sociology of the movement is difficult to summarise briefly, in that he does not highlight a synthesising definition which draws these strands together because 'with no central authority, New Age is not doctrinaire and consequently means many things to many different people' (York 1995: 35).

J. Gordon Melton et al. in *The New Age Almanac* write:

The New Age Movement is an international social movement which emerged in Western society in the late 1960s . . . the movement has become an important new force in the development of the ever-changing Western culture. As a unique movement it is quite recent, but the New Age has emerged from older movements, always integrating long-standing ideas and trends in the West. While freely accepting new perspectives from the East, the movement has deep roots in Western philosophy and life.

The New Age Movement can be defined by its primal experience of transformation. New Agers have either experienced or are diligently seeking a profound personal transformation from an old, unacceptable life to a new, exciting future. One prominent model for that transformation is healing, which has given rise to what is possibly the largest identifiable segment of the movement, the Holistic Health movement. Having experienced a personal transformation, New Agers project the possibility of the transformation not of just a number of additional individuals, but of the culture and of humanity itself. More than a possibility, it is, they claim, a present reality: the New Age is emerging in this generation. This affirmation, this hope, that the New Age is imminent gives the movement its name. Healing projected into the larger social context has become a movement to heal the earth, the ideological foundation for the movement's support of peace and ecological activism. (Melton et al. 1991: 3; original emphasis removed)

— DEFINITIONS BY CHRISTIANS —

The New Age first entered the Christian collective consciousness through the warnings of Constance Cumbey in 1983:

> According to New Age sources, the New Age Movement is a worldwide network. It consists of tens of thousands cooperating organizations. Their primary goal or the secret behind their 'unity-in-diversity' is the formation of a 'New World Order'. The Movement usually operates on the basis of a well-formulated body of underlying esoteric or occult teachings . . .
> Carefully structured along the lines set forth in the Alice Bailey writings, it includes organizations teaching mind control, Holistic Health, esoteric philosophy; scientific workers, political workers; and organizations dedicated to peace and world goodwill. It also includes many consumer, environmental and nutritional organizations as well as religious cults of every shade and description. (Cumbey 1983: 54)

Texe Marrs cites a thirteen-point New Age Plan by Satan for world domination, which includes:

> Point #1
> The principal aim of The Plan is to establish a One World, New Age Religion and a one world political and social order.
> Point #2
> The New Age World Religion will be a revival of the idolatrous religion of ancient Babylon in which mystery cults, sorcery and occultism, and immorality flourished.
> Point #3
> The Plan is to come to fullness when the New Age Messiah, the Antichrist with the number 666, comes in the flesh to lead the unified New Age World Religion and oversee the new one world order.
> Point #4
> Spirit guides (demons) will help man inaugurate the New Age and will pave the way for the Antichrist, the New Age man-god, to be acclaimed by humanity as the Great World Teacher.
> Point #5
> "World Peace!," "Love!" and "Unity" will be the rallying cries of the New Age World Religion . . .
> (Marrs 1987: 16–17; original emphasis removed)

Cumbey and Marrs provide examples of the more extreme Christian definitions of New Age – more nuanced definitions by Christians are considered in Chapter 8. A good example of a Christian definition of New Age that avoids such extremes is that of Russell Chandler, a journalist:

> New Age is a hybrid mix of spiritual, social, and political forces, and it encompasses sociology, theology, the physical sciences, medicine, anthropology, history, the Human Potential movement, sports, and science fiction.
>
> New Age is not a sect or cult, per se. There is no organization one must join, no creed one must confess. Identifying individuals as 'full-blown' New Agers is baffling . . . Although 'new' in style and vocabulary, the movement is in many ways as old as the Eastern religions of Hinduism and Buddhism, Western occultism, and the mystical oracles of ancient Greece and Egypt. New Age has simply recast the theory of reincarnation into the language of Western humanistic psychology, science, and technology . . .
>
> Remember, 'New Age' is an umbrella term. A precise definition is a chimera. (Chandler 1989: 17–18)

– FAMILY RESEMBLANCE THEORY OF DEFINITION –

Given the wide range of extant definitions already seen, New Age is rightly described as an umbrella term for a wide collection of phenomena. One way of uniting disparate phenomena into such an overarching schema is to use what has been described as a polythetic (Needham 1975; Southwold 1978) mode of definition. A number of scholars have already applied this method of definition to New Age (e.g. Barker 1992: 189; Prince 1992). Adam Possamaï (1998), although not developing the concept, describes New Age as a 'meronymy' or the single descriptor for a range of distinguishable religious phenomena.

Unlike a conventional definition, a polythetic definition does not rely on one-to-one correspondences between the definition and the phenomenon. Rather, it employs one-to-many relationships, with many characteristics answering to a singular definition. Thus there are multiple possible characteristics which make up the definition of a single phenomenon. In any one instance of the phenomenon, only a limited number of these characteristics will be present. It may well be that there is no extant example of the phenomenon containing all the possible characteristics outlined in the polythetic definition.

Another way of describing this mode of definition was sketched in outline form by the philosopher Ludwig Wittgenstein (1889–1951) in *Philosophical Investigations* (1953). Family resemblance theory draws its name from the nature of resemblances between family members. For instance, my daughter has one of my dimples, but she also has her mother's chin. I clearly resemble my brother, but it is not readily apparent that he is Jasmina's uncle. Family resemblance theory therefore allows for a pool of 'common core' characteristics from which resemblances are inferred, but also allows for dissimilarities between phenomena united by the same definition.

It may still be asked, however, whether a polythetic or family resemblance definition of New Age actually defines anything that has not previously been defined in other ways. For example, Colin Campbell's term 'cultic milieu' (Campbell 1972) has many similarities with New Age. Campbell introduced this term to provide a lasting reference point which scholars could latch onto in the ever-shifting world of ephemeral religious cults. In non-academic parlance, the cultic milieu may be similar to what many people mean when they talk about the 'occult scene'. This was given an academic flavour by Martin Marty with the idea of an 'occult establishment' (Marty 1970). New Age is akin to these ideas, too.

− PAGANISM −

Pagans are often concerned to distinguish themselves from New Agers. Michael York distinguishes between the sociology of the New Age and Neo-Pagan movements (York 1995), although noting the overlap. Most Christian critiques of New Age, however (e.g. Cumbey 1983; Groothuis 1986), include Paganism under the New Age umbrella. Tanya Luhrmann also comments, 'In whatever form magicians practise magic, they situate it within what is proclaimed the "New Age"' (Luhrmann 1989: 32). A successful definition of New Age will have to take both these viewpoints into account.

Amy Simes lists a number of reasons for distinguishing between New Age and Paganism (Simes 1995: 489ff). Firstly, New Age shamanism is described as 'a secular activity' while Pagan shamanism is 'a religious act'. Secondly, Pagan spirituality is said to be less 'vague' than New Age. Thirdly, Pagan interpretations of reincarnation are said to have a simpler view of natural cycles that is more suggestive of the eternal round than vertical planes, whereas New Age interpretations are said to emphasise karmic law, judgement and hierarchical planes. Fourthly, it is claimed that Paganism prefers the material to the spiritual, whereas for New Agers the reverse is the case. Fifthly, Paganism is described as more democratic than New Age. Sixthly, Paganism is said to have more ritual activity than New Age. Seventhly, Pagan groups are claimed to evidence more commitment and community than New Age groups. Finally, New Agers are said to construe their movement as modern, while Pagans emphasise historical continuity. Simes denies that 'any sort of significant crossover of identity exists between these two movements' (ibid.: 497).

Joanne Pearson (1998) devotes a whole article to denying that Wicca is New Age. Wicca, modern witchcraft deriving from the influence of Gerald Gardner (1884–1964), is usually understood to be Pagan, although again there are qualifications to this categorisation (see Pearson 2000). The majority of Wiccans surveyed by Pearson did not regard Wicca as part of the 'New Age movement'. Pearson analyses the possible reasons for this by comparing Wicca to Heelas' portrayal of New Age, concentrating on three principles: 'Your lives are not working'; 'You are gods and goddesses in exile'; and 'Let go/drop it' (Heelas 1996a: 18–20). The first principle is said to be neither a central theme nor a starting point for entry into Wicca. The second principle is rejected with the claim that, although a small number of Wiccans do not believe in the gods as external realities, the majority do worship gods and goddesses through invocation with an external and inner aspect. The third principle is admitted to be partly applicable to Wicca.

Pearson suggests two further principles that differentiate Wicca from New Age: authority and commitment. Wiccans acknowledge the authority of the high priestess and high priest, and also of other Wiccans with areas of expertise, such as Qabbalah or tarot. While New Agers are typically serial seekers (see Chapter 9), lacking commitment to any particular organisation, Wiccans are often committed long-term through their initiation into and membership of an individual coven.

Reender Kranenborg (2001) suggests that, while Wicca is a kind of New Age, Neopaganism itself is an independent movement. Reasons given include the generality of New Age views of the divine compared to the concrete specificity of the Neopagan pantheons. New Age has a hierarchical view of reality populated by spiritual beings (see Chapter 4), while nothing of the kind exists in Neopaganism. The New Age notion of karma (see Chapter 4 again) is absent in Neopaganism, Kranenborg claims, although present in Wicca in the Netherlands. The understandings of evil are different, with New Age viewing it as a means to spiritual development and Neopaganism viewing it as a natural part of the world. Neopaganism does not have the New Age expectancy of a new era, he claims.

The complex New Age esoteric anthropology with various forms of bodies – physical, astral, ethereal and causal; or ego, mind, soul and divine spark – do not exist in Neopaganism, according to Kranenborg. New Age seeks deliverance or self-realisation through various techniques; neither the goal nor the techniques are present in Neopaganism. New Age holism (see Chapter 4) is partial, in that the world is often said to be illusory, while Neopagan holism is more firmly grounded. The Christ, often encountered in New Age, is not important in Neopaganism. The importance of revelation or channelling (see Chapter 7) is not mirrored in Neopaganism, claims Kranenborg.

Kranenborg argues that the most important differences between New Age and Neopaganism are their respective practices – with the closed circles and textual and symbolic rites of Neopaganism rarely encountered in the open gatherings of New Age. Likewise, the seasonal Neopagan festivals and rites of passage are not present in New Age. Nevertheless, Kranenborg does acknowledge some similarities between New Age and Neopaganism, including the concept of spiritual energy, the use of magic, and the importance of nature.

The question of the relation between New Age and Paganism is an important one in New Age studies, and of practical value to accommodate the sensitivities of practising Pagans. Since I have undertaken no fieldwork in any form of Paganism, I do not feel qualified to reach a final conclusion, but hope that the opinions set out above will be helpful. I have also taken up in this book the terminology of Pearson et al. (eds 1998: 1), using 'Paganism' as the preferred emic term over the scholarly usage of 'Neopaganism', etc. (except where the latter term is used by other authors, as in York and Kranenborg above).

– SYNOPSIS –

This introductory chapter has briefly demarcated the field to be covered by this guide to New Age, emically and etically, with examples of definitions of New Age given by New Agers themselves, by scholars and by Christians – and consideration of claims by Pagans of what New Age is not. The underlying framework through which this book will approach New Age is family resemblance theory, and although it will not feature again much in the text, it should be borne in mind at all times.

The second chapter takes a practical example of New Age, the channelled text A Course in Miracles (1985). This is explored in the ways that will be detailed in later chapters, including through the history of ideas, philosophy, anthropology, sociology and psychology.

A brief history of New Age is given in the third chapter, starting with true New Age in its manifestations after World War II and looking at earlier roots in pre-war, pre-industrial and ancient times. This is then extended to look at mythical roots of New Age.

The fourth chapter considers the philosophy of New Age, including its metaphysics, its understanding of God and other beings, of salvation and death, and of history. A vignette is used to demonstrate the application of a philosophical approach to New Age through brief consideration of the relation between New Age and postmodernism.

A basic anthropological or phenomenological approach is taken in the next chapter, which depicts a range of examples of New Age, grouped under the headings of events, rituals and practices.

The sociological structure of New Age is considered in Chapter 6, which emphasises the importance of qualitative and statistical studies in formulating sociological theories such as cult–sect–church theory, NRM theory, SPIN theory, NSM theory and NSRM theory. (All these abbreviations will be explained!) Three New Age groups are considered as vignette examples.

The final scholarly discipline considered for its approach to New Age is psychology, which has had an important historical influence on New Age. Attempts at psychological profiles of New Agers are reviewed before a description of a typical New Ager. Two vignettes are given in this chapter – the application to New Age of conversion theory, and questions about mental health in relation to channelling.

Importantly, Chapter 8 considers non-academic approaches to New Age, starting with emic approaches by New Agers themselves before considering media and Christian approaches. Other non-academic approaches covered include rationalist, Native American, feminist, Jewish, Sufi and local community approaches.

A more detailed academic literature survey is given in the penultimate chapter, with an emphasis on as yet unpublished doctoral theses, which are in many ways the most authoritative studies of New Age. It is argued that, just as some have suggested New Age is itself a publishing phenomenon, so market forces impact on the academic understanding of New Age.

The final chapter collects together various views on the future of New Age. Some British scholars claim New Age has never existed; an American scholar claims it is already dead; while Italians have described a new stage of New Age, known as Next Age.

The book does not end with the last chapter, as the bibliographic references are as important as the body of the text for students of New Age. Just as there is no substitute for real-life fieldwork in New Age, so there is no substitute for reading the full original texts, both primary and secondary, that describe the phenomena. It is hoped that this book will facilitate further investigation of New Age. In this sense, it really is only a guidebook – a starting point and not the final word on the subject.

– NOTE –

1. In studies of New Age, the most prominent example of this distinction is made in Hanegraaff (1996: 6–8).

CHAPTER 2

The Course – A Case Study

This chapter applies the approaches of later chapters – history of ideas, philosophy, anthropology, sociology and psychology – to a specific case study, showing how each discipline can be applied in practice by the student of New Age.

The initial choice of which facet of New Age to investigate further is fundamental to a successful study of New Age. No single student of New Age can hope to study the whole panoply of groups and practices in detail. A broad picture may be painted, but this should always be based on sound knowledge of a smaller number of typical groups. There is a methodological problem here: for how is the student to know which groups are typical of New Age, at the outset of investigation into the field, before logical inferences are drawn from the study of the particular group as to the nature of the larger field? There is no way around this problem. The 'bootstrap' theory (whereby one pulls oneself out of the swamp by tugging on one's bootstraps) is perhaps the best solution that has been found. This is similar to the 'cybernetic loop', which provides feedback on the interim results of a system as the process runs, and inputs these back into the system, producing more accurate results for the duration of the study.

A choice faces the student: whether to read the existing secondary literature on New Age before commencing fieldwork, or whether to commence fieldwork 'blind', without the insights of extant studies. The first approach has the advantage that the choice of fieldwork location is more likely to be consistent with the approaches of earlier students, although the flipside is that this approach may overlook new or alternative approaches to the field. The second, 'blind' approach has the advantage of avoiding possible clichés and biases in earlier studies, but carries the risk of not focusing on the central issues identified by the graft of more seasoned scholars of the field. The approach chosen will in practice depend on the demands placed on the student: whether there is a need to engage in fieldwork immediately, through institutional or personal pressures, or whether there is time to spend in the library and armchair beforehand.

Prior to this case study, I had already completed a detailed survey of Christian approaches to New Age (Kemp 2003a) and thus took the first approach. Building on my existing knowledge, I chose for this current chapter to investigate further a text which uses Christian vocabulary but is usually described in the secondary literature as New Age: A Course in Miracles (the Course), channelled by Helen Schucman (1909–81), and first published in the USA in 1975. Schucman is said to have understood the channelled entity to be the historical Jesus, although she was uncomfortable about her relationship with Jesus and with the dictation.

Many Course students will object to my inclusion of the Course as a case study of New Age: the Course is not New Age, they protest.[1] This was the response I encountered when negotiating fieldwork access to a Course study group: they were unhappy to be included in a book on New Age. Kenneth Wapnick (b. 1942), a central teacher of the Course, claims: 'The Course's profound metaphysical foundations . . . [are] certainly a far cry from the more worldly emphases and less demanding nature of many contemporary New Age approaches' (Wapnick 1999a: 363). Such concern with 'New Age' reflects Schucman's avoidance of the 1970s vogue term 'psychic' (ibid.: 304, 369). From an etic viewpoint, Massimo Introvigne questions whether the Course truly represents New Age, suggesting that its adaptations by personalities such as Marianne Williamson (b. 1952) are more suited to the label (Introvigne 2000: 221). Wouter Hanegraaff (1996: 115) points out that the Course is unique in his selection of New Age source texts, in that it is the only example of true other-worldliness (see Chapter 4).

As will be discussed in Chapter 8, while self-understandings of religious phenomena are important, they are not conclusive – indeed, I will suggest that no single approach to New Age, not even the academic approach, should assume prime position in a definition. My hope is that in the description of the Course that follows, developed along the disciplinary lines indicated later in this book, it will become clear why I understand the Course to be a typical manifestation of New Age.

– HISTORY OF IDEAS –

Helen Schucman received the channelled text of A Course in Miracles between 1965 and 1972, when she was a research psychologist, assistant professor and later associate professor in the Department of Psychiatry at Columbia-Presbyterian Medical Center, New York. She initially asked her academic supervisor, Bill Thetford (1922–88), for advice on how to deal with the inner dictation. Thetford had grown up in Christian Science, although he was now agnostic, and affirmed her experiences, typing up with Schucman her notes on the channelled text.

Kenneth Wapnick describes Schucman as a 'very closet Christian' (1999a: 410), although she was born Jewish and maintained a persona of scientific atheism in her professional life. As a child, her Catholic governess would secretly take her to church on Sundays, and as an adult Schucman left her husband Louis while he was asleep to attend late-night services at St Patrick's Cathedral, New York. The Course contains over 800 quotations from and allusions to the Bible (ibid.: 459).

Wapnick, like Schucman Jewish by birth, and a convert to Catholicism, undertook the final editing of the channelled text with Schucman, in consultation with Thetford. Under instructions from Jesus, personal material relating solely to Schucman and Thetford was removed from the published text. Judy Skutch Whitson (then Judy Skutch), also from a Jewish family and interested in parapsychology, had founded the Foundation for Parasensory Investigation in 1971, renaming it the Foundation for Inner Peace (FIP) in 1975 following a vision experienced by Schucman. Wapnick founded the Foundation for A Course in Miracles (FACIM) in 1983 as a sister, teaching arm of FIP. Skutch, Wapnick, Thetford and Schucman decided to finance the publication of the Course and were surprised to receive a large contribution from Reed Erickson, a wealthy industrialist who had read an early manuscript.

There have since been a number of bestselling popularisers of the Course, including Gerald Jampolsky and Marianne Williamson. The copyright of the Course has in recent years been the subject of a number of court cases, and is now strictly monitored. A version of the Course, without the final redactive alterations, known as the *Jesus Course in Miracles* (JCIM), appeared on the Internet in December 1999. The Course in Miracles Society published a print version of the *JCIM*, comparing in an appendix the *JCIM* with the 1975 published edition. Copyright litigation arising from these actions is ongoing at the time of writing.

– PHILOSOPHY –

The Course explicitly distinguishes itself from philosophy or theology: 'This is not a course in philosophical speculation, nor is it concerned with precise terminology ... A universal theology is impossible' (Manual: 73). (References to A Course in Miracles are quoted in the format used by students of the Course. The Course contains three volumes, previously published separately: the Text, the Workbook and the Manual for Teachers. The page numbers used here are from the first edition of the Course.) Elsewhere, however, the Course does claim to be '[a] unified thought system in which nothing is lacking that is needed, and nothing is included that is contradictory or irrelevant' (Workbook: 66).

These statements may be reconciled if we understand that the Course is depicting a state of mind which is to be achieved, rather than constructing a logical system to be analysed and debated. To discuss the 'philosophy' of the Course may therefore be somewhat missing the point in the eyes of students of the Course; but students of philosophy know of no subject which is not amenable to evaluation and critique and it is from the point of view of a philosopher and not a student of the Course that this analysis is written.[2]

A similar paradox is apparent in the Course's view of truth: on the one hand, the Course claims to be the only truth – 'Complexity is not of God ... He knows of one creation, one reality, one truth and but one Son.' (Text: 508) It is probably in this vein that the Manual for Teachers claims that 'there are only two thought systems' (Manual: 1), namely the true thought system of the Course and all other, false thought systems.

Yet again, the Manual (pp. 3–4) describes the Course as but one version of the universal course; other pupils are called to different teachers who teach a form of the universal teaching that is appropriate for their level of understanding. 'Are other teachers possible, to lead the way to those who speak in different tongues and appeal to different symbols? Certainly they are' (Manual: 56). The Course also emphasises the importance of being non-judgemental, while at the same time describing itself as a 'required course' (Text: Introduction). Kenneth Wapnick, following Helen Schucman, interprets this as meaning the Course is required only for only for those for whom it is the appropriate path (Wapnick 1989: 10). Other commentators have described the Course as a manifestation of the perennial philosophy (see Chapter 4).

The Course in many ways parallels the methodology of René Descartes' (1596–1650) seminal Discourse on Method and The Med-

itations, which set the scene for all subsequent Western philosophy. Central to this methodology is the so-called 'method of doubt'. Compare:

> I had long ago noticed that, in matters relating to conduct, one needs some-times to follow, just as if they were absolutely indubitable, opinions one knows to be very unsure . . . but as I wanted to concentrate solely on the search for truth, I thought I ought to do just the opposite, and reject as being absolutely false everything in which I could suppose the slightest reason for doubt, in order to see if there did not remain after that anything in my belief which was entirely indubitable. (Descartes 1968: 53)

with:

> When every concept has been raised to doubt and question, and been recog-nized as made on no assumptions that would stand the light, then is the truth left free to enter in its sanctuary, clean and free of guilt. (Text: 613–14)

In both these methodologies doubt is applied to all concepts. Another parallel between the Course and Descartes is use of the analogy of the dream. The passage from the fourth part of the *Discourse* taken above continues:

> And finally, considering that all the same thoughts that we have when we are awake can also come to us when we are asleep, without any one of them being true, I resolved to pretend that nothing which had ever entered my mind was any more true than the illusions of my dreams. (Descartes 1968: 53)

The Course similarly uses the analogy of the dream to question conventional perceptions of truth and reality (e.g. Text: 351, 541). Yet different conclusions are drawn. Descartes coins the famous formula 'cogito, ergo sum' – 'I think, therefore I am' (ibid.: 53) to prove the existence of the individual. The Course, however, dwells on the fundamental doubt rather than inferring real individual existence: in the Course, reality as currently perceived is an illusion. Descartes was able to dismiss this fundamental doubt because he retained, or claimed to retain, belief in a Christian-type God who does not deceive (ibid.: 158). In this way, the Course's doubt in conventional reality is more far-reaching than Descartes's, who retained the notion of individuality distinct from an honest, personal God.

If the Course shows some similarities to Descartes, it also shows debts to that other foundational Western philosopher, Plato (427–348 BCE). The analogy of the shadow is used (e.g. Text: 541), reminiscent of Plato's famous analogy of the cave in the *Republic*, where prisoners strung up in a cave believe the shadows dancing on the wall opposite

them are all there is to reality; they are ignorant of the real world outside the cave of shadows. Again, the Course claims that life's problems
stem from the fact that we cannot recognise (or 'know again') ourselves, our brothers or God – implying that we already knew reality,
but have since forgotten it. This is a Platonic doctrine, known as *anam-
nesia*. The Course also claims 'I do not perceive my own best interests'
(Workbook: 36). This is the idea that individuals do not fully comprehend the situation they are in and need external moral guidance. Again
this is a Platonic doctrine, only in Plato it was the philosopher-king
who perceived our best interests for us, rather than Jesus through the
Course.[3]

The underlying similarity between the Course and Platonism is the
notion of the fundamental reality of the idea: 'God is an idea . . . *you*
are an idea' (Text: 293). In Platonism this is known as the theory of
forms, and may be explained simply by saying that the world we perceive is but a reflection of heavenly forms or eternal ideas, which alone
have true existence. This philosophy can also be described as idealism,
and the Course is in a some ways an example of such a philosophy,
although it denies reality even to these eternal ideas.

The Course introduces a variation to Platonic idealism through the
influence of modern psychology. 'Real ideas', as they are known in the
Course ('eternal forms' in Plato) are distinguished from 'false ideas'
(Workbook: 13, 15). The purpose of the Course is to empty the mind
of false ideas and replace them with real ideas. This 'conversion' is
discussed below in the section on the psychology of the Course.

Wapnick (1989) explores the Course in the light of ancient
Gnosticism (see Chapter 3), also making comparisons to Platonism and
Christianity. Originally, Wapnick saw the Course as complementary
to traditional Christianity,[4] but by the time he wrote *Love Does Not
Condemn*, he came to speak of Jesus in the Course 'redefining' and
'correcting' traditional Christian thought (ibid.: 13). An interesting passage in Wapnick's deposition in some copyright litigation explains the
modification of terminology:

> Even before the course was actually published, without mentioning the course by
> name, I would use the New Testament Jesus as a vehicle for conveying what it was
> we wanted to say. I actually ended up being rather good at it in the sense that tak-
> ing statements that my audience and my students and patients could understand
> and relate to and giving them a different meaning that would be more consistent
> with what I took to be a more loving message. (Wapnick 1999b: 93–4)

The Course also exhibits similarities to the existentialism of Jean-
Paul Sartre and others, which was popular in the period Schucman

channelled the text, with its emphasis on the importance of meaning. Lesson 2 in the workbook reads: 'I have given everything I see in this room [on this street, from this window, in this place] all the meaning that it has for me.' (Workbook: 4 [brackets in original]) The process of worldview change outlined in the workbook is described as working 'toward the goal of separating the meaningless from the meaningful' (Workbook: 6). In some ways, Sartre's concept of consciously choosing the meaning we give to the world is upheld in the Course, since we are exhorted to follow the path that is right for us. 'Purpose is meaning', as the workbook explains (Workbook: 38).

– ANTHROPOLOGY –

Although the Course is often studied by lone students without contact with other readers of the text, it is difficult to get a feel for the Course as part of a substantive movement without engaging in fieldwork. There are a great number of private study groups concentrating on the Course and many of these are listed on the Internet. Thus examination of just one study group will not be representative of the Course as a whole.

New Age meetings often begin with those present introducing themselves to others, much in the style of encounter-group therapy. So, on my first visit to a meeting of a local group (which I will here call the study group) studying the Course, I made a point of introducing myself as a researcher, who was just as interested in the interaction of the members of the group, as in the text the group was studying. Here, as with other groups I have researched, I was told that, while I might think I was researching for a critical book, the Course has mysterious methods, and in fact this could merely be the Course making itself available to me in a more personal, spiritual way.

The study group I attended meets on average one Friday per month. The leader, Rosie,[5] conducts a large number of study groups and therapies from her home, not just concentrating on the Course. The first reception room in her house is set aside for New Age merchandise, including books, newsletters, tapes and cards for sale, and a small library of New Age books to borrow. The main reception room is where the meetings are held, and is decorated in a New Age style with ornaments such as statues of Buddha, Chinese paintings and burning incense. In the background, while people arrive for the meetings, soft New Age music is playing – with the CD case displayed in case you would like to purchase a copy. As people arrive, they are invited to make themselves a cup of herbal tea or decaffeinated coffee (with soya or organic milk) in the kitchen. On the first evening that I met the study group, there was little conversation or chit-chat before Rosie started the meeting and asked us to introduce ourselves.

There was Tina, a 30-ish office worker who had attended some of Rosie's other groups, and had read the Course in some detail; Connie, a middle-aged black lady who had travelled some distance by public transport to be at the group; Fiona, also middle-aged, who found it difficult to read the Course by herself and hoped the study group would help; and of course Rosie herself, meticulously presented and perhaps younger than Connie and Fiona. As is common in New Age groups I have studied, there were no men – apart from me. At the first meeting the previous month there had apparently been three more people, but they had made various excuses and were not seen again.

The first hour and a half of the meeting was taken up by watching a professional video introducing the Course. We then broke for coffee and chatted for a while. Fiona was interested in my book, which gave me an opportunity to expand on what I hoped to cover and the approach I was taking. Soon Rosie started proceedings again, and we gave our reactions to the video. Connie was impressed by the ease with which the American presenters and commentators had expressed complex spiritual ideas – and others agreed that Americans often have such a facility in comparison to the more intellectual approach often taken by British presenters. My opinion, though I did not express it at the study group, was that the video was being used by Rosie as a way to grant an aura of established authority to both the text and the study group.

Rosie then asked us how we would like to proceed – watch another video, listen to a tape or 'draw a card'. We chose the last, and Rosie passed round a box of small cards written by Gerald Jampolsky and based on the Course. Tina reminded us to pick a card – at random – with our non-dominant hand. The reason for this, I supposed, was based on the common New Age distinction between logical left-brain thinking and mystical right-brain thinking. The card I drew read, 'I am not the victim of the world I see.' On the reverse was a brief explanation of this quasi-proverbial statement. Rosie asked us to think about our cards each day until the next meeting, when we would report on our progress. Another example of a card I drew on a later evening is 'I am determined to see things differently'.

The study group then naturally progressed to a discussion of our initial perceptions of the Course. Rosie explained some of the concepts to us in more detail, giving what Fiona later commented to me was a more psychological slant than she was used to from other Course meetings she had attended. We all had questions, and when Rosie was slow to answer, each of us tried to explain to the enquirer what we thought the answer could be. Soon Rosie drew the study group to a close and we paid the modest fee to Rosie for the evening.

This was very much the normal pattern of the study group evenings, although the order was sometimes changed, with a video watched at the end, for example. In later weeks, we also reported on what was jokingly called our 'homework': the Jampolsky cards. Tina was the most conscientious and kept a diary of her thoughts on the cards she selected, from which she sometimes read to us. Rosie also set herself 'homework', and reported back to the group on her progress – indicating to me that, although she was regarded as an authority on the Course by the study group, she was still on the path of learning.

The use of the non-dominant hand to pick the Jampolsky cards is a small example of modern-day magic, or belief in the effect of prescribed ritual behaviour. Nowhere is such ritual magic suggested in the Course; it is an accretion which may be unique to the study group, but is probably more widespread. I will now turn in the rest of this section to a consideration of the understanding of magic, a traditional anthropological concept, in the Course.

'Magic is the mindless or the miscreative use of mind. Physical medications are forms of "spells," but if you are afraid to use the mind to heal, you should not attempt to do so' (Text: 21). Illness is 'a form of magical solution. The ego believes that by punishing itself it will mitigate the punishment of God' (Text: 78). The Course teaches that theological salvation is achieved through magic, just as psychological intervention uses magic: both heal through the ego (Text: 160). Magic is an attempt at reconciling the irreconcilable thought systems of sickness and perfection (Text: 173). Belief in magic is sustained by the illusion that it works (Manual: 40).

The miracle is distinguished in the Course from magic; it is in effect magic that really works because it is based on the true nature of things rather than the illusory ways of the world.

> A miracle is a correction. It does not create, nor really change at all. It merely . . .
> reminds the mind that what it sees is false . . . The miracle is taken first on faith,
> because to ask for it implies the mind has been made ready to conceive of what
> it cannot see and does not understand. (Workbook: 463)

The centrality of miracles to the Course is observable by their appearance in the title: *A Course in Miracles*. Yet it is not immediately clear from the Course itself – at least to me – exactly what a miracle is. Along with many traditional words used in the Course, its meaning is modified from the conventional sense.

W. Norris Clarke, a Jesuit who has some difficulties with the relationship of the Course to traditional Christianity, interviewed Kenneth Wapnick:

> [Clarke:] On one hand, I am hearing you say that it does not make any difference if you project a parking space or what you do as long as you do not attribute that to the Holy Spirit. But now you are saying the opposite, which is do not project parking spaces or any such thing, they are all in the mind.
>
> [Wapnick:] Right, I am saying both things. I am saying that the best thing is not to use magic at all, but most of us are not up to that all the time. The best thing would be to ask the Holy Spirit, "What should I do?" rather than to project the parking spot. (Wapnick & Clarke 1995: 81–2)

Wapnick appears to be warning against the use of base magic; but his admonition to ask the Holy Spirit for guidance implies that, if the Holy Spirit tells us to use 'magic' to project a parking space, such 'magic' is in fact an acceptable miracle.

Miracles are also central to Chuck Spezzano's vision. In *Awaken the Gods*, a collection of aphorisms for daily meditation, the following are included:

> To have a miracle know who you are and share that knowledge.
> To create a miracle change your mind.
> Creating a miracle is not believing an illusion through affirming the truth.
> (Spezzano 1991: 86–7)

These aphorisms conform to the general import of the Course. The practical effect of such aphorisms on miracles is demonstrated through a number of 'miraculous' (in the conventional sense, that is, without scientific explanation) healings: Spezzano has told audiences that he has seen, for example, cancer and haemorrhoids cured through use of his Psychology of Vision, which is influenced by Course material.

Marianne Williamson, another important interpreter of the Course, also retains the distinction between magic and miracles:

> Magic is when we focus the mind on a desired manifestation, giving our shopping list to God and telling Him what we want Him to do for us. Miracles are when we ask God what we can do for Him . . . If we write affirmations for a brown Mercedes Benz, the power of the subconscious mind is such that we will probably get it. The point is, we won't necessarily be happy once we do. The miracle-minded perception would be to make happiness itself our goal and to relinquish the thought that we know what that would look like. (Williamson 1992: 181–2)

Again, though perhaps flippant in tone, this passage demonstrates a real belief in mind altering reality (the core idea of magic), and implies that if a brown Mercedes-Benz really would make us happy, then manifesting a brown Mercedes-Benz is a valid miracle.

In the early days of the Course, this process of requesting magical miracles was known as 'asking' for specific help. Jesus or the Holy Spirit was often asked, through Schucman, for specific advice 'in matters such as times to meet, street corners to stand on for taxi-cabs, whether to attend certain meetings, and the like' (Wapnick 1999a: 442). Wapnick describes soon becoming uncomfortable with such a 'magical' or 'psychic' process, which he describes as reflecting the lower rungs of the ladder of true prayer – '"asking-out-of-need" . . . always involves "feelings of weakness and inadequacy, and could never be made by a Son of God who knows Who he is"' (ibid.: 453).

Thus the concept of magic in the Course, in its original form and as interpreted by some contemporary leading teachers, is ambiguous. On the one hand it is rejected along with the illusory material world; but on the other hand, in the form of the miracle, or true magic, it is affirmed. Another way of looking at this is that a miracle is magic that works because it accords with the true nature of things. Ultimately, however, according to the Course, neither magic nor miracle has any real existence.

– SOCIOLOGY –

D. Patrick Miller provides a survey of the Course network (Miller 1998: 61–78). It includes the Miracle Distribution Center, in Fullerton, California, founded in 1978, which sends a free bimonthly newsletter, *The Holy Encounter*, to 10,000 people and maintains a database of Course study groups with 2,100 such groups listed worldwide in 1996. The Foundation for Life Action, Los Angeles follows Tara Singh, a former student of Krishnamurti and convert to the Course. The Interfaith Fellowship, in New York, is a congregation of 150–200 people following Revd Jon Mundy, a former Methodist preacher, and Revd Diane Berke. The Circle of Atonement, in Sedona, Arizona, was founded by Robert Perry and in 1994 established a teaching wing with a school called Learning Circle. The California Miracles Center, in San Francisco, was incorporated in 1987 by Revd Tony Ponticello, holds Sunday morning services and publishes the *Miracles Monthly* newsletter. Endeavor Academy, in Baraboo, Wisconsin, is described by Miller as 'the most controversial' Course centre, in that it has been described as a 'cult' following Chuck Anderson, known as 'Dear One'. In London there is the Miracle Network, run by Ian Patrick, with its *Miracle Worker* newsletter and Miracle Café. Miller also points to the frequency with which the Course is encountered in Unity church circles (see Chapter 3) and in recovery groups following the twelve-step model of Alcoholics Anonymous.

In Chapter 6 we will see that New Age tends to cut across traditional typologies of new religious movements. It is obvious that the Course is not a cult (in the non-pejorative sense) – there is not enough control over members. Nobody would claim it is large enough and well-established enough to represent a sect, even less a church – although these remain possible outcomes for its future development. Under another typology, we may describe the Course as rejecting the world we currently live in, affirming the world we should live in with the right miracle consciousness, and accommodating traditional Christian language to achieve this transformation. Under yet another typology, we would probably describe the Course as manipulationist, in that it attempts to alter reality through altering the mind;[6] or perhaps thaumaturgical, in its emphasis on miracles.

Originally, Helen Schucman believed the Course was intended only for five or six disciples – 'was for only very few, and certainly not the masses' (Wapnick 1999a: 304) – since it was so difficult truly to understand. The Course was first circulated in manuscript form among Schucman, Bill Thetford and Kenneth Wapnick's circle of friends. At this point in time, it may be seen in many ways to be a private phenomenon (see Chapter 6). As soon as it was published, the Course became an audience phenomenon. Once practitioners, such as Gerald Jampolsky and hundreds of others less well-known, began to offer services based on the teachings of the Course, these aspects may be seen as client phenomena. More recently, with the success of organisations such as Foundation for Inner Peace and the Foundation for *A Course in Miracles*, the Course has exhibited movement phenomena.

The Course also fits into the SPIN model of NRMs – a segmented, polycentric, integrated network (see Chapter 6). It is not represented by a monolithic organisation, but has a cell-like, 'segmented' structure of representatives from well-established foundations to loose-knit Internet-based groups and small home-study circles, almost entirely independent of each other. This structure is also 'polycentric', in that while FACIM is an important node in the Course network, it is not the only important node. It is not quite so easy to describe the Course movement as 'integrated', unless we mean by this that it is focused around a central vision, namely that vision presented in the Text. The Course is well described as a 'network', however, rather than as a more traditional sociological structure.

While there are some reservations in describing the Course as a SPIN, it is also difficult to describe it as a new social movement (NSM), mainly because it lacks the broad social support typically seen in NSMs such as the green movement or anti-nuclear movement. Again, this does not preclude the Course from being an NSM in its early developmental stages, before broad social support is achieved; but this is probably unlikely. If it lacks the characteristics of an NSM, the Course similarly lacks the characteristics of a new socio-religious movement (NSRM), again through the lack of broad social appeal.

These sociological models are further explained in Chapter 6.

– PSYCHOLOGY –

Just as the Course denies it is a form of philosophy, it also denies that it may be understood psychologically: 'The structure of "individual consciousness" is essentially irrelevant because it is a concept representing the "original error" or the "original sin". To study the error itself does not lead to correction' (Manual: 73). Nevertheless, the Course was channelled through a professional psychologist (Helen Schucman), who was encouraged to accept and transcribe the material by another psychologist (Bill Thetford), and the text was edited by a third psychologist (Kenneth Wapnick). It would therefore be surprising if there was not a strong psychological influence in the text, and indeed this is the case. Wapnick is reportedly preparing for publication a work on the Course and psychology, including a comparison of the Course with the thought of Sigmund Freud and Carl Jung.

The Workbook explicitly describes itself in the introduction as a manual for psychological change: 'It is the purpose of this workbook to train your mind to think along the lines the text sets forth . . . The purpose of the workbook is to train your mind in a systematic way to a different perception of everyone and everything in the world' (Workbook: 1).

Meanwhile, the Manual for Teachers describes teaching, that is, living life as described in the Course, as 'a method of conversion' (Manual: 1). 'It cannot be too strongly emphasized that this course aims at a complete reversal of thought' (Manual: 57).

The workbook sets out to achieve this aim through the daily repetition of mental exercises. These 'lessons' are meditations on short sentences reflecting the teaching of the text. For example, Lesson 1 is a meditation on the idea 'nothing I see in this room [on this street, from this window, in this place] means anything' (Workbook: 3 (brackets in original)). It is recommended that the first three lessons should not be meditated upon more than twice each day, ideally in the morning and evening, and not for longer than a minute at a time.

The duration and frequency of meditation upon each day's lesson is gradually extended, so that Lesson 20, 'I am determined to see', is repeated at least twice an hour (Workbook: 31); Lesson 31, 'I am not the victim of the world I see' (Workbook: 48), the text I drew at the study group, is recommended for two extended periods of three to five minutes in the morning and evening, as well as continued repetition as often as possible during the day; and Lesson 93, 'Light and joy and peace abide in me' (Workbook: 159), should be repeated for the first five minutes of every hour during the day. Potential converts to the worldview of the Course are encouraged with exhortations that they must 'want' the lessons to be true (Workbook: 42). The lessons may seem 'silly, irreverent, senseless, funny and even objectionable' (Workbook: 45).

The goal of the course is described in traditional Christian terminology as 'salvation', but this word is used to mean something quite different, namely escape from the cause of the world. The cause is identified, 'let go' of and replaced (Workbook: 34). The goal is also described in more psychological terms as 'healing and wholeness' (Text: 66–83). 'To heal is to make happy' (Text: 66).

'Sanity is wholeness' (Text: 82) epitomises the influence of psychological terminology in the Course. False ideas (i.e. belief in the real existence of the material world and its ills) are described as 'delusions' or 'irrational', accompanied by feelings of guilt and fear. The 'ego's voice', which tells us this world is real, is described as a 'hallucination' (Text: 128). The ancient Greek maxim 'Know thyself' (Text: 142) is repeated. Separation from the real self is described as 'dissociation' (Text: 136) – the mind is 'split' (Text: 148);[7] identification with the material body is said to cause 'depression' (Text: 140, 175). Teaching the Course is said to diminish 'self doubt', another core psychological concept (Workbook: 1).

The mental state of those not following the Course is labelled 'insanity': seeing what is not there (because the world is illusory); hearing what makes no sound; manifesting emotions (fear, guilt) the opposite of true emotions (love, happiness); communicating with no one (true communication is through ideas, such as the idea of peace (Text: 294)); being isolated from reality (separated from God); seeing your split mind everywhere (distinguishing between self and other); and being preoccupied with your own voice (rational thought) so that you do not hear God's voice (the Course) (Text: 231–2). In contrast, the Manual answers the question 'What are the characteristics of God's teachers?' (Manual: 8–15) by emphasising that all teachers appear different on the surface, having different worldly backgrounds and superficial 'personalities'; but these differences are viewed as temporary, since in time advanced teachers will demonstrate the following characteristics: trust, honesty, tolerance, gentleness, joy, defencelessness, generosity, patience, faithfulness (adherence to the Course in all aspects of life) and open-mindedness (open to the teachings of the Course).

An appendix to the Manual clarifies a number of key terms used in the Course. The first of these is 'Mind – Spirit' (Manual: 75–6), the second 'The ego – The miracle' (Manual: 77–8), the third 'True perception – Knowledge' (Manual: 81–2); these are all psychological terms (the remaining two terms clarified, Jesus Christ and Holy Spirit, are Christian in origin). Mind is described as 'the activating agent of spirit, supplying its creative energy' (Manual: 75); when the term is capitalised in the text, it refers to God or Christ. 'Right-mindedness' is defined as listening to the Holy Spirit; 'wrong-mindedness' as listening to the ego and making illusions, experiencing anger and guilt. In Freudian psychology the ego represents reality, mediating between the demands of the id and the superego in light of the 'reality principle'; in the Course, this definition of the ego is modified to mean the perceiver of the illusory 'world', a non-existent sham. The ego is also defined in the workbook as 'idolatry; the sign of limited and separated self, born in a body, doomed to suffer and to end its life in death . . . The ego is insane' (Workbook: 457). True perception, or forgiveness, salvation or atonement, is defined as the perception that sin – and the world with it – does not exist.

– CONCLUSION –

The various approaches that will be taken in this book – history of ideas, philosophy, anthropology, sociology and psychology – have been applied to the Course. Other approaches, such as media, rationalist and the approaches of other religionists, especially Christians, could also be profitably explored. As yet, there is little academic work on the Course.[8]

It is perhaps rash to claim that the Course is a typical example of New Age, since both students of the Course and many scholars will contest such an identification. But there are at least useful similarities to note, and this chapter has illustrated how a study of field phenomena can be undertaken in an interdisciplinary fashion.

– Notes –

1. In 1991 the Foundation for *A Course in Miracles* wrote to the Library of Congress requesting that the Course not be catalogued under 'New Age', but rather under 'spirituality' and 'A Course in Miracles', citing sharp disagreement with New Age thinking and giving the following examples: the Course is based on non-dualistic metaphysics; the Course does not support prosperity consciousness; the Course does not overemphasise positive experiences but rather guilt; the Course teaches we are not God, but God is our source; and the Course draws on Freudian psychoanalysis and the Neoplatonic tradition. The Library of Congress has reportedly acceded to this request.

2. D. Patrick Miller, author of *The Complete Story of the Course* (1998) comments that 'to merely read the Course without experiencing its discipline firsthand is to miss its essential "mind-training" aspect. It is not meant to be taken as a set of ideas from which one can learn by comparing it to other sets of ideas, but as a set of ideas that is literally activated within one's consciousness by an accompanying mystical discipline. Without that activation, the Course's metaphysical ideas can appear as an impenetrable tangle of mystifications' (Personal communication, 25 October 2002). I have always been perplexed by such comments, since I was told at school that 'theology is faith seeking understanding'.

3. As Rosemarie LoSasso, director of publications at FACIM points out, according to the Course, Jesus merely reflects the truth that is in us – there is no difference between Jesus and us, the difference being apparent only within the illusion of time (Personal communication, 14 February 2003).

4. LoSasso: 'Right from the beginning he [Wapnick] saw the two as mutually exclusive thought systems' (Personal communication, 14 February 2003). Although I do not have access to all the material available to LoSasso, from the published material I have reviewed, I disagree with her interpretation.

5. Where only first names are used in this book, these are pseudonymous.

6. As D. Patrick Miller has pointed out to me, in fact the Course does not attempt to alter reality since it holds that reality does not in fact exist. However, I am sure many students of the Course suffer from the same misunderstanding as I fell into.

7. A phrase reminiscent of the medical term 'schizophrenia', derived from the Greek *schizein*, 'split'. See Chapter 7.

8. Ruth Bradby is currently undertaking doctoral research on the Course at Chester College, England and Gaia Zanini in Bologna, Italy. See also Pollock (forthcoming).

CHAPTER 3

History of Ideas

It is tempting to paint a picture of unseamed historical development of New Age from ancient times to the present day. This is often how New Agers themselves present their history, emphasising continuity with the past and rediscovery of hidden traditions that have been perpetuated esoterically. However, it is important not to overemphasise historical continuity in New Age. There are two ways of approaching the history of ideas: one is to examine the broad continuity and development of ideas throughout history, neglecting tangible historical events; the other is to examine in detail the physical history of personal influences and interactions within a given period. The first method misses much in historical detail, while the second method is so focused that it can miss larger trends.

In this chapter, I will try to indicate broad trends in the history of New Age ideas, moving back from the present to ancient and even mythical traditions; but there will also be reference to historical events and influences, to emphasise the fact that all ideas are transmitted through real people and happenings. At some times the account may therefore seem to brush over huge periods of history, connecting trends separated in time and geography; and the account may seem to be disjointed, jumping from one historical personage or group to another with little tangible historical evidence for a connection other than the similarity of the underlying ideas. The most useful picture lies in a combination of these methods in the history of ideas.

− POST-WAR −

The Penguin Book of New Age and Holistic Writing (Bloom ed. 2001), an anthology of New Age texts, was first published simply as *The Holistic Revolution* (2000): William Bloom, the editor, uses 'the two terms "holistic" and "New Age" interchangeably, as referring to the same general phenomenon . . . in the long-term . . . the phrase "New Age" will pass out of common usage as the culture inevitably becomes less new and as the significance of the term "holistic" becomes better appreciated' (Bloom ed. 2001: x–xi).

Holistic Health overlaps with New Age and in its own right is the immediate predecessor of New Age. Holistic Health crystallised into a discernible movement a decade or so earlier than New Age, and is now more mainstream. Evidence of this can be seen in the United Kingdom House of Lords Science and Technology Committee's Sixth Report of 21 November 2000 on complementary and alternative medicine (CAM) (part of Holistic Health), which considered CAM from the point of view of public health policy in the light of its increasing widespread acceptance by the public.

The varieties of holism as a philosophical viewpoint are mentioned in Chapter 4 and discussed in detail by Wouter Hanegraaff (1996). Essentially, the central idea is that to be healthy, fulfilled individuals, we need to be 'whole', that is, well rounded in body, mind and spirit. Whereas conventional notions of health concentrate on absence of illness and disease, Holistic Health is concerned with the whole person and their wellbeing. Conventional remedies may subdue medical afflictions, but they do not necessarily make a person feel 'whole' and healthy. Hence Holistic Health practitioners often turn to what are termed 'alternative' or, more recently, 'complementary' remedies. These include the panoply of traditional folk remedies from all traditions, along with more recent techniques. Chinese traditions are especially popular, such as acupuncture and herbal medicine, and may now be found on offer in some conventional medical establishments. Chiropractic, which manipulates the spine, is now also available on some health insurance schemes. Reiki, a Japanese practice where energy is channelled into the body, is extremely popular but not as mainstream. Other Holistic Health techniques include aromatherapy, where essential oils of plants are used to stimulate well-being; homeopathy, developed by Samuel Hahnemann (1755–1843), which uses 'potentised', minute dosages of toxins in order to effect a cure; Bach flower remedies, thirty-eight preparations first used in the 1930s; and reflexology, where meridian lines on the feet are massaged to heal other areas of the body. There are many more Holistic Health techniques, and new techniques are still being developed.

Hanegraaff (1996) distinguishes Holistic Health from 'Human Potential' (see Chapter 7), which emphasises psychological healing over physical healing. Human Potential is further subdivided by Hanegraaff into transpersonal psychology and a shamanic consciousness movement. While it is possible to discern trends in healing techniques according to these divisions, it is not clear how useful it is to describe these trends as 'movements'.

One well-documented new social movement that overlaps with New Age is the environmental movement, also known as the ecological movement (McCormick 1989). This movement has, since the political successes of Green parties across Europe from the 1980s and culminating in the Earth Summits of 1992 (Rio de Janeiro) and 2002 (Johannesburg), gained much mainstream acceptance. It may now seem strange to describe environmentally conscious policies such as sustainable development as 'alternative', but when they first entered the public conscious in the 1960s, that is what they were. Rachel Carson's *Silent Spring* (1962) powerfully evoked the spectre of a dawn without a chorus of birds due to the overuse of pesticides. More weighty reports followed, including *The Limits to Growth* (Meadows et al. 1972) from the so-called Club of Rome and *Blueprint for Survival* from *The Ecologist* magazine, published in the same year (*The Ecologist* 1972).

The early environmental movement overlapped with campaigns for nuclear disarmament. Greenpeace, a membership network which pioneered high-profile activism, was founded in the early 1970s and shot to the headlines with the sinking at Auckland, New Zealand in 1985 by the French intelligence service of the ship *Rainbow Warrior*, which was protesting over French nuclear tests at Mururoa Atoll, near Tahiti. Friends of the Earth, another environmental interest group, was founded by David Brower in 1969, a splinter movement from the Sierra Club, which had been founded way back in 1892. In the 1990s radical environmentalists in Britain developed a tradition of direct-action occupations of development sites, notably public road projects, with 'Swampy', real name Daniel Hooper, becoming a household name.

New Age has sometimes been described as the 1960s revisited (e.g. Dery 1996: 21). Wade Clark Roof et al. (1993) investigated the suggestion that New Age is a latter-day manifestation of 'baby boomer spirituality', that is to say, the spirituality of those born after the Second World War and before the assassination of President Kennedy, who had their formative teenage and young adult life in the 1960s. The similarities between the ideals of New Age and the ideals of the 1960s are obvious. Both are associated with alternative lifestyles and rejection of mainstream culture which involve, *inter alia*, Eastern religion and other non-conventional philosophies, radical politics, peace campaigning, feminism, 'coming out' and civil rights.

What happened in the 1960s has been the subject of both glorification by its protagonists – especially in the music business – and demonisation by its detractors – notably the New Right during the leaderships of Ronald Reagan and Margaret Thatcher. In many ways, the 1960s were the culmination of the trends of previous decades. Many women had been 'liberated' during the Second World War when they took up what had previously been 'male' roles. Youth emerged as a significant market force in the relative affluence of the 1950s and the expansion of the educational system, and was quickly condemned by its elders. Rock 'n' roll music also took off in the 1950s, with stars such as Elvis Presley, Little Richard and Bill Haley.

Stephen Kent (1993) has suggested that alternative spiritualities emerged in response to the decline of the anti-Vietnam War movement, when campaigners internalised their political radicalism out of disillusionment. American conscripts were selected by a lottery, and burning or otherwise avoiding the draft was a very visible form of protest. Open troop deployment began in 1965, and in response the first 'teach-ins' were organised in universities across America to inform students about the war. Demonstrations quickly crossed the Atlantic. In the United Kingdom, the anti-war protestors were building on the work of the popular Campaign for Nuclear Disarmament (CND), which had first been organised in 1958. CND gained notoriety with its Aldermaston marches, which attracted between 50,000 and 100,000 participants in each of the three years from 1959 to 1961, the majority of marchers being under the age of twenty-one. But there was never a strong anti-nuclear campaign in the United States, and in Britain, CND lost momentum in the 1970s.

The 1960s are also known as the era of the 'permissive society'. Above all, this meant sexual permissiveness, which was enabled by the advent of the female contraceptive pill, Enovid, which was declared safe for human use in 1960. By 1967 there were six million users in America, although take-up in Britain did not begin until the end of the decade. Hugh Hefner's *Playboy* empire started with the production of its first magazine in 1953 in Chicago. Some women fought back against the 'partner-swapping' mentality, with their own form of sexual liberation, typified in Germaine Greer's *The Female Eunuch* (1970). Homosexuality became more socially acceptable, with significant liberalisation in the legal consequences.

Drugs were an essential ingredient of the 1960s, reaching the height of their influence with the so-called 'summer of love' of 1967. The use of cannabis rocketed from the early 1960s, but remained illegal in both the USA and the United Kingdom despite concerted campaigns by users.[1] LSD – lysergic acid diethylamide-25 – was first manufactured in Switzerland in 1943, and continues to circulate on the black market. Use of LSD was promoted by Timothy Leary (1920–96), a Harvard academic who championed its spiritual effects and suffered imprisonment for his efforts. Aldous Huxley (1894–1963) documented his experiences on mescaline in *The Doors of Perception* (Huxley 1954), having met Humphry Osmond (b. 1917), who coined the term 'psychedelic' to mean 'mind-manifesting'.

The 1960s counterculture has been theorised by Theodore Roszak in *The Making of a Counter Culture* (1969) and Milton Yinger in *Countercultures* (1982). The question occurs as to what extent today's myth of the 1960s was ever grounded in reality, but it is undeniable that, whatever its truth, this myth has some currency in the historical tradition of New Age.

Perhaps the most durable legacy of the 1960s has been its music, but Jonathon Green argues (1999: 418–44) that the rock bands of the era were not heavily involved in its countercultural aspects. Nevertheless, the Beatles were associated in the popular press with the new permissiveness, along with the Rolling Stones, The Who, Jimi Hendrix, Pink Floyd and the Grateful Dead, among many others. The festivals at the end of the decade – famously, Woodstock (1969) and the Isle of Wight (1968–70) – evolved into the free festivals of the 1970s and the commercial events of the 1980s and 1990s, especially Glastonbury and rave culture. In this way, they led into the phenomenon of New Age travellers.

The festival scene may be traced to the US folk and jazz festivals, coming to the United Kingdom in the mid-1950s (Clarke 1982). The Woodstock festival of 1969 provided a new paradigm for such festivals. Kevin Hetherington, who completed a doctoral thesis on New Age travellers (Hetherington 1993), traces the travellers' historical origins to the free festivals of the 1970s, in turn a by-product of the 1960s hippie music and drug culture. Free festivals were both a critique of the commercialisation of 1960s music festivals and a result of the failure to organise, fence and thus successfully charge admission for commercial festivals.

The first Glastonbury free festival was held in 1971, although it was later to become a successful commercial venture continuing throughout the 1990s and into the new millennium.[2] The People's Free Festival was held in Windsor Great Park each year from 1972 to 1974, when it was stopped by the police. In 1975 the prehistoric monument at Stonehenge became the location for the free festival event of the year. From around this time, people began to travel between festivals in convoy, often in large old buses, camper vans and caravans.

Free festivals were often illegal and unregulated, occupying land without permission, breaching noise and health regulations and allowing open trading in drugs. In 1984, the police estimated that more than 30,000 people had attended the festival at Stonehenge. In response to complaints, the police attempted to prevent the 1985 festival at Stonehenge by stopping New Age travellers from getting to the monument. They used tactics developed in the miners' strike of 1984–5, with the result that the country lanes in Wiltshire came to a standstill. Legislation was passed in 1986 and 1994 in the United Kingdom which made festivals more difficult to hold legally.

Despite the new legislation, New Age travellers attempted to hold a festival at Stonehenge from 1987 to 1989. Around this time, festival culture was influenced by a new phenomenon, acid-house and warehouse parties, or 'raves', which were heavily drug influenced. In 1992 a rave with over 20,000 people was held in Castlemorton, Gloucesterhire, which attracted many New Age travellers. The 1994 legislation, however, effectively eradicated the free festival and rave tradition in Britain, with the result that many New Age travellers have moved into continental Europe (Hetherington 2000: 128–30). Since 2000, Stonehenge has again been opened for midsummer gatherings, but these have been heavily regulated and have not attracted much media attention.[3]

While New Age travellers and those interested in New Age spirituality are, in the popular conception, closely associated, it is far from clear why the two groups should share the same tag. New Age spirituality is not an essential part of New Age travellers' culture, although there are similarities between the two worldviews. My research has found few New Agers who have ever been New Age travellers, and in my interviews with those interested in New Age spirituality, people often distanced themselves from 'the travellers'. A member of the Findhorn Community, for example, comments 'The description by journalists of some groups of British travelling people as "new age" adds to the confusion. As far as we know these groups do not espouse any spiritual cause at all' (Walker ed. 1994: 24n1). According to Hetherington, travellers are just as likely to distance themselves from

New Age spirituality proper. However, Hetherington argues th
the term 'New Age' to describe both movements is apt (Hethe
2000: 12), since both share core values associated with individu
dom and expressivism. There is some overlap in sites of central significance, such as Stonehenge, Glastonbury and Totnes in South West
England. Many New Age spiritualities are of interest to some New Age
travellers – such as Paganism, the Druid tradition, astrology, Earth spiritualities and a 'back to nature' approach to living.

The best scholarly historical examination of New Age before the
1960s is contained in Steven Sutcliffe's *Children of the New Age*
(Sutcliffe 2002). Sutcliffe mentions a wealth of alternative spiritual
activity in Britain from the 1920s, including Theosophy, Anthroposophy,
New Thought, Christian Science and Frank Buchman's Oxford Group,
later renamed Moral Re-Armament (MRA).

It is significant that Peter and Eileen Caddy, founders of the Findhorn
Foundation, the New Age community in Scotland, first met in connection with MRA. 'Armchair religiosity' (Sutcliffe 1998: 38) is the
name Sutcliffe gives to this kind of 'seekership' (see Chapter 9). He
suggests it was driven by 'the wider print culture of periodicals, book
clubs, bookshops, publishers and lecture circuits' (ibid.: 38). Christoph
Bochinger (1995) has forwarded a similar thesis concerning the spread
of New Age ideas in contemporary Germany.

Sutcliffe (2002) examines the origins of the Findhorn Community.
Peter Caddy (1917–94) had a career in alternative spirituality, beginning
with the Rosicrucian Order, Crotona Fellowship and the works of
Alice Bailey. From 1947, Caddy followed society mystic Sheena Govan
(1912–67) (later marrying her) in a spirituality which was influenced by
the Evangelical Protestantism of her father John Govan, founder in
Scotland in 1886 of the Faith Mission. Govan's flat in Chelsea, London,
became a centre for a select few who 'raised vibrations', 'received messages' and attended to the 'Christ within' (Sutcliffe 1998: 52). Dorothy
Maclean, an initiate of Hazrat Inayat Khan's Western Sufi Order, and
Eileen Combe (later also to marry Caddy) joined Govan's circle.

The influence of Govan on the Caddys and Maclean is central to
understanding the spirituality of Findhorn as it emerged in the 1970s,
argues Sutcliffe, summarising Govan's group's characteristic traits as:
the functional marginality of the actors' life journeys; an interest in the
non-rational, inner, intuitional, esoteric or spiritual; the mutation of
sexual and marital relationships; women in positions of power; and
association in a small group rather than a denomination, sect or
movement (ibid.: 68).

Another important actor in these early days of New Age was Sir George Trevelyan (1906–96) (see Farrer 2002), who as principal of Shropshire Adult Education College at Attingham Park organised a number of courses in esoteric religion and compiled a mailing list of around 1,000 people for these courses. On his retirement in 1971, the Wrekin Trust continued this work. The Wrekin Trust survives to the present day, and still promotes the esoteric spiritualities Trevelyan was interested in.

Peter Caddy attended a weekend at Attingham Park in 1965 entitled 'The Significance of the Group in the New Age'. Sutcliffe speculates that the Attingham Park gathering

> more-or-less directly represented a wider constituency of New Age interest and affiliation in Britain in the mid-1960s. Some several hundred or more individuals in various informal interest groups and networks of a 'spiritual', religious, and recreational nature must have been involved . . . we might estimate that no more than a few hundred people were actively involved with Universal Link in Britain. The empirical influence of the Universal Foundation is even harder to gauge, but probably far slighter . . . we can estimate that the total figure of those engaged with New Age in Britain in the early-to-mid 1960s was not more than a few thousand. (Sutcliffe 1998: 92)

Actors in this milieu include Liebie Pugh (1888?–1966) and Anthony Brooke (b. 1912). Pugh experienced psychic visions of a Christ-like figure, and circulated a newsletter in the 1960s known as *Universal Link*, the mailing list for which was transferred to Findhorn on her death. Brooke and Monica Parish founded Universal Foundation in the mid-1960s to promote his lectures across the world on spiritual matters. Brooke was a 'close associate' of the early Findhorn community and also promoted Pugh's *Universal Link*. It was Brooke that introduced David Spangler's booklet *The Christ Experience and the New Age* to Findhorn, having met him in 1967.

In 1999 Channel 4 television in the UK ran a series of programmes entitled *Far Out: The Dawning of New Age Britain*, which uses oral history to present a history of New Age back to 1914. It is striking that the spiritual impact of the Second World War is significant to many of the respondents. Miriam Akhtar and Steve Humphries (1999) published an illustrated transcript of many of the testimonies, including brief accounts by Doreen Valiente, Benjamin Creme and Maclean. Although there is some evidence that other individuals interviewed, who are generally unknown to the public, saw themselves as part of a New Age – for example, The White Eagle Lodge is described as 'Church of the New Age' (Akhtar & Humphries 1999: 89) – Sutcliffe's thesis that New Age was used merely as an emblem in these times is perhaps more convincing. Further, it is not made clear why, for instance, a Hare Krishna devotee or the Brotherhood Church, a Christian anarchist community, should be regarded as New Age. Nevertheless, Akhtar and Humphries' is an invaluable introductory collection of primary material on this period of New Age broadly understood to include forms of Eastern mysticism, Spiritualism and other alternative lifestyles.

– PRE-WAR –

Spiritualism was at its height after the First World War and has been authoritatively studied by Geoffrey Nelson (1969a, 1969b). The Spiritualist movement had entered public consciousness with the famous spiritual 'rappings' heard by the Fox sisters from 1848 in Hydesville, New York. Prior to the Fox sisters, Andrew Jackson Davis (1826–1910) received communications from Galen and Emanuel Swedenborg (see below), publishing *The Principles of Natures, Her Divine Revelations, and a Voice to Mankind* in 1847. He had first encountered animal magnetism (see below) in 1843. Spiritualist séances involve communication via a medium with the spirit of a dead person, often a relative of a member of the audience, either verbally or through some other form of communication such as automatic writing or drawing. Spiritualism remains common today, and should be distinguished from New Age.

Soon after Spiritualism became popular, in 1862 Mary Baker G. Eddy (1821–1910) received healing for a nervous condition from Phineas Parkhurst Quimby (1802–66). Quimby coined the phrase 'Christian Science' but how much Eddy's system owes to Quimby is hotly disputed. The main distinction between the two systems is usually said to lie in the fact that Quimby used mesmerist direct-touch healing techniques, while Eddy's system is entirely mental.

Eddy's healing works by elimination of belief in a mortal world; only 'Divine Mind' has ultimate existence, and thus each of us consists entirely of Divine Mind. This entails the denial of the existence of evil. Nevertheless, Eddy had a paranoid fear of 'malicious animal magnetism' (MAM), a malign influence which is said to be directed at Christian Scientists by their enemies. MAM, or hypnotism, as it is also known, is belief in the real existence of things other than Divine Mind. Ontological monism, as belief in the sole existence of Divine Mind may be classified, also logically entails belief in the immortality of the soul. Christian Science grew through the establishment of churches and reading rooms and an international hierarchy and journal. Registered practitioners can perform healing for Christian Scientists.

New Thought grew in parallel to Christian Science. This movement of mental healers was very similar to Christian Science, but lacked the cohesive organisation of that movement. Many of its members derived their beliefs direct from Quimby and other mesmerists, or had previously been students of Eddy. The International New Thought Alliance (INTA) was created in London in 1914, and continues today. A distinguishing doctrinal difference between Christian Science and New Thought is that New Thought regards the mortal world as merely an educational means to greater understanding, not evil or merely illusory. Sickness, for New Thought, is an actual condition that may be healed by the power of the mind.

New Thought includes the Unity School of Christianity founded by Charles Fillmore (1854–1948) and his wife Myrtle, a student of Emma Curtis Hopkins (1853–1925), who was in turn a student of Eddy. *Modern Thought* magazine began in 1884, and in 1890 the Society of Silent Help, later Silent Unity, advocated distant healing through 'silent soul communion' (Braden [1963] 1966: 235). The United Church of Religious Science, Religious Science International and the International Divine Science Association are further examples in the New Thought tradition. Revd Nona Brooks (1861–1945), who co-founded Divine Science, also came to New Thought through healing by Hopkins. Malinda Cramer, however, claimed original inspiration for *Divine Science and Healing*, published in 1904. Divine Science Federation International united such independent Divine Science groups in 1957.

New Thought is by its sociological nature and philosophical approach very open to New Age. However, Melton et al. report (1991:347) that INTA and Association of Unity Churches speakers criticised the New Age Movement at conferences in the late 1980s. Christian Science too has preserved its boundaries with New Age. Although Christian Science has been represented at the New Age Mind-Body-Spirit Festival in London, for example, there was a distinct consciousness amongst the stallholders that this was part of an outreach programme to convert New Agers to Christian Science rather than an acknowledgement of the New Age nature of Christian Science.

Dell deChant (forthcoming), in a useful summary of the history of and relationship between New Thought and New Age, cites a survey in 1988 that found forty-four per cent of Unity churches (about 150) held *A Course in Miracles* (see Chapter 2) groups in their buildings.

The definitive study of New Thought was first provided by Charles Braden ([1963] 1966), whose work contains an extensive bibliography.

Around the same time that Christian Science and New Thought were becoming popular, Helena Petrovna Blavatsky (1831–91), a Russian emigrée, founded the Theosophical Society in New York in 1875. The large tomes of *Isis Unveiled* (2 vols, 1877) and *The Secret Doctrine* (2 vols, 1888) were received in communication from the Mahatmas, a spiritual group of masters directed by Lord of the World (formerly from Venus), who lives at Shamballa in the Gobi desert. Buddha, Jesus, Confucius, Plato, Manu and Maitreya are his helpers, with Master Morya or Master M., and Master Koot Hoomi or Master K. H.. The society's motto is 'There is no religion higher than Truth' and its aims are:

1. the formation of a universal human brotherhood without distinction of race, creed, sex, caste or colour;
2. the encouragement of studies in comparative religion, philosophy and science; and
3. the investigation of unexplained laws of nature and the powers latent in man.

(Quoted in Washington 1993: 69)

Blavatsky crystallised the occult and cultic milieu at the turn of the century. She influenced, among others, Evelyn Underhill (1875–1941), author of *Mysticism* (1911), which is still found in New Age bookshops; Anna Kingsford (1846–88), who gave lectures on the 'new gospel' proclaiming reincarnation, published as *The Perfect Way; or, the Finding of Christ*; Annie Besant (1847–1933), author of *Esoteric Christianity*; and Revd Charles Leadbeater (1854–1934), a bishop in the Liberal Catholic Church. Besant and Leadbeater championed the cause of Jiddu Krishnamurti (1895–1986), an Indian boy, as World Teacher or Maitreya and future Mahatma from 1911 through the Order of the Rising Sun, later the Order of the Star in the East. Krishnamurti eventually rejected this position to create a following as a spiritual teacher in his own right.

Leadbeater's promotion of Krishnamurti led to the breakaway of Rudolf Steiner (1861–1925), leader of the German Theosophists, from the Theosophical Society in 1909. In 1913 Steiner formed the Anthroposophy movement. Steiner believed that the Christ spirit had descended into Jesus of Nazareth because humankind had lost contact with the spiritual realm. Now the Christ seeks to 'mass incarnate' into all humankind, in the real 'second coming'.

Alice Bailey (1880–1949), another follower of Blavatsky, is credited by William Bloom, a leader of New Age in Britain, and others with inventing the modern meaning of the term 'New Age'. In 1919 she contacted the spiritual entity, The Tibetan, or Djwhal Khul, from whom much of her vast corpus was communicated. Bailey founded the Arcane School in 1923, and this is still a vibrant movement with a correspondence course consisting of suggested readings from Bailey's works with 'seed meditations' for individual work. She also founded a number of other groups, including the New Group of World Servers, World Goodwill, Triangles and Lucis Trust.

Two further new religious movements that are important predecessors of New Age, and yet remain outside the Spiritualist, Christian Science and Theosophical movements, include Gurdjieff's Work and the Hermetic Order of the Golden Dawn.

George Ivanovich Gurdjieff[4] (1866?–1949) was born on the Russian–Armenian border and travelled extensively through North East Africa and the Middle and Far East, returning to Russia around 1911. He taught a cosmological and psychological system of ideas which, together with sacred dancing and manual labour, formed the basis of his teaching at his Institute for the Harmonious Development of Man, near Paris. Founded in 1922, it was fully active till 1924, when he began to put his teaching into written form. Gurdjieff made at least eight visits to America, establishing his teaching in New York and Chicago.

In Search of the Miraculous (1987) gives an account by Gurdjieff's pupil P. D. Ouspensky of the first seven years of Gurdjieff's teaching. First published posthumously in 1949, it has probably been more widely read than Gurdjieff's own texts, most of which were likewise published posthumously, between 1950 and 1975 (Gurdjieff 1950, 1963, 1975). Gurdjieff's teaching, known as the Work, has had an important influence on New Age, combining and connecting with other new religious movements, and giving rise to independent teachings on the Enneagram of personality (see Chapter 5). For the reader who wishes to know more about Gurdjieff and his work, Moore (1991) expresses the 'myth' of his life, using extensive quotations from Gurdjieff's and other writings. Wellbeloved (2002) explores the Theosophical, modernist and oral traditions which influenced Gurdjieff's writings and gives an analysis of his major text. Wellbeloved (2003) is an accessible dictionary of Gurdjieff's teaching terms.

The Hermetic Order of the Golden Dawn was founded in 1888 by William Wynn Westcott (1848–1925), Samuel Liddell MacGregor Mathers (1854–1918) and William R. Woodman (1828–91), all three Freemasons. Famous members included W. B. Yeats (1865–1939), the poet, who also joined the Theosophical Society; Aleister Crowley (1875–1947), the black magician notorious for his sex magic; and Dion Fortune (Violet Penry-Evans, née Firth) (1891–1946), who later founded the Fraternity of the Inner Light. The Golden Dawn was a ritualistic magical lodge, based on the Qabbalah with Christian and Eastern input, and structured hierarchically with secret chiefs, inner and outer orders and ten initiatory grades related to the Qabbalistic Tree of Life.

Two well-written historical enquiries which bring this pre-War period of alternative spiritualities to life are Martin Green's *Prophets of a New Age* (1992) (see further Chapter 7), and his *Mountain of Truth: The Counterculture Begins* (1986), which examines the loose community at Ascona, Switzerland, from 1900 to 1920. Green has a broad understanding of New Age, which he applies to revolutionary radicalism throughout modern history. New Age phenomena are said to occur in all periods, although Green reserves usage of the term to describe periods when they are unusually concentrated, such as 1880–1910 and 1960–90. This diachronic conception of New Age is not common in New Age studies, and indeed Green is not influential in this respect, but his understanding of the notion, based on detailed historical research, is a useful counterbalance to Steven Sutcliffe's dismissal of the term (see Chapter 10).

– PRE-INDUSTRIAL –

Mary Baker Eddy, Phineas Parkhurst Quimby and Andrew Jackson Davis all ultimately derived their theories of animal magnetism from the work of Franz Anton Mesmer (1734–1815), who is now also claimed as a progenitor of conventional psychotherapy and psychodynamic psychology. Thus on important counts, Mesmer may be considered as significant in the history of New Age ideas. Mesmer healed his patients through the removal of blockages in the circulation of magnetic fluids, manifested by *crises* (French for 'attacks' or 'fits'). In 1784, the French Royal Academy of Sciences and the Paris Faculty of Medicine were commissioned to investigate mesmeric healing. The commissioners, who included Benjamin Franklin, found no evidence for Mesmer's magnetic fluid and claimed instead the results were explicable by the imaginations of his patients.

Christoph Bochinger (1995: 520–4) claims that William Blake (1757–1827), a near contemporary of Mesmer, was the first to use the term in today's sense. Wouter Hanegraaff (1996: 95–6) acknowledges that Blake may have been the first to speak of a New Age with an esoteric meaning, but counters that this is not sufficient to credit Blake as a historical precursor of contemporary New Age. Nevertheless, Blake's poetry is often cited by New Agers, and is in many respects similar in outlook. Furthermore, Kathleen Raine, in *Blake and Tradition* (1968), argues that Blake was inspired by 'the tradition', which Désirée Hirst (1964) has described as 'the hidden stream', of Neoplatonic, hermetic, Qabbalistic and Boehmenist thought (see below). Yet there is little hard historical evidence that Blake had actually read at first hand any authors from such traditions; his knowledge of the traditions may have been derived from immersion in popular culture. In this way, Blake's spirituality is similar to the New Ager's spirituality in that it is reminiscent of many historical movements without owing any firsthand historical debts to them.

In *Witness against the Beast* (1993), E. P. Thompson suggests that Blake knew of the Muggletonian sect through his mother's influence. The followers of Ludowick Muggleton (1609–98) were unorthodox Christians with leanings to Ranting, Quakerism and Boehmenism. They were anti-authoritarian and anticlerical, meeting in pubs and singing hymns to contemporary tunes. They saw Satan as the God of Reason, just as Blake identified Jehovah with his mythical character Urizen ('your reason' – depicted on the cover of this book).

Blake was at one point a member of a Swedenborgian church in London, where the first independent Swedenborgian congregation was established in the 1780s. The Swedenborg Society was formed in 1810 and still advertises in the New Age Mind-Body-Spirit Festival magazine. The New Jerusalem Church is now known simply as the New Church, and regards Swedenborg's writings as divinely revealed. Swedenborg has influenced many New Age writers both directly and indirectly through authors such as Ralph Waldo Emerson (1803–82).

Emanuel Swedenborg (1688–1772) was the son of a Lutheran bishop. His early career was as a successful scientist, before he turned to anatomy and underwent a religious crisis, documented in his *Journal of Dreams* (1743–4). Thirty volumes of religious writings followed, including the eight-volume *Arcana Coelestia* and four-volume *Apocalypsis Explicata*. *On Heaven and Hell*, written in 1758, is perhaps his best-known theological work. Swedenborg's writings were based on personal experiences which revealed the imminent commencement of a fifth age, which would be a new age of reason and truth in religion. He understood this revelation to be the Second Coming. Each of the five ages was said to begin with divine revelation and decline into corruption.

Another influence on Blake, Jacob Boehme (1575–1624), by profession a shoemaker and small-time merchant, was jailed for the publication of his first mystical book, *Aurora*. He taught the existence of two parallel worlds, the first an eternal, celestial heaven, the second this earth, features of both of which are to be found in human nature. The second nature, which is chaotic, will be destroyed to reveal the glorious first nature. God is thus born into the hellish worlds, revealing himself, or rather his perfect twin, Sophia (Greek for 'wisdom') to us through his works in a seven-part cycle. Humans will be reborn in the heavenly world in a second birth, he taught, and a new age would be revealed on this world when the celestial nature was realised. Boehme's thought attracted a following around John Pordage (1608–81) and the Philadelphian Society, and Arthur Versluis (1999) has described a 'Christian esoteric tradition' around Boehme.

Before Boehme was known as a mystic, Giordano Bruno (1548–1600), an Italian polymath and occultist, devised memory techniques and advocated a post-Copernican infinite universe of multiple worlds. Giordano is the name he adopted as a Dominican, with whom he was ordained in 1572. After a colourful career lecturing and advising in the universities and courts of France, England and Germany he returned to Italy in 1591, where he was denounced to the Venetian Inquisition the following year for heresy before being extradited to Rome. Frances Yates (1964) depicts Bruno as a key Elizabethan occult figure in the tradition of pseudo-Hermes Trismegistus (see below), where his affinities with New Age may be clearly identified.

Paracelsus (Philippus Aureolus Theophrastus Bombastus von Hohenheim) (1493–1541) was a strong influence on Boehme. He is said to have attended the universities at Basel, Tübingen, Vienna, Wittenberg, Leipzig, Heidelberg, and Cologne, and to have travelled throughout Europe, Russia, Egypt, Arabia and the Holy Land in his search for what were in his time unconventional medical cures. His adopted name means 'above or beyond Celsus', a famous early Roman physician, and for a few years between 1524 and 1528 he enjoyed renown as a doctor and lecturer at Basel, returning to fame after a further period of wandering with the publication in 1536 of *Der Größen Wundartzney*. Paracelsus was a successful physician, documenting syphilis and suggesting a mercurial treatment, for example, and is best known in New Age circles for anticipating homeopathy by advocating administration of toxins in small doses.

Heinrich Cornelius Agrippa von Nettesheim (1486–1535) expounded his Qabbalistic, numerological and magical philosophy in

De Occulta Philosophia (1510–33). Despite publishing around 1530 'Of the Vanitie and uncertaintie of artes and sciences', an attack on occultism and other sciences, Agrippa was jailed for his heretical beliefs and is chiefly remembered in New Age circles for his magical system.

Meister Eckhart (c. 1260–1327/8) was a Dominican theologian and mystic, whose writings were found to contain heretical propositions and who was condemned by a bull of Pope John XXII in 1329. During his lifetime, however, Eckhart was a successful scholar, preacher and administrator. Robert Forman (1991) distils Eckhart's teachings into an evolutionary system of transformative experiences, beginning with attachment to worldly objects in the fallen state, through letting go of these attachments and attaining detachment, untroubled by the world. The fourth and final stage is rapture or mystical experience, which if experienced permanently can be described as a breakthrough to the Godhead.

The unorthodox Christian sect known as the Cathars (from the Greek for 'pure') have been the subject of much esoteric speculation. Most famously, Arthur Guirdham claimed in *The Cathars and Reincarnation* (Guirdham 1970) that some of his friends were reincarnations of Cathars. A scholarly introduction to Cathar history is found in Stoyanov (2000: 186–216). The Cathars or Cathari arose in the twelfth century CE, with the first report of a Cathar bishop dating from 1143 in Cologne. Catharism was established among the aristocracy in Languedoc, southern France, by the end of the twelfth century, perhaps partly due to Cathar anticlericalism, which allowed the nobles to usurp land and tithes from the Catholic Church. Cathars were anathematised in a papal decree of 1184. A Cathar Council met at St-Félix, near Toulouse, sometime between 1166 and 1176 to institute Cathar bishops and dioceses. At its height, Catharism stretched from the Rhineland to Lombardy.

Cathars who had received initiation or spiritual baptism by the laying on of hands, *consolamentum*, wore a black robe and were known by their coreligionists as *perfecti*, practising strict asceticism including abstention from sex and meat eating. The *consolamentum* reunited the soul, which had become lost in the evil material world, with its heavenly spirit. Cathars believed that the evil demiurge was inferior to the Father God. Following the Council at St-Félix, Catharism tended to an absolute dualism under Papa Nicetas, bishop of Constantinople.

The Languedoc Cathars were severely persecuted, with public burnings of *perfecti*, by northern French nobleman under the authority of

Pope Innocent III in the Albigensian Crusade of 1208 and subsequent inquisitions by Dominicans. The final bastion of Languedoc Catharism was the castle at Montségur, which fell in 1244 with the burning of over 200 Cathars.

It may be difficult to see how this potted history of Western esotericism relates to New Age. Claims sometimes encountered among New Agers that there is direct historical continuity should be rejected. The most detailed historical examination of Western esotericism in relation to New Age has been undertaken by Hanegraaff (1996), who further suggests that New Age has resulted from the secularisation of Western esotericism through the impact of theories of causality; evolution; the study of religions and theosophy; the psychologisation of occultism; and the capitalist market economy (Hanegraaff 2002). Similarly, Hill (1993) argues that New Age is not new because its features – individualism, idealisation of human personality, tolerance, syncretism, monism and empowerment of individuals – have been seen in earlier forms of alternative spiritualities. Possamaï (2001) counters that New Age is a new development in esotericism, mainly because of the renewed importance in everyday-life practice of knowledge of the self, what he calls the Human Potential Ethic.

– ANCIENT –

There is some evidence that Cathars derived their views from Bogomils and Paulicians, and thence perhaps even from ancient Gnostic sects (see Stoyanov 2000). Raschke (1980) and Zoccatelli (1998), among many others, claim that New Age is a contemporary form of Gnosticism. Both are salvation religions with sharp dichotomies between spirit and matter, radical ethics, an openness to new revelations, an open canon of religious texts, and both give the individual self central importance.

Gnosis, the Greek word for 'knowledge', is a form of spiritual awareness that has been carefully studied by Dan Merkur in *Gnosis: an Esoteric Tradition of Mystical Visions and Unions* (1993). It has been defined as 'knowledge of the divine mysteries reserved for an elite';[5] Merkur describes it as 'an esoteric practice of visionary and unitive mysticism' (ibid.: 116). Gnosis was key to a large number of religious groups in the Mediterranean arena around the turn of the Common Era, into the fourth century CE, and perhaps beyond. Their origins may be found in Judaism, although this is disputed (Filoramo 1992: 144–6). They were perceived as a threat by what became the orthodox catholic

Church, and one of the most important sources for our knowledge of gnosis is a Christian heresiologist, Irenaeus, Bishop of Lyons (c. 140/50–200 CE), in his *Adversus Haereses*. More recently, the collection of texts found at Nag Hammadi in Egypt have added to our knowledge of the people who sought gnosis.

The Nag Hammadi library contains thirteen books with fifty-three texts (some of which are not core Gnostic writings), including *Apocryphon of James*, *Apocalypse of Adam*, *Hypostasis of the Archons*, *Trimorphic Protennoia* and *Zostrianos*. They include secret revelations, letters, treatises, prayers and gospels, many attributed (as was common in the ancient world) to famous Christian personages. Perhaps the most commonly cited Gnostic text in New Age is the *Gospel of Thomas*, a collection of hidden sayings by Jesus which are said to have been compiled by Didymus Jude Thomas. The earliest manuscripts date from c. 200 CE, but otherwise it is difficult to pinpoint the origin of the text. Similarities to the canonical gospels, especially those of Luke and Matthew, may be found in many of the sayings.

Valentinus (*fl.* 150 CE) is one of the best-known Gnostic leaders and teachers, both from hostile sources and extant texts. Educated in Alexandria, he taught in Rome and was considered for the papacy before being denounced as heretical. According to Irenaeus,[6] Valentinus' student, Ptolemy, taught that there is a male principle called Pre-Father or Deep, and a female principle known as Thought, Silence or Grace. Among many unions to constitute the divine pleroma (Greek for 'fullness' or 'perfection'), Silence is inseminated by Deep and bears Mind and Truth. Mind begets Word and Life, who in turn produce Human and Church. In all, there are thirty principles, known as aeons or eternities, in the pleroma. Only Mind after Deep and Silence could understand Deep. Wisdom, the last aeon, sought to experience Deep without her consort Desired, and was stopped by Limit or Cross. However, this effort had given birth to an imperfect essence, Achamoth (from the Hebrew for 'wisdom') which was therefore thrown out of the pleroma by Limit. Christ and Holy Spirit were then born to Mind, to re-order the other aeons, who created Jesus. Christ brings Achamoth back to the pleroma. Achamoth produces the soul of the cosmos and fashions the lower demiurge or creator God. The demiurge does not know the Deep nor even Achamoth and so claims to be God (Isaiah 45: 5): it is this God that conventional Christians were thought by Gnostics to worship, rather than Deep. The demiurge went on to create human beings, but unknowingly included a spiritual spark.

Irenaeus wrote that Ptolemy divided believers into the spiritual Valentinians, who will be saved independently of their ethical behaviour; the psychical Christians, who should be ascetic in order to be saved; and the material Pagans, who will not be saved.

It is impossible to reconcile all these texts – as well as other Gnostic sources – into a united religious vision. Indeed, Michael Allen Williams (1996) has argued that we need to 'rethink Gnosticism' and dismantle the category. For the word 'Gnosticism' is a modern invention; nobody in antiquity described themselves as belonging to a movement of Gnosticism. Williams demonstrates that Gnostics may be seen as parasites or innovators; anticosmic world rejecters or sociocultural accommodators; haters of the body or perfectors of the human; ascetics or libertines; deterministic elitists or inclusivists. Such arguments sound very similar to arguments about the status of contemporary New Age. Just as with Gnosticism, so very few people actually describe themselves as New Age; and each of Williams' above-mentioned contrasting attributes applies equally well to New Agers of various ilk.

The Gnostic aeons were related to the known planets, which form the basis of all systems of astrology. Many newspapers today contain brief astrological horoscopes foretelling the prospects for people born under the influence of these twelve zodiacal star signs, which are in fact derived from the ancient understanding of the movements of the planets, the sun and the moon in relation to the earth. Astrology is one of the most popular mantic arts in New Age, reflecting its longstanding tradition, which dates at least to the civilisation of Sumeria in 4300 BCE, and probably earlier still (see e.g. Campion 1994). Another ancient tradition that impacts on New Age is the Hermetic tradition, associated with the Emerald Tablet and the legendary Hermes Trismegistus, influenced by the traditions around the Greek god Hermes and Thoth, the Egyptian god of wisdom.

– Mythical –

New Age does not share the concerns of Western historiography over historical factuality. If something is true for the individual, that is all that matters in New Age. Such an approach to history widens the scope of cultures that can be admired and used as role models. New Agers have no methodological problems citing the (historically questionable) practices of ancient Celts, Essenes, Egyptians, Atlanteans or even aliens in order to justify their New Age position today.

For example, there is a strong Celtic tradition in New Age that is also popular in many Christian churches. Yet our knowledge of pre-Christian Celtic culture is minimal, if we limit ourselves to sources valued by conventional scholarship. New Agers, however, have rebuilt a whole Celtic tradition which has then been adopted as a spirituality more ancient, and therefore more appropriate, than Christianity or other later traditions. One important example of such reclamation is the widespread celebration of solar and lunar festivals, from the winter solstice through Oimelc to the spring equinox, to Beltain, the summer solstice, Lughnasadh, the autumn equinox and Samhain. However, as Hutton (1991) has shown, there is little evidence for the celebration of these festivals in ancient Britain. Marion Bowman describes such speculation as 'Reinventing the Celts' (Bowman 1993; see also Bowman 1995): 'You can choose to be Celtic if it feels right for you: spiritual nationality is a matter of elective affinity' (Bowman 1995: 145).

Similarly, the Essenes are strong cultural markers in New Age. Matthew Wood, for example, has studied a New Age group known as the Essene Meditation (Wood 1999), which explicitly calls upon this inter-Testamental sect as a role model for their current spiritual practices (see Chapter 9). Since Helena Petrovna Blavatsky, there has been a popular notion that Jesus was a member of the Essenes, tracing his teachings to Pythagoras, the Egyptians and Buddhists. Reender Kranenborg, however, has examined the presentation of the Essenes in Western esotericism (Kranenborg 1998) and concluded that 'The ideas about the Essenes are a product of Western esotericism which have little, if any, historical validity' (ibid.: 245). Kranenborg acknowledges that the historical existence of the Essenes is 'beyond any doubt' (ibid.: 248) – they were a Jewish sect originating approximately 167 BCE and possibly had some connection with the Dead Sea Scrolls, which were discovered in Qumram. Modern esoteric ideas about the sect, however, are traced by Kranenborg to Karl Friedrich Bahrdt (1741–92) and earlier writers.

Another culture that is popular in New Age circles is the ancient Egyptian tradition, and more specifically, the pyramids. Pyramids are credited with special preservatory powers – for example, in a Mind-Body-Spirit festival I encountered a salesman selling 'Pymats', which are cloths printed with a picture of a pyramid to put under your pillow at night in order to facilitate more healthy sleep. Peter Lemesurier (1990) is one of the better-known exemplars of an esoteric tradition, popular in New Age, which reads history and predicts the future from the dimensions of the Great Pyramid.

Other cultures that are valued by New Age include those of Atlantis and Lemuria. These are said to be lost continents once inhabited by an advanced civilisation that communicated telepathically. Again part of the Western esoteric tradition, these cultures were popularised by Blavatsky and remain influential in New Age.

An interesting question is why certain cultures are valued above others in New Age. For example, the Nilitic Nuer have been famously documented by Edward Evans-Pritchard, but his works are not part of the New Age canon. Similarly the Trobriander Islanders have been documented by Bronisław Malinowski, but their culture is not assimilated by New Agers. Conversely, another great, early work of anthropology, James Frazer's *The Golden Bough* (1890) is greatly revered in some Pagan quarters.

The final example of mythical cultures having an influence on New Age that I will give here is that of aliens, that is, extraterrestrial cultures. There is a great industry in alien literature, from pictures of UFOs to accounts of alien abductions and conspiracies to take over the world. Aliens have even become mainstream, in popular films such as the *Alien* series and the television series *The X-Files*. That New Age should be so open to the influence of alien culture is not surprising when put alongside the influence of channelled entities and other discarnate beings in New Age. It is part of the importance given to individual experience above traditional, scientific measures of factuality. Consequently, if a New Ager experiences an alien being, this is all that matters to them. Studies of UFO spirituality include James R. Lewis's *Encyclopedic Sourcebook of UFO Religions* (Lewis ed., forthcoming b) and *The Gods Have Landed: New Religions from Other Worlds* (Lewis ed. 1995).

– CONCLUSION –

This chapter begins firmly in the discipline of scholarly historiography, with descriptions of Holistic Health and the 1960s, New Age travellers, the Children of the New Age at Findhorn, and earlier movements such as Theosophy, Christian Science, Swedenborgianism, Blake and Boehme. Somewhere after these well-documented historical traditions, perhaps even as early as our understanding of Meister Eckhart, mythological traditions become more dominant. The Cathars, Gnostics, Celts, Essenes, Egyptians – are all historical societies or groups, but historical evidence is less substantial and mythologising is more influential. With Atlantis, Lemuria and alien traditions, we are of course firmly within New Age mythologies.

Tracing the history of New Age ideas sometimes blurs the distinction between etic scholarship and emic mythologising. Of course there are historical precursors to contemporary New Age ideas – this is a tautological premise. Historiography, however, must draw a line between describing probable historical antecedents of New Age ideas – even when tangible historical evidence of direct influence is difficult to unearth – and the sort of New Age propaganda exercise that attempts to reveal hidden esoteric lineages preserving a perennial tradition intact from ancient and mythical times – or even outside the history of the Earth.

– NOTES –

1. In May 2002, a report from the Home Affairs Committee of MPs recommended that cannabis be downgraded in the UK from class B to class C, but did not call for legalisation or decriminalisation. As this book went to press, changes were not expected to come into effect until 2004.
2. The Glastonbury Festival did not take place in 2001 due to concerns over an alleged breach of the local authority licence during the 2000 festival, but resumed again in 2002.
3. See e.g. *The Independent*, 22 June 2002, where it was reported that 22,000 'revellers' welcomed the summer solstice at Stonehenge, with eleven arrests. 'English Heritage had allowed the celebrations on condition that people did not bring in glass bottles or fireworks and did not climb on the stones.' There were few reports in broadsheet newspapers in 2003.
4. I am most grateful to Sophia Wellbeloved for assistance with this section on Gurdjieff.
5. An international colloquium at Messina, Italy, in 1966, quoted in Merkur (1993: 111).
6. As summarised in Williams (1996: 14–18).

CHAPTER 4

Philosophy

Philosophy is about thinking logically and critically around a subject. Philosophy was the first science to emerge in the ancient Greek world, and still today higher degrees in many disciplines retain the title 'Ph.D.' or 'doctorate in philosophy'. Philosophy can be engaged in without much empirical or first-hand knowledge of the subject under discussion – this is both its strength and its Achilles' heel.

There is no one such thing as New Age philosophy, though there are many examples of New Age philosophies. Christian critics of New Age and philosophers commenting on New Age often speak of 'the New Age worldview', but the reality is that there are as many New Age worldviews as there are New Agers. Olav Hammer (forthcoming) suggests that this diversity of philosophical positions in New Age is a result of the fact that it is written by entrepreneurs from within the cultic milieu: committed New Agers establish themselves as experts within a particular field (such as astrology, healing or tarot) and work as self-employed practitioners rather than as part of a regulated profession. Of course, in line with the polythetic definition or family resemblance model of New Age outlined in Chapter 1, these New Age philosophies do share many similarities as well as many differences. This chapter seeks to explore some of the common core family members of New Age philosophical worldviews.

Another caveat is that, while the themes outlined in this chapter are of common concern among many New Agers, they may not be articulated in the ways presented here. This chapter uses technical philosophical terminology, and while many New Agers are well educated (indeed, Kemp (2003a) found that up to half of New Age Christian respondents had completed a further degree or professional qualification), not all New Agers express their beliefs in philosophical language. Nevertheless, these beliefs may be analysed usefully as expressing the essential ideas underlying such philosophical terminology and, as seen in the previous chapter, there may be direct historical debts to some of the movements of thought mentioned here.

There are two distinct groups of philosophical analysis of New Age. The first analysis to appear, historically, was the Christian rationalist critique, which was constructed with explicit reference to the heresiological writings of the Fathers of the Church. A more objective philosophical analysis of New Age did not appear until 1995, when Wouter Hanegraaff completed his doctoral thesis on the subject, and this remains the main example of such an analysis. In this chapter I will seek to combine the insights of both approaches. (Other rationalist approaches, including those of Basil (ed. 1988), Gordon (1988), Hess (1993) and Gardner (1988, 1996), are less philosophically structured and are considered in Chapter 8.)

Douglas Groothuis published a very popular Evangelical series on New Age in the 1980s (Groothuis 1986, 1988, 1990). Building on previous critiques of New Age by fellow Christians, he defined New Age according to its treatment of articles of Christian doctrine. His analysis was therefore akin to the debates in the ancient world between Christians and non-Christians. Groothuis summarises the constituent elements of New Age philosophies in the following table:

Table 4.1   New Age beliefs according to Groothuis

	New Age
1. Metaphysics	God is the world, pantheism
	God is impersonal/amoral
	All is spirit/consciousness, monistic
2. Epistemology	Man is all things, truth within
3. Ethics	Autonomous and situational (relative)
4. Nature of Humans	Spiritual being, a sleeping God
5. Human Problems	Ignorance of true potential
6. Answer to Human Problems	Change of consciousness
7. History	Cyclical
8. Death	Illusion, entrance to next life (reincarnation)
9. View of Religion	All point to the One (syncretism)

(from Groothuis 1986: 167)[1]

Hanegraaff (1996), meanwhile, structures his analysis of New Age with the following concepts: holism and evolution; meta-empirical and human beings; the philosophy of mind; death and survival; good and evil; visions of the past; and the idea of a New Age.

If we combine the insights of both apologetic and philosophical approaches, the following themes emerge as key considerations in the discussion of New Age worldviews: fundamental metaphysics; understanding of God, human nature and meta-empirical beings; notion and means of salvation, and understanding of death; concept of history and the idea of a New Age. These will each now be considered in turn, before final consideration of another common philosophical theme in relation to New Age, namely postmodernism.

– METAPHYSICS –

It is a common New Age observation (e.g. Capra 1982) that most Westerners view the world in the way set out by René Descartes (1596–1650): a fundamental metaphysical dualism, with a strict division between the spiritual and the material. Descartes outlined this philosophical system in his *Discourse on Method* and *The Meditations*, which employed the methodology of mechanical rationalism. New Agers often use this observation on Western metaphysics to call for a return to a pre-Cartesian worldview, what Thomas Kuhn (1962) called a 'paradigm shift'. Indeed, Lynn White Jr (1967) has claimed that Cartesian dualism is to blame for the present ecological crisis. While it is not necessary for philosophers to join in this call for a change in worldview, it is probably correct to typify in general terms conventional metaphysics as dualist and mechanical, and New Age metaphysics as monist and holistic.

Monism is the idea that there is just one substance underlying the many objects we see in the world. For example, rocks, trees and humans may be understood to be simply manifestations of a more real substratum of 'spirit', out of which everything is made. This contrasts with the more conventional Cartesian worldview that reality consists of dual substances, one tangible and the other spiritual; and with the materialist view (also, paradoxically, a form of monism) that all objects are reducible to subatomic particles and there is no spiritual substance.

Holism (sometimes, especially earlier, spelt 'wholism') is a modern word for a worldview which claims ancient roots. It is the idea that for anything to be 'healthy', the whole perspective must be taken. Holism is often encountered in healing movements, where it espouses the notion that the whole person must be treated: body, mind and spirit. But holism is also the root philosophy underlying the modern ecological movement, which is a concern for the whole environment rather than one (human) species within it. The phrase 'the whole is greater than the sum of its parts' is a key holistic concept; contrast this with mechanical rationalism, which breaks down large entities into individual parts for analysis.

Hanegraaff (1996) provides a detailed exposition of both monism and holism, identifying a number of distinctions within these philosophical trends. Holism is defined, according to Hanegraaff, in common opposition to non-holistic views, particularly dualism and reductionism. These are further defined as: the distinction between creator and creation, between man and nature, and between spirit and matter; the tendency to fragmentation; and the tendency to reduce spirit to matter. Hanegraaff argues:

> Holism can be conceived in abstract terms as: 1. based on the possibility of reducing all manifestations to one 'ultimate source'; 2. based on the universal interrelatedness of everything in the universe; 3. based on a universal dialectic between complementary polarities; 4. based on the analogy of the whole of reality, or of significant subsystems with organisms. (ibid.: 120, original emphasis removed)

Since Hanegraaff's discipline is the history of ideas, it is hardly surprising that one of his central tools of analysis comes from A. O. Lovejoy: the distinction between this-worldliness and other-worldliness. Hanegraaff further distinguishes 'strong other-worldliness', which regards the world as an illusion; a position which accepts this world is real but claims it ought never to have come into existence; and those who refuse to discuss the nature of the world because this is irrelevant to the aim of salvation. This-worldliness is divided into 'strong this-worldliness', which includes many Pagans, and 'weak this-worldliness', which envisages a better 'this world' either on this Earth (i.e. millenarianism) or beyond death. Most typical of New Age, according to Hanegraaff, is weak this-worldliness – this world is regarded as a place for learning and growth.

– GOD AND BEINGS –

There is no one New Age God or pantheon. Indeed, it may even be possible to be New Age without believing in the existence of any God or gods at all. The theological position of New Agers ranges from scientific atheism through agnosticism, primeval animism, Pagan polytheism, Judeo-Christian-Islamic monotheism to a compromising panentheism and full Eastern pantheism. Virtually any position on the nature and existence of God and or the gods is possible from a New Age perspective. Christian critics often claim that New Agers are by definition pantheist, but this is by no means true of all New Agers. In this section, I will give some examples of the wide spectrum of New Age views on the nature of God.

Kemp (2003a) compares the beliefs about God of three New Age Christian groups with statistics from a New Age lecture series, Alternatives (York 1995), two evangelical Anglican congregations and available national statistics.

Table 4.2 *What do you believe God is?*[a]

What is God?	Christaquarian	Alternatives	Evangelical
Real personality	18	6	58
Fiction	1	0	2
Impersonal force	19	33	17
Personality and force	2	-	2
Don't know	5	13	2
Other	53	52	17
No answer	2	-	2

(adapted from Kemp 2003a, citing York 1995 for Alternatives)

[a] Figures expressed as a percentage of the total return. Return and sample size: Christaquarians 286/601 = 48%; Alternatives 48/121 = 40%; Evangelical 53/114 = 46%. Columns do not necessarily total 100% owing to rounding of figures.

What emerges from this analysis is that New Age-oriented groups are less likely than the comparative Evangelical congregations to view God as a real personality. The view of God as a real personality is held by roughly the same number of New Age-oriented believers as the view of God as an impersonal force. The most common description of God for the New Age groups could not fit into any of these categories, while for the Evangelical dataset, this indecision or non-alignment was considerably less marked. This gives some indication of the range and variety of individual New Agers' understandings of God.

Donahue's consideration (1993) of the 'Prevalence and Correlates of New Age Beliefs in Six Protestant Denominations' is one of the first published statistical enquiries into New Age. The most common image of God was panentheism (the belief that all is in God, and God is in all), held by between thirty-nine and forty-nine per cent of the six congregations; twenty-four to thirty-four per cent subscribed to theism; and between six and thirteen per cent to pantheism. However, neither pantheism nor panentheism correlated with the seven New Age beliefs that were tested.

I have not encountered in the literature on New Age any acknowl-edgement that New Agers do not have to believe in the existence of any God or gods. But there are many New Agers who are extremely scepti-cal about the existence of any deity or deities. Such New Agers tend to be those attracted to New Physics, but they may also have other inter-ests, including, for example, New Age rituals. This may seem para-doxical, but it is no more paradoxical than the section of Christians represented by the publication God in Us (Freeman 1993) by an Anglican vicar (at the time, though later defrocked), denying the exis-tence of God.[2] Elsewhere, the Scientific and Medical Network admits to full membership only those with professional scientific qualifica-tions. Members' interests include parapsychology, quantum physics, environmentalism, holism and reincarnation. These are typical New Age beliefs. Yet many members are also either extremely sceptical or agnostic about the existence of God, or are definitely atheist. Similarly, Marilyn Ferguson's The Aquarian Conspiracy ([1980] 1989) was a sum-mary of the scientific literature she edited for her Brain/Mind Bulletin and contained relatively few references to religious concepts.

Contrary to the claims of some Christian critics, many New Agers have a view of God which is remarkably similar to that of more con-ventional Christians. Indeed, many New Agers are Christians (Kemp 2003a). Many people who describe themselves as having adopted New Age beliefs and practices have no qualms in reciting the Apostles' Creed, for example. As seen above, Donahue (1993) also found that a number of Protestant congregations held some New Age beliefs.

If we are to consider the Pagan influence on New Age, it is clear that New Agers may also be polytheistic, believing in the existence of many divine beings from Pan or the Horned God to Thor or Odin. These are invoked in elaborate rituals, often in the open air, sometimes naked ('sky-clad'). Nevertheless, New Age polytheism is not necessarily to be understood in exactly the same way as ancient polytheism, since many New Agers interpret the existence of the gods psychologically. Vivianne Crowley is a prime example of this approach, taking the Wiccan gods to represent Jungian archetypes.

Equally, New Agers may often be considered pantheist. This is most apparent in traditions derived from New Thought (see Chapter 3), such as A Course in Miracles (see Chapter 2) or Louise Hay's You Can Heal Your Life (1984). Such traditions are both pantheist and monist, in that everything is believed to be part of the One God or Reality. God is to be found in each individual, each animal, each star, each tree. All is God. Again, New Age pantheism differs from conventional notions of pantheism since, at the same time as holding that everything may be worshipped as God, New Age pantheism often denies that anything other than God really exists.

A compromise position, espoused by many Christian New Agers such as Matthew Fox, is panentheism. This is the belief that while God may be found in everything, God is something more than the totality of all things. Panentheism thus attempts to retain Christian notions of a fundamental divide between God and creation, while at the same time emphasising their unity and interactivity.

New Age worlds are often populated by a variety of other beings in addition to God or the gods, and under various guises. *Devas, Fairies and Angels: a Modern Approach* (Bloom 1986) and *Working with Angels, Fairies and Nature Spirits* (Bloom 1998) are classic explanations of the panoply of New Age beings and how to work with them. Bloom emphasises that he is 'not describing something that happens simply in the human mind' (1998: 2), but this does not prevent him from having a playful attitude to the real existence of such marvellous beings. His ideas are derived from the writings of Alice Bailey (see Chapter 3) and influenced by Pagans, and try to instil a sense of the reality of ambience and atmosphere through personification.

A parallel New Age understanding of beings occurs in the channellers (see Chapter 7). These are modern-day mediums, who speak or write, often under trance, with the voices of discarnate spirits, such as Jesus (as in *A Course in Miracles*), extraterrestrial entities (as in Bloom's *The Christ Sparks* (1995)), or Atlantean warriors (as in Ramtha, channelled by J. Z. Knight). These New Age beings thus never manifest themselves alone, as do devas, fairies and angels, but only through the channeller. The existence of these discarnate beings is often tied up with belief in reincarnation, in that their spirits are understood to have once been incarnate and now to be living in another realm. This is similar to Spiritualist notions of contacting the spirits of dead relatives from the other side, but typically differs in the type of information relayed. Channelled messages tend to be lengthy passages of wisdom, *A Course in Miracles* being a case in point. Spiritualist messages tend to be comforting words of consolation from departed loved ones.

These two understandings of New Age beings, which may be called the nature tradition and the channeller tradition, may of course be held together by one New Ager, although they tend to divide between what Paul Greer (1994) called the ecological and patriarchal poles of New Age (see Chapter 9).

New Age understandings of the human being are more unified. A very common idea among New Agers is the notion of a higher personality or self, which guides individuals to their true destiny. This may be personified as a guardian angel, or simply understood as a division of the psyche akin to Freud's ego, id, and subconscious. New Agers often talk about following the higher self, in a way similar to that in which evangelical Christians will ask for a word from the Holy Spirit in order to determine their actions. The higher self is accessed through relaxed states which may be achieved by meditation, aromatherapy or other New Age techniques.

Two of the most venerated New Age beings are Christ and the Buddha. These beings are typically understood to have resonated with their higher selves to an unprecedented extent, with the result that they achieved quasi-divine status. Many New Agers believe that the Buddha and Christ are incarnations of the same spirit. Some New Agers believe that this spirit will reincarnate in the near future. Benjamin Creme (b. 1922) famously believes that the Maitreya has already incarnated in East London and is teaching followers again. Other New Agers believe that everyone has the potential to incarnate the Christ spirit within them, and thus achieve salvation.

– SALVATION AND DEATH –

New Age understandings of salvation differ from conventional Western and conventional Eastern notions of salvation, in their understandings both of the end of salvation and of the means of attaining it. The Western Judaeo-Christian-Islamic tradition (grossly simplified) teaches that if we lead a good life in accordance with God's holy word, we will be rewarded in the life to come. New Agers tend to reject rule-based religiosity in favour of a situationist spirituality which locates more importance in what ethical action means to each individual.

New Agers tend to emphasise well-being in this lifetime as the goal of their spirituality, whereas traditional Western religiosity has held out promises of an improved life to come, whether in heaven, paradise or a bodily resurrection. Indeed, New Agers are often criticised for the immediacy of their goals: a spiritual technique can be bastardised into a 'quick fix'. For example, the Qabbalistic tradition of Judaism does not advise practice of its techniques until after middle age, and then there is a lifelong practice to follow. Contrastingly, a New Ager may visit a spiritual fair with the intention of buying some books, and happen instead to purchase a session of reflexology in the expectation that the foot massage will leave her feeling reinvigorated and perhaps cure her troublesome back.

It will be seen that this New Age understanding of the means and end of salvation differs also from traditional Eastern notions. This is despite the fact that New Agers are often highly conversant with Eastern traditions and may use their terminology. For example, the notion of karma is often used by New Agers. They may take it to mean something akin to destiny, or perhaps relate it to actions undertaken in past lives having an effect in the current life. Very seldom, however, do New Agers simply take over traditional Hindu or Buddhist understandings of karma. The idea of escaping from the suffering, *dukha*, of the earthly cycle of birth and death, *samsara*, is not a typical New Age concept. Neither do New Agers typically share the Buddhist notion that the *atman*, soul, is non-existent and non-transferable at death; New Agers tend to believe in a perennial human spirit or essence which transfers from body to body at death and birth.

Tony Walter has investigated the understanding of 'Death in the New Age' (1993; see also Walter & Waterhouse 1999). He argues that New Age beliefs and practices concerning death and after can be understood as resacralising death in response to the modern tendency to secularise death through medicalisation, privatisation, individualism and expressivism. His findings contain the warning that most New Agers have yet to reach old age, so not too many have died. (As we shall see in Chapter 7, Walter may underestimate the average age of a New Ager.) Walter also includes the caveat that many New Agers construct their own individual beliefs about death.

Walter uses an implicit family resemblance categorisation theory to define New Age beliefs. One 'core belief' of New Agers is in an inner essence or soul. From this belief it follows that, for New Agers, it is only our material body that dies. Walter points out that reincarnation also provides reassuring memories from past lives and deaths. Some New Agers believe that the soul chooses the moment to reincarnate and become discarnate. Walter observes that many New Agers are not bothered by the risk of their present actions affecting a future life, as in traditional doctrines of karma. He also recognises that some New Agers do not subscribe to reincarnation, but believe simply in a continuation of life after death. Other New Agers are less concerned about long-term future life, but are comforted by their beliefs about the immediate period after death. Walter is here referring to near-death experiences (NDEs), famously investigated by Elizabeth Kübler-Ross.

The New Age idea of a soul is said to be similar to the Neoplatonic version of Christianity in which only the soul, and not a unified person (body and soul) continues after death. However, two differences

..om the Neoplatonic idea are that the New Age soul is not identified with the mind, and that the soul can also leave the body for short journeys to other realms before returning to the body.

Walter and Waterhouse (1999) observe that there are more people in the West now believing in reincarnation than there are Western adherents of Eastern religions or New Age. Furthermore, many people combine belief in reincarnation with a worldview which has traditionally excluded it, namely Christianity – only six in ten people who indicated in a survey that they believed in reincarnation explicitly rejected belief in the resurrection of the dead (Kemp 2003a).

– History and a New Age –

New Age theories of history are multiple. The centrality of these theories to New Age is revealed in the movement's very name, referring to a new epoch of time. They are, however, difficult to reconcile with each other, and indeed, under traditional philosophy, would be seen to be mutually incompatible.

Wouter Hanegraaff asserts that all forms of New Age thinking share at least two general assumptions about the nature of reality: that reality is an unbroken, unified whole and that it is engaged in a process of evolution (Hanegraaff 1996: 158), which he calls the holistic assumption and the evolutionistic assumption respectively. The paradox that New Agers can believe both in evolution over time and in the nature of time as an illusion is not lost on Hanegraaff. Cyclical evolutionism is pictured as a downward process of emanation of duality from a primeval singularity. Random (Darwinian) linear evolutionism is generally rejected in New Age because it precludes ultimate meaning. Teleological, open-ended or creative linear evolutionism is, however, common in New Age. Hanegraaff adds the further possibility of a teleological spiral.

Some of the earliest twentieth-century thinkers to be associated with contemporary New Age proper had well-developed theories of history. Pierre Teilhard de Chardin (1881–1955), for example, who was the most influential author in Marilyn Ferguson's survey of 'Aquarian Conspirators' (Ferguson [1980] 1989: 463), taught in *The Phenomenon of Man* (1955) and *Le Milieu Divin* (1957) an evolutionary view of history through genesis, cosmogenesis, noogenesis (from the Greek for 'mind') and Christogenesis to the 'Omega Point' of unification before God. Teilhard's evolutionary theory of history was taken up more recently by Peter Russell in *The Awakening Earth: The Global Brain* (1982).

Fritjof Capra (1982) reviews some of these New Age theories of history and, using Arnold Toynbee's graphical illustration of the rise and fall of historical cycles, suggests that we may be at a 'turning point' in history. 'Turning Points' had a currency in New Age circles prior to Capra's publication: it was the name of the lecture series at St James's church, Piccadilly, London, which preceded the current Alternatives series (see Chapter 6).

Christian New Agers often coalesce theories of a New Age in history with classical theological notions of a second coming or kingdom of God. Thus Fr Diarmuid Ó' Murchú speaks of the *basilea* (Greek for 'kingdom') rather than referring to a New Age, although his writings are firmly within the New Age camp. Revd Adrian Smith, another New Age Christian, similarly refers to the Aquarian Age (Smith 1990) almost as a synonym for the kingdom of heaven.

Despite the complexity of these understandings of history, there is an unexamined problem at the heart of many of these New Age theories. They purport to be cyclical, and indeed are usually based on the astrological cycle of ages derived from the precession of the equinoxes, by which the ruling sign of an age changes every 2,000 years or thereabouts. Eventually, this cycle should therefore return to its origin. However, contemporary notions of a New Age rarely refer to past transitions between astrological signs into previous New Ages, nor do they envisage a further New Age when the current New Age begins to decline. There is a tension between a cyclical and a linear conception of history, which is perhaps best resolved by Hanegraaff's suggestion of a spiral theory of history. Such a construct is however rarely encountered in primary New Age sources.

The idea of a new age is a common theme throughout the history of ideas (see e.g. Levin 1994). One of the earliest examples is to be found in Iranian Zoroastrianism, which taught of a battle between good and evil at the end of history. The Jews took over the Zoroastrian end-history while in captivity in Babylon, and at the same time absorbed from Babylonian astrology the notion of the seven planets ruling over thousand-year periods. There were Jewish apocalyptic sects before Jesus, preaching a Messiah who would usher in the end of the world. The most important expression of this view before Jesus is the Hebrew Bible's *Book of Daniel*.

According to the Gospel accounts, Jesus foretold a time of strife and suffering, false Christs and false prophets, which would be followed by the coming of the Son of Man in glory from heaven. It is the *Revelation of John*, or the *Apocalypse*, that develops the imagery to its fullest in the

New Testament, but it is interesting to note that there was much debate as to whether the book should be admitted to the Christian canon.

Irenaeus and Hippolytus in the early Church thought that world history would total 6,000 years, followed by a seventh millennium under the rule of Christ. Irenaeus thought this millennium would be followed by the kingdom of God the Father, which would last forever. Prophecies of the forthcoming millennium were found in otherwise non-Christian sources, including Virgil's fourth *Eclogue*, and the Sibylline oracles.

After early influence in the Church, the idea of a new age or millennium became heretical by the fourth century CE unless it was interpreted allegorically or spiritually. However, the theme was to return. Joachim of Fiore (c. 1135–1202), an Italian abbot and mystic, divided history into three periods: the age of the Father and of the law, the age of the Son and the Gospel and faith, and the age of the Holy Spirit and of direct knowledge of God. Each age was to last forty-two generations of thirty years apiece. As the Second Age had begun with the birth of Christ, it followed that the Third Age would begin in 1260.

When the End failed to materialise, the dates were revised. Adam Nachenmoser, in his *Prognosticum Theologicum*, arrived at the year 1587 by counting the 1,260 years from the death of Constantine, the first Roman Emperor converted to Christianity, in 327 CE. The Antichrist would rule until 1600, when the new age would begin. Paracelsus (see Chapter 3) claimed that an 'Elias the Artist' would appear fifty-eight years after his death, which occurred in 1541. According to Simon Studion (b. 1543) in his unpublished *Naometria*, written in 1604, the last generation that Joachim predicted would end in 1620. He identified the new order with the Confederation of Militiae Evengelicae, a Protestant alliance of 1586.

In the seventeenth century, many people were predicting the imminence of the Last Day, which would usher in the kingdom of God. Heinrich Vogel, a Protestant pastor, published in 1605 the *Revelation of the Secrets of Alchemy*, which predicted that the uniting of the Gospel and of alchemy would reveal the Antichrist. Julius Sperber described the new age in his *Book of Wonders*, complete with a new religion. The Puritans proclaimed that the New Jerusalem would be founded soon in England, and gained the confidence of Oliver Cromwell before the success of his revolution. Similar millennial ideas were carried to America in 1694 when a German mystical community led by Johannes Kelpius emigrated to Pennsylvania. William Blake (1757–1827) and Emanuel Swedenborg (1688–1772) (discussed in Chapter 3) also foretold a new age. In more recent times, the idea of a new age has been taken on by

The Church of Jesus Christ of Latter-Day Saints, formed by Joseph Smith (1805–44) after a series of visions beginning in 1820 and translated as the *Book of Mormon*. Fundamentalist Christians have revived the division of history into seven ages, now called dispensations. Myths of a new age were also found in Adolf Hitler's vision of a thousand-year Third Reich.

But while this history of the idea of a new age shows its widespread acceptance in Western thought, it does not follow that New Age proper derives its eschatology directly from any one of these new age mythologies. Direct historical influence can only safely be shown from Alice Bailey's writings (see Chapter 3) about a New Age of global understanding.

– VIGNETTE – POSTMODERNISM –

As a vignette demonstrating the possibilities of a philosophical approach to things New Age, I will reconsider the relation between New Age and postmodernism (see also Kemp (2001)).

Postmodernism has been defined in many ways and under various guises, including post-modernism (with a hyphen), postmodernity, high modernity and late modernity (see Best & Kellner (1991) and Lyon (1994) for good introductions). At its simplest, postmodernism is what comes after modernism. It usually has philosophical implications, but can be used to refer simply to societal trends. These include the increasing globalisation of national economies and cultural capital, and the ensuing plurality of choices facing the individual. Long-established traditions or 'meta-narratives' are replaced by a smorgasbord relativist approach to truths.

Aldo Terrin subtitles his work on New Age *La Religiosità del Postmoderno* (1992), and comments that New Age appears simply as the spirit of the new postmodern culture (Terrin 1992: 246). Anthony D'Andrea similarly asserts that 'just as Protestantism was the "spirit" of modernity, the NAM [New Age movement] is the "spirit" of late modernity (or of post-modernity)' (D'Andrea 1997: 69, my translation).

David Lyon suggests that both postmodernity and New Age may be seen as responses to a perceived 'crisis of modernity', since both herald a new era, reject traditional truths, emphasise self and consumption, avoid party politics, adopt new organisational structures, are implicated in globalisation, and may be understood in terms of the *fin de siècle* (Lyon 1993: 117). Lyon develops this approach in *Jesus in Disneyland: Religion in Postmodern Times* (2000), often taking New

Age as an example. While mainly coming from a Christian (or post-Christian) viewpoint, Lyon suggests that postmodern religion, or more correctly, postmodern spirituality, is flourishing in new forms. In a similarly Christian analysis, John Drane discusses spiritual seekers in the context of what he calls *The McDonaldization of the Church* (2001).

Anna Kubiak (1999) treats New Age as a 'postmodern conspiracy', part of postmodern culture. New Age lacks a clear definition, is structured as a network, and avoids the extreme cultural categories of high/low culture, East/West, ritual/game, global/local, body/soul and inside/outside. Further, New Age popularises the esoteric, is individualistic, rejects tradition, is relativist and is perennialist.

Christopher Partridge (1999), while agreeing that there are postmodern elements within New Age, claims that its epistemology (theory of knowledge) is essentially modernist. Shirley MacLaine's espousal of the 'you create your own reality' New Age dictum is taken by Partridge as a postmodern rejection of modernist epistemology. There is an emphasis in New Age on choice and consumerism, he says. But while New Age is admittedly characterised by diversity, in fact generally New Age thought requires the modernist notions of the self, truth and authority, and also constructs meta-narratives. For example, most New Agers believe in an evolving consciousness, which derives from modernist evolutionary progress theory.

Paul Heelas, whose work on Self spirituality is discussed in Chapter 7, is also concerned with the relation of New Age to modernity and postmodernity, as the subtitle to *The New Age Movement* (Heelas 1996a) shows – *The Celebration of the Self and the Sacralization of Modernity*. Two further articles by Heelas (1993 and 1996b) deal with similar themes. In the latter article, he defines postmodern as de-differentiated, consumer-oriented, relativist, concerned with utilitarian selfhood, expressivist and having a periodised view of history. Having compared New Age to this definition, he concludes that New Age is not postmodern, because it amplifies an experiential meta-narrative or overarching philosophy of life – for example, an 'inner tradition' of 'timeless wisdom'.

What really matters in these analyses is not the final answer to the question of whether New Age is postmodern or not, but the fact that all authors acknowledge at least some similarities and connections in the worldviews. In this way, exploring the philosophical problems of postmodernity can illuminate the philosophical structures of New Age.

– CONCLUSION –

The debate over whether New Age is postmodern is just one example of the use of the discipline of philosophy in New Age studies. Other examples considered in this chapter include the very concept of a 'new age' and fundamental philosophical themes such as metaphysics, God, beings, salvation, death and history. There is less of a distinction between New Age philosophy and philosophy of New Age than between emic and etic usage of other disciplines by New Agers or with reference to New Age. This is perhaps partly because of the 'armchair' nature of philosophy, which makes it accessible not just to academic scholars trained in its techniques but also to the independent researchers, often self-taught, found in New Age; and also because the sociological characteristics of professional and lay philosophers may be similar to those of New Agers (see Chapter 7). Another discipline that is accessible to autodidacts is anthropology, the concern of the next chapter.

– NOTES –

1. Groothuis' original table also included columns for secular humanist and Christian worldviews, and a tenth category, 'View of Jesus Christ'.
2. See also research by Peter Brierley of Christian Research, reported in the *Daily Telegraph*, 31 July 2002, p. 5, which found in a survey of 2,000 Church of England clergy that one-third doubt or do not believe in the physical resurrection, and only half are convinced of the truth of the virgin birth.

CHAPTER 5

Anthropology

Anthropologists have often been the first scholars to document alien traditions. In some ways, this has remained true with New Age, even though New Age is close to hand for most Westeners, and not to be found on a distant tropical island, as often used to be the case with alien traditions. There has also been some use of anthropologists' work by New Agers themselves – Frazer (1890), for instance, has been used as a compendium of alternative religious practices by many New Agers and Pagans. This chapter employs a basic anthropological approach: relating in a scientific fashion observed phenomena such as religious events, rituals and practices. The crucial step of providing an interpretation of such material is not attempted here – some anthropological interpretations of New Age phenomena by other scholars are considered in Chapter 9.

Many religious traditions have distinctive practices which may be observed by outsiders. These include the Christian mass, the Muslim prayer and the Jewish sabbath meal. New Age does not have practices which are quite so definitively central to its tradition; however, there are many practices, followed by a great number of New Agers, which may be seen to be akin to the distinctive practices of the great religious traditions. Typical New Age practices include channelling, meditation and healing. Typical New Age rituals include the circle dance, invocations and hugging. Typical New Age events include workshops, festivals and environmental action. Of course, there are many more examples of New Age phenomena, but in accordance with the family resemblance or polythetic mode of definition outlined in Chapter 1, I hope that sufficient understanding of New Age from an anthropological perspective can be gained by exploring a limited number of examples from fieldwork in England in 1995 and 1996 (see Kemp 2003a), categorised here as events, rituals and practices.

– EVENTS –

For a New Ager, the whole of life is sacred and so in some ways it is artificial to single out certain events and describe them as New Age. For example, the regular working day of a lawyer or secretary may be described as full of opportunities to develop the inner self and show love to fellow beings and devas. However, from an outsider's perspective, certain events do appear to hold more religious significance for New Agers. These include gatherings around a camp fire, story-telling and musical performances. In this section I describe New Age workshops and New Age festivals.

The cultic milieu has long supported the existence of psychic fairs (see Jorgensen 1982; Jorgensen 1983; Jorgensen & Jorgensen 1982). A more recent study of a psychic fair has been conducted by Matthew Wood (1999). Although both Jorgensen and Wood relate psychic fairs to New Age, this relationship has been questioned by some scholars. Certainly, at my local psychic fair, some stalls do sell New Age-type goods such as books by New Age authors, tapes, crystals and indigenous craft products. However, the majority of stalls are manned by traditional psychic readers, such as palm readers or tarot card readers. Some of those attending are regular followers of the psychic fair circuit, but many are simply weekend shoppers intrigued by the posters outside the hall. Quite where the dividing line between traditional spiritualism and contemporary New Age should be drawn is difficult to determine.

Danny and Lin Jorgensen conducted participant observation of tarot card readers in Florida in the late 1970s. Danny Jorgensen's analysis of psychic fairs found three segments of the 'esoteric community':

1. a 'psychic' network of cult-like churches, business and practitioners;
2. an 'esoteric' network of cultic study groups, quasi-religious groups, medical clinics and associations;
3. a 'spiritual' network of cult-like religious groups using extraordinary practices to achieve spiritual enlightenment. (from Jorgensen 1983: 59)

Jorgensen divides psychic fairs into large – attracting 1,000 to 3,000 people – or small – attracting a few hundred people. Large psychic fairs are designed to produce a profit, whereas small psychic fairs are intended to produce economic support for a particular group. Small psychic fairs attract only friends, seekers and the regular clientele of guest readers, and tend to be relatively homogeneous in terms of social characteristics. Large psychic fairs, however, attract quite a diversified audience. There are both insiders and outsiders to the esoteric community. Community members distinguish between 'students', who conduct casual study of esoteric literature, 'explorers', who move from group to group, and 'denouncers', characterised by extreme scepticism.

Jorgensen highlights the importance of psychic fairs for the esoteric community in their facilitation of direct contact between esoteric and exoteric social networks, which may result in the recruitment of new members and participants. Psychic fairs and esoteric communities compensate for the anonymity of urban groups and serve as the basis for intimacy, identity and social solidarity.

The most successful New Age fair in Britain is the Festival for Mind-Body-Spirit, which has been studied by Malcolm Hamilton (2000). The festival was started by Graham Wilson in 1977 and reached a peak of 88,000 visitors in London in 1979, at which point it was exported successfully to Australia and the United States. Attendance dipped in the early 1980s only to rise again, so in 1988 Wilson instituted the Healing Arts Festival and by 1996 a second Festival for Mind-Body-Spirit was booked each year.

The Festival for Mind-Body-Spirit attracts stallholders such as New Age booksellers, sensory deprivation hood practitioners, Reiki therapists, astrologers, sellers of natural products, dietary technicians, established NRMs such as the Aetherius Society and the National Federation for Spiritual Healers, and independent facilitators such as Matthew Manning. Wilson reported to Hamilton (ibid.: 190) that the festival has shifted from the esoteric fringe to an almost mainstream position. For example, the Body Shop, Anita Roddick's successful beauty care franchise, dropped out after the early festivals because it no longer considered itself alternative. Hamilton describes this shift as from a 'conversion' to a 'consumption' orientation, from influencing visitors (e.g. Rajneeshees) to selling products and services. A further change, for example, has been the decline in stalls with global or environmental concerns, which have been replaced by those concerned with personal development.[1]

Hamilton surveyed 402 visitors to the Festival in 1990. He found that forty-seven per cent of visitors sampled had attended previous festivals, and forty per cent had previously visited similar types of event elsewhere. Women were generally involved in more alternative activities than men. There was a general trend for increasing involvement up to about the age of fifty, after which involvement dropped off. Hamilton reports, 'The figures show a fairly high degree of immersion in the New Age subculture and a considerable overlap between this and related concerns such as environmentalism, vegetarianism, animal rights and so on' (ibid.: 196) (see Table 5.1).

Table 5.1   Involvement in alternative activities by sex and age (% of festival sample)

Activity	Women	Men	16–25	26–35	36–45	46–55	56+
Use of therapies	89	76	78	80	88	92	89
Health magazines	65	49	39	55	72	70	69
Human potential groups	51	39	35	44	56	56	40
Human potential magazines	71	63	57	65	72	78	77
Sects and cults	14	24	4	20	17	20	34
Green	65	59	64	62	66	60	51

(Hamilton 2000: 196)

New Age festivals such as these, inspired by the psychic fair tradition, are to be distinguished from those inspired by the free rock music festivals associated with New Age travellers, and considered in Chapter 3. There is undoubtedly some overlap in audiences and organisers, but my impression is that the flow of ideas is almost entirely one-way, from the psychic-type festivals to the traveller-type festivals.[2]

Most New Age festivals present opportunities for attending workshops, which is certainly part of what it means to be a New Ager. Of course, there are also many New Agers who would never attend a workshop. But most New Agers have attended at least a couple of workshops, and some New Agers are serial workshop attendees. Often, a workshop is the first serious point of contact with New Age. What tends to happen is that two friends will attend a workshop together, one being a newcomer to New Age and the other more experienced. In this way, workshops are one of the most important networking events for New Age. Workshops differ from public lectures in that there is more involvement by and engagement of the individual, and more commitment in the form of time and expenses. The first workshop is almost an initiatory rite, and may confirm a career of workshop attendance or signal the beginning of an individual's private spiritual quest undertaken through personal reading.

Those who are not invited to workshops by friends may come across advertisements at religious centres or in the spiritual press. This was the way I found out about my first New Age workshop, through *Vision* magazine, an annual directory of Christian retreats.[3] Many Christian retreat centres now hold New Age-influenced retreats, and indeed some Christian retreat centres devote their entire programme to New Age-style retreats. Enneagram retreats are particularly popular among Catholics, despite the lack of obvious connection with the Catholic tradition.

The Emmaus Retreat Centre[4] holds a year-long programme of retreats. In the year I attended, these included a mid-life directions workshop, spiritual insights from the Christian East, a traditional Holy Week retreat, 'An invitation to explore through scripture, prayer and clay', icon painting, twelve-step spirituality and a workshop on dreams and the imagination. The facilitators were often community sisters or priests, although for the Enneagram course the facilitator, Karen Webb, was non-Christian.

Webb has taught the Enneagram in the oral tradition since 1991. She began her career as a management trainer in human resource development before completing an undergraduate degree in religion[5] and graduating from the Enneagram Professional Training Programme under Helen Palmer in California. Webb is also the author of the Enneagram volume of the popular Thorsons New Age series, *Principles of . . .* (Webb 1996).

The workshop I attended began on a Friday evening with an open session where people introduced themselves to each other. There were about twenty of us, varying in ages from early twenties to retirement age, but mostly middle aged and about two-thirds were women. There was an industrial chaplain whose wife had encouraged him to take the course; a social services inspector who had been on a spiritual quest since a bout of depression; an animal welfare officer who was cross-training to become a counsellor; a former hippie now in his forties; a high-school principal who had travelled to the workshop from his school in Belgium; a sixty-five-year-old teacher at a Catholic teacher-training college; a retired teacher from Kent; and a trainee accountant on a career break.

The first session of the workshop, after we had got to know each other, introduced us to the idea of the true self, which is larger than the personality worn as a mask in everyday life. We were encouraged to shift our focus of attention and be more conscious of our potential for self-growth. Loosening awareness, focusing our attention on the 'belly centre', which has no thoughts, and letting things happen without conscious direction would open us up to the divine within. The

Enneagram was to be used as a spiritual tool to achieve this change in consciousness.

The origins of the Enneagram are disputed, but may be Sufi, from G. I. Gurdjieff or from Oscar Ichazo of Arica.[6] The Enneagram is a nine-pointed diagram within a circle. Each point is connected to others with a line, and represents a personality type. Each of the nine personality types is said to be equally distributed throughout the population. The personality types, with their various qualities, are defined by Webb as shown in Table 5.2.

Table 5.2   Enneagram qualities according to Webb

No.	Type	Passion	Holy idea
1	The Perfectionist	Anger	Perfection
2	The Giver	Pride	Freedom
3	The Performer	Deceit	Hope
4	The Romantic	Envy	Origin
5	The Observer	Avarice	Omniscience
6	The Questioner	Fear	Faith
7	The Epicure	Gluttony	Work
8	The Boss	Lust	Truth
9	The Mediator	Sloth	Love

There are a wealth of further correspondences among and between the personality types, and the following sessions started to fill out these bare descriptions. Of course, there was plenty of detail that Webb could not cover in this introductory workshop and there was often a forward-looking focus on what could be achieved with further workshops. No theoretical analysis of this bare anthropological description of a New Age workshop is offered here, except to say briefly that in many ways, workshop protocol may be thought of as ritualistic – akin to the mien adopted when entering a Christian church or Islamic mosque. New Age, however, has developed and adapted a great number of rituals in much more obvious ways.

– RITUALS –

At first thought, the idea of New Age rituals may seem incongruous, given the free-thinking and liberal approach of most New Agers. However, the appropriation of traditional rituals, and recontextualising them in a modern setting, is typical of New Age.[7] This occurs across the board with Native American rituals, Christian rituals, Masonic rituals, Celtic rituals – and indeed any other accessible tradition – all of which are reset in postmodern style. New Agers are not afraid of inventing new rituals, without claiming traditional roots, either. In this section I will explore two forms of New Age rituals: circle dance and invocations.

Circle dances are frequently used in a New Age context, often to start or end a workshop or ritual event. There are a variety of forms of circle dance, some quite different from others. Many draw consciously from traditional folk dances, but others have been choreographed more recently. One New Age Christian religious community which I researched often includes a circle dance in its Sunday worship. Those not chair-bound stand in the centre of the chapel in a circle, holding hands. The leader explains the moves: forward to meet you, backward to greet you, sideways to let you pass. Music starts at a slow pace, and newcomers quickly get the hang of the simple steps. The dance is tame enough to allow the many elderly worshippers to participate, but is also accessible to younger visitors.

A more racy circle dance is the energetic spiral dance led by the witch Starhawk (Miriam Simos). True to its name, the spiral dance is not in the form of a traditional circle, but begins as a line of people holding hands. In the dance I participated in, the evening was very well attended so the line was not very straight! Starhawk started to trace a spiral around the room. At first this was a very loose spiral, but as the dance progressed, Starhawk wove her way nearer and nearer to the centre and the spiral became tighter. All the time, we were chanting, providing a rhythm to the dance, and much merriment. At the end of the dance, everyone was closely bound together in a dense spiral within the room.

Invocations form a similar function to well-known prayers such as the Lord's Prayer or the Grace. Perhaps it is simply that New Agers do not like the Christian overtones of the designation of 'prayer' that they have adopted an alternative term. They are recited with eyes open or closed according to the practice of the invoker, standing or seated. Hands are rarely held together as in Western Christian prayer, but may sometimes be held in the lap with palms facing up to the heavens (as is common in charismatic circles) or down to the Earth (as is common in Pagan circles). The tone of voice used is similar to that of spoken prayers in Christian churches – neither prose nor poetry or chant, but respectful, quiet and meaningful.

Alice Bailey's invocation is used by the Arcane School at its conferences and in its local meetings as well as in private usage. It has been translated into almost seventy languages and has become popular beyond the bounds of the Arcane School. Indeed, some anti-New Age Christian tracts warn against use of the 'occult' invocation by unaware Christians in church settings.

> From the point of Light within the Mind of God
> Let light stream forth into human minds.
> Let Light descend on Earth.
>
> From the point of Love within the Heart of God
> Let love stream forth into human hearts.
> May the Coming One return to Earth.
>
> From the centre where the Will of God is known
> Let purpose guide the little human wills –
> The purpose which the Masters know and serve.
>
> From the centre which we call the human race
> Let the Plan of Love and Light work out.
> And may it seal the door where evil dwells.
>
> Let Light and Love and Power restore the Plan on Earth.
> (Adapted version,[8] *World Goodwill* newsletter 2000.4, p. 4)

William Bloom describes a technique of invocation in *Meditation in a Changing World* (1987). There are nine steps, which may be summarised as follows:

1. Become aware of the planetary environment from a centred meditation space.
2. Imagine a source of pure love and healing in the crown of your head.
3. Lift your consciousness up and touch this pure source on behalf of the planet.
4. Hold this peak for as long as you can – probably between thirty seconds and five minutes.
5. Relax and let the energy subside.
6. If it feels right, reach up again to the pure source.
7. Imagine the energy flowing down through you.
8. Imagine the energy flowing out from you to where it is needed.
9. Sound out the Aum mantra, which will ensure that all energy is distributed.

Bloom describes invocation as part of the whole process of meditation. Invocations are also used at the lecture evenings he directed, Alternatives, where the angel spirits of the four corners are often invoked before or after the lectures. It is suggested that invocations are more powerful if used at the time of the full moon, when the vibration of matter is said to be slightly accelerated. Bloom has written a prayer called 'A Glastonbury Invocation', inspired by the Lord's Prayer and Alice Bailey's invocation.

> There is a Source of Love which is
> the Heart of All Life.
> Let that Love flow
> Source to Earth
> Heart to Heart.
>
> There is a Source of Light which is
> the Mind of All Life.
> Let that Light flow
> Source to Earth
> Mind to Mind.
>
> There is a Source of Power which is
> the Purpose of All Life.
> Let that Power flow
> Source to Earth
> Purpose to Purpose.
>
> We are that Love
> We are that Light
> We are that Power.
>
> Peace and Healing on Earth.
>
> (Bloom 1990: 125)

Again, no theoretical analysis of these descriptions is offered here except to point out, as a link to the next section, that dance and invocation are bound up in New Age with concern for unity and healing of body, mind and spirit.

– PRACTICES –

Healing in New Age is undertaken not just to cure afflictions, but to engender a more healthy and satisfying lifestyle. The holistic philosophy underlying this approach was explored further in Chapter 4. New Agers typically teach that everyone has the power to heal, but only certain people tap this potential. Accordingly, there are as many varieties of New Age healing as there are New Agers. They vary from quasi-charismatic laying on of hands, through other non-physical approaches using chakras and auras, to tactile bodywork techniques such as Rolfing and Feldenkrais. In this section I describe the techniques of the National Federation of Spiritual Healers and of New Age healers in a Christian church.

The National Federation of Spiritual Healers (NFSH) was founded in 1955 and now has more than 7,000 members working individually and in centres throughout the United Kingdom, with a growing overseas membership. It is a registered charity, but does not associate itself with any religion. According to a 1994 promotional leaflet:

> It does see the source of healing as divine, but respects the right of every individual to his or her own interpretation of that source. The word 'spiritual' in the title refers to that quality of spirituality implicit in the healing process.

There is a training programme and scheme of development for probationary healers, leading to full registration. The NFSH also publicises spiritual healing to the general public and receives referrals from general practitioners. NFSH-registered healers work in their own and patients' homes, in doctors' surgeries, in hospitals and in local health centres.

> Spiritual Healing is the channelling of healing energies through the healer to the patient. It re-energises and relaxes the patients to enable their own natural resources to deal with illness or injury in the best possible way. By 'attunement' – perhaps best described as a combination of empathy and intent – either in the presence of the patient or at a distance – and by directing energy, usually through the hands, the healer seeks to supplement the depleted energy of the recipient, dealing with stress at whatever level it exists and releasing the body's own recuperative abilities to deal with the problem in the most effective way for that individual.
>
> Patients receiving healing tend to experience sensations of being re-energised or relaxed, 'pins and needles', heat or coolness, and pain coming to the surface and dispersing, indicating that the energies are indeed 'going to work'. Healing can be given for any illness, stress or injury as a therapy which is completely natural, has no side effects and is complementary to any other therapy. (Promotional leaflet, 1994)

One NFSH healer I interviewed conducts healing sessions in the nurses' hall of the local hospital.

> I always start off by telling them to take three deep breaths, 'love' for the first breath, 'peace' the second breath, 'tranquillity' the third breath. To hold it for a count of three and on the outbreath, whatever their problem is, to visualize it being blown away in a big bubble . . . Then I tell them to completely relax and close their eyes and try to go in their imagination to a place where they are happy. (Interview, 10 July 1996)

The healing continues with the channelling of healing energies through the hands, which are held slightly above the chakra centres of the patient. Another NFSH healer distinguishes between spiritual healing and Spiritualist healing, the former channelling energy and the latter channelling discarnate entities. Harry Edwards (1893–1976), the founder of the NFSH, was a Spiritualist and used mediumistic techniques at a time when they were still illegal in England.[9] Clients, however, are not asked to believe in anything, save that there is something better than mankind. If the client expresses an interest, this is explained in terms of the life energy that makes the flowers grow, or as unconditional love. Most patients are long term and the NFSH is their last port of call. About seventy per cent of my interviewee's clients are over retirement age, and for this reason are unlikely to be New Age, he said. Nevertheless, his spiritual healing technique is based on the chakras and the emotional, astral and spiritual bodies which have been proven, he claimed, by Kirlian photography. Spiritual healing is a matter not just of rebalancing energy, but also of teaching the patient how to maintain that balance by 'personal responsibility'. For example, resentment can lead to rheumatism. On the other hand, recognising the cause of rheumatism may not cure it, but can create a peaceful mind.

The chairman of a local NFSH centre first became interested in spiritual healing through meeting a numerologist his wife had consulted at the Festival for Mind-Body-Spirit in London. Brought up nominally Christian, he has been a member of Friends of the Earth since its early days, and was greatly influenced by Marilyn Ferguson's *The Aquarian Conspiracy* ([1980] 1989). After several years of practising Spiritualist healing, he took a part-time course in humanistic counselling and psychotherapy. He was at the time of the interview also a member of the Association for Therapeutic Healers and described his healing technique as 'co-creationist': 'Healing work is done very much as an equal-partnership project and relies both on the healers' facilitating role and the recipients' willingness to work at what they need to work at in healing themselves' (Interview, 25 July 1996). He distinguished this tradition of healing from the technique of channelling healing power down to the patient, a tradition that used to dominate the NFSH. It is this 'co-creationist' tradition of spiritual healing that is now growing in the NFSH and is likely to appeal to the New Agers it attracts at its exhibitions at festivals such as Mind-Body-Spirit, he said.

Healing has always been part of the Christian tradition since Jesus performed his healing miracles. Since the turn of the twentieth century, alternative healing traditions have made increasing inroads into mainstream Christianity (see Gartrell-Mills 1991). The churches reacted to the healings of Christian Science and New Thought by developing their own healing ministries. More recently, since the ascendancy of New Age from the 1970s, many churches have adopted New Age healing techniques. This tradition is now distinguishable from charismatic healing techniques, which arose at a similar time and may once have been connected (see e.g. Lucas 1992).

For example, one Anglican church in London housed for a number of years an alternative healing centre. Consultations were available by appointment and on a drop-in basis, free of charge, although donations were encouraged. The healing techniques used included Reiki, hypnosis, past-life regression and various forms of channelled healing. The centre proved very popular and moved to larger premises at another London church.

When I attended for a healing session, after waiting in a busy reception area, I was shown to a darkened room. The therapist sat in front of a bright desk lamp so that his face was obscured from me. After a general discussion of my health problems (which were genuine), the healing session began. I sat upright on a chair and the healer stood behind me. He told me to close my eyes and imagine a peaceful colour. From his explanations, observation of other healing sessions (and peeking through my closed eyes), I know that what he did next was to hold his hands flat out slightly above various areas of my body. Beginning with the crown of the head, he moved down past the eyes, shoulders and heart to the solar plexus, knees and feet. All this took about ten minutes and was conducted in silence. When he was nearly finished, he told me to imagine the peaceful colour again and, on the count of five, open my eyes. The result was that I felt very relaxed and possibly more full of energy.

The church that housed this healing centre also conducts spiritual healing after Sunday services once a month. The healers, five or so in number, are commissioned during the service by the officiant. After the service, over half the congregation queues up to receive healing in a side chapel. Again the 'patient' sits on a chair while the healer conducts healing from behind. Outwardly, it looks very similar to healing conducted in charismatic churches. However, from speaking to the healers, I know that they have been trained in traditions such as Reiki and the spiritual-healing tradition of the NFSH.

If healing is a central New Age therapy, meditation is its counterpart for individual practice. Meditation is a universal religious practice and exists in manifold forms. There is no agreed definition of the different varieties of meditation, and each tradition classifies them in its own way. In a useful discussion of terminology in relation to Indian Buddhist meditation, Paul Griffiths ([1993] 1994) distinguishes *inter alia* between the term 'meditation' as used by some Christian ascetical theologians, where it means discursive and repeated consideration of central religious images; a general usage of the term to refer to any deliberate consciousness-altering technique that does not use external chemical substances; concentration or 'one-pointedness of mind'; *dhyāna* states, aimed at withdrawal from the world and stopping all thought; *bhāvanā* or 'cultivation', which refers to specific techniques also aimed at reduction of thought; and 'mindfulness', in which one pays attention to one's thoughts and actions.

As with Buddhist meditation, so with most New Age phenomena: there is not just one New Age form of meditation. New Agers meditate in many different ways, drawing from many different traditions – including, but not limited to, each of the Buddhist traditions described above. Indeed, it is distinctive of New Age that it does not limit itself to one tradition or set of traditions. In this section, I will describe the form of New Age meditation set out in William Bloom's *Meditation in a Changing World* (1996).

Meditation in a Changing World explains Bloom's approach to meditation. Meditation is described as allowing the 'inner personality' to become fully present. This is achieved through relaxation and holding a focus as the observer. Observing our breath is said to be an easy way into focus and relaxation. It is envisaged that the beginner in meditation will find it easier in a quiet spot in his/her home. Daily practice of a minimum of twenty minutes is recommended. The ideal posture is to have a straight spine.

Bloom outlines six aspects of meditation: centring, alignment, review, expansion, awareness and service. He emphasises the importance of grounding meditation, that is, sensing 'the energy of our body going down beyond our feet and deep into the earth' (Bloom 1996: 36). Centring is the achievement of a calm, relaxed and observant state of mind without the endless chatter usually engaged in. Techniques for centring include mantrams (repeated words or phrases), babbling in a 'foreign' language which we do not understand, or self-reflection. Alignment is an attunement with our inner self, attained through concentrating on the 'third eye' behind our physical eyes. This can also be helped through an exercise known as 'The Perfect Being in the Heart', which is the imagination of a being of spiritual perfection inside your own heart. Another method is to 'Climb the Planes', as outlined by Alice Bailey: the physical plane, emotional, mental, intuitional, spiritual, monadic and divine. Alternatively, invoking and radiating helpful atmospheres is said to help alignment. Review is the coming to an understanding of our own faults and behaviour patterns, similar to the Christian confession. It is simply a run-through of the previous twenty-four hours in our mind. Various exercises are suggested to amplify this review. Expansion of consciousness is a method of embracing our inner self fully. It is said that, after many years of practice of meditation, the distance between the silenced personality and the inner self decreases until it can be achieved permanently. The 'peak experience' may become a plateau. Part of the process of expansion is also to expand out into the cosmos, both in geographic and consciousness terms. Again, a number of exercises are outlined. Awareness includes ecological awareness of the environment around us, and a compassionate sense of the interconnectedness of all life. Meditation is said to be of very practical service, both through natural radiation and through deliberate invocation, channelling and radiation.

Group meditation is said to have a ripple or wave effect which multiplies the beneficial quality of individual meditation. It can be undertaken prior to any form of collective work. There is said to be a planetary network of light, a conscious telepathic and intuitive linking of meditators throughout the world which joins together daily. It is hoped that this will affect the atmosphere of the whole planet. The Harmonic Convergence, a worldwide group meditation, was orchestrated by José Argüelles on 16–17 August 1987 and was practised by many groups monthly for some years afterwards, possibly continuing today. In this way, the solitary practice of meditation is given social significance.

– CONCLUSION –

This chapter has documented in bare ethnographic or phenomenological style an observer's account of what are considered typical New Age events, rituals and practices. Little interpretation has been offered, but these typical New Age phenomena may be understood on a scale varying according to the number of people involved, from large crowds (festivals), to smaller congregations (workshops, rituals), intimate groups (healing) and finally small-group or solitary practices such as meditation. In this way they cut one slice of New Age cake and, I hope, show some internal characteristics which are not immediately obvious if viewing the cake externally only. To apply another metaphor, this is one branch of the family resemblance tree of New Age: a number of core family members have been described, in the hope that we may better understand the family (New Age) as a whole.

Of course, this is not to deny that other anthropological slices can be cut – and indeed many have been (see Chapter 9); nor to deny that core family members can be described under other approaches – one of which, sociology, will be considered in the next chapter.

– NOTES –

1. See further Massimo Introvigne's comments about the personalisation of New Age into Next Age, discussed in Chapter 10.
2. For a full discussion of New Age festivals in the free tradition, see St John (2000).
3. Produced by the Retreat Association and now known as *Retreats*.
4. West Wickham, Kent, England.
5. Under Paul Heelas. It has been shown (e.g. York 1995: 190–1) that New Agers often have a further degree. It is not surprising, therefore, that many have a further degree in religion, psychology or an associated field. New Agers often attend academic conferences. Indeed, at the 1996 Nature Religion Today conference hosted by Lancaster University, a significant proportion of the attendees were New Agers rather than academics, and some of the speakers were 'New Age leaders' rather than academics. Conversely, it is often possible to spot a number of research students or academics at New Age events. For example, at a lecture given by Starhawk in 1996, I encountered Eileen Barker, Michael York and two further research students in addition to myself.
6. Sophia Wellbeloved writes (in Lewis 2003):

    Enneagram of Personality publications usually give secret Sufi origins for the Enneagram. This appropriation of the Enneagram, stems from the Sufi Idries Shah who convinced the Gurdjieff teacher J. G. Bennett of its truth. Although there is no record of any direct evidence offered for this view, the mythology of Sufi origins is now well-established.

    In *The Theory of Celestial Influence: Man the Universe and Cosmic Mystery* (1954) Rodney Collin, who learned about the Enneagram from Gurdjieff's pupil P. D. Ouspensky, re-introduced Gurdjieff's cosmic laws in his own synthesis which makes evident their zodiacal and astrological foundations. His Enneagram of planets, related to planetary types of people, provides the link between 'Gurdjieff's Enneagram' and the 'Enneagram of Personality' which developed from the teaching of Oscar Ichazo at his Arica Institute in Chile. In 1970 this course was taken by Claudio Naranjo, a psychiatrist and LSD researcher, together with others from the Esalen Institute in California. Kathleen Riordan Speeth and Bob Ochs were pupils in the group which Naranjo taught on his return to the US. Ochs, a Jesuit with a Ph D in Theology from Paris, adapted the enneagram types into 'the nine faces of God'. He taught this version of the enneagram at Loyola University in Chicago and also at the University of California at Berkeley (see Beesing, Nogosek and O'Leary 1984). These classes are the direct origin of the introduction of the Enneagram into Jesuit retreats and indirectly of Helen Palmer's *The Enneagram:*

Understanding Yourself and the Others in Your Life (1995), who based her book on the material in his classes as did Don Riso for his *Personality Types: Using the Enneagram for Self Discovery* (1987).

7. See also the alternative worship movement in Evangelical and charismatic Christian circles, studied in Guest (2002).
8. The original version used gender-specific language and referred to the Christ rather than the Coming One.
9. Under the Witchcraft Act 1736, which was repealed in 1951.

CHAPTER 6

Sociology

Awareness of New Age as a distinct sociological phenomenon crystallised with Marilyn Ferguson's *Aquarian Conspiracy* ([1980] 1989), which applied sociological and other scientific theories to a collection of observations on what were acknowledged to be diverse spiritual phenomena. New Agers themselves have not often employed sociological theory since then, in contrast to their use of the fruits of other disciplines such as anthropology, philosophy and psychology. It is remarkable, then, that the sociology of New Age was one of the first, and is now one of the most developed, scholarly approaches to New Age.

Sociologists have developed a number of models for analysing religious phenomena. One of the earliest and most successful models, to be discussed in this chapter, is known as the church–sect theory. This has been modified many times since its inception in the late nineteenth century to account for new socio-religious developments. In particular, the notion of a new religious movement (NRM) was developed to replace pejorative use of the word 'cult'.

More recently, Michael York (1995) has pointed out the shortfalls in applying this traditional sociological theory to New Age. He took up Ferguson's application ([1980] 1989) of Luther Gerlach and Virginia Hine's model (Gerlach & Hine 1968) of a SPIN of SPINs, where a SPIN is a segmented, polycentric, integrated network (see below). Another sociological model which can usefully be applied to New Age is social movement theory. In Kemp (2003a) I suggested that social movement theory could be combined with church–sect theory in order to describe New Age as a new socio-religious movement (NSRM) (see below).

This chapter also considers a long-debated sociological theory, the so-called secularisation thesis, which claims that society is becoming more secular and less religious. This is relevant to New Age studies, because the popularity of New Age is sometimes said to refute the secularisation paradigm. I will then examine three New Age social groups in the light of these sociological theories: Ramtha's School of Enlightenment at Yelm, Washington; Alternatives, a New Age lecture series in London; and the Findhorn Community in Scotland. First, however, we must consider that from which all sociological theory should be derived: qualitative and statistical data.

– QUALITATIVE AND STATISTICAL STUDIES –

Most extant sociological studies of New Age are based on qualitative participant observation. This is first-hand fieldwork by the researcher studying New Agers on their own ground. The diversity of definitions of New Age makes scientific study of it difficult: what are we to observe? It is not always easy to delimit a sample of New Agers, although this can sometimes be ascertained by membership of a New Age group or NRM. For example, in Kemp (2003a) I carried out field-work with three New Age Christian groups. However, since some who many observers agree are typical New Agers in fact deny the label applies to them, self-profession of New Age is not a reliable indicator.

Statistical study of New Age populations is in its early stages, despite the voluminous amount of qualitative comment. It would be assisted by the agreement of a tool for measuring New Age affiliation, in order that studies can be compared on a similar basis. Useful attempts at a survey to measure New Age affiliation have been put forward by Stuart Rose (1996), Dick Houtman and Peter Mascini (2002), Pehr Granqvist and Berit Hagekull (2001) and Michael Donahue (1993).

Rose's scale measures participation in New Age activities. It can produce a numerical indicator of the average number of New Age practices the population engage in. However, Kemp (2003a) found that an Evangelical Christian population scored higher than expected on the same scale: the tool must therefore be used with caution. The list of practices surveyed is as follows:

Have you ever participated in or used any of the following?
Acupuncture/shiatsu
Alexander Technique
Aromatherapy
Buddhism
Channelling
Colour therapy
Creative visualisation
Crystals

Dance therapy
Earth mysteries
Ethical investing
Flower remedies
Green politics
Healing workshops
Herbalism
Homeopathy
Hypnotherapy
Massage
NLP
Past-life therapy
Psychotherapy
Rebirthing
Reflexology
Recycling
Shaman/Pagan rituals
Sound therapy
Spiritualism
T'ai Chi Ch'uan/Yoga
Transactional analysis
Veganism
Vegetarianism
Women's Studies groups
(Kemp 2003a, adapted from Rose 1996: 363)

Houtman and Mascini (2002) analysed a sample of 1,848 respondents to a 'telepanel study' or computer-driven population. New Age was operationalised by asking to what extent respondents had been involved in five practices closely related to New Age: reincarnation, astrology, New Age, yoga, and oriental religions. Additionally, five Likert-type[1] questions were asked, expressing four core ideas of New Age:

One's character is strongly determined by the stars and planets;
One can predict one's future to a large extent by reading the lines in one's hand;
After death, one's soul passes to another human being or animal;
One should search in different religions oneself to make one's own religion;
The one and only true religion does not exist, but there are truths one can find in all religions of the world.
(from ibid.: 462)

Those involved with the five practices also agreed most strongly with these five statements, but it must be questioned whether such a simple operationalisation accurately captures New Age or is wide enough to include, for example, Spiritualists and followers of some Eastern religions.

Granqvist and Hagekull have developed a more sophisticated instrument for measuring New Age affiliation: the 'New Age Orientation

Scale (NAOS)'. It was tested on a sample of fifty participants selected from vegetarian cafés, alternative bookstores and health centres assumed to attract New Agers. Mathematical analysis of the results supported the construct validity of the scale and showed that one large factor summarised the New Age items reasonably well.

The New Age Orientation Scale (NAOS)

Instructions: Below are listed a number of statements describing different ideas in relation to issues such as spirituality, philosophy of life, knowledge, and mental capacities. Please mark each statement by indicating the extent to which it corresponds to your opinion. Write *one* number in the space preceding the statements. Use the following response scale:
1 = strongly disagree 2 = disagree 3 = partly disagree 4 = partly agree 5 = agree
6 = strongly agree

___1) I am convinced that thought transference and/or the ability to move things by mere thinking actually do work.

___2) I've read some of the new, 'alternative' books that deal with how to reach spiritual or personal development (e.g. *The Celestine Prophecy, A Course in Miracles, The Sacred Self, Out on a Limb*).

___3) The position of the stars at birth affects how one will live one's life or how one's personality will develop.

___4) I think that we are now approaching an entirely new age, that will *radically* change our view of science, spiritual knowledge, or the true nature of man.

___5) To reach one's personal, spiritual insight, every individual should combine or mix the truths that are hidden within different old traditions (e.g. Shamanism, the religions of native people, astrology, Eastern wisdom, Kabbala).

___6) There are some objects or places that have a special spiritual meaning, for instance being surrounded by a certain type of energy.

___7) I am convinced that at least two of the following phenomena occur: dreams reveal what will happen in the future, one receives premonitions of what is to occur, or there are people who can 'see' the future.

___8) With the assistance of a 'medium', it is possible to get in touch with dead people or with life on other planets.

___9) There are many 'alternative treatments' (e.g. Reiki healing, Rosen-, Zone-, Aura-, Primal-, Reincarnation-, Crystal-, and Chakra therapy) that are at least as effective as the regular medical treatments for bringing about human well-being and health.

__10) I regularly use some specific technique (e.g. Yoga, rebirthing, meditation, massage) to become a more harmonious human being or to reach spiritual development (do *not* include prayer as a technique).

__11) Everything that happens in an individual's life has an underlying meaning that it is important to try to comprehend.

__12) The whole cosmos is an unbroken, living whole, that the modern man has lost contact with.

__13) Things that happen (e.g. divorce, death) in a house or room leave a certain 'atmosphere' that affect the people who subsequently move in.

__14) A problem with the established health care system is that science has priority over intuition or old wisdom.

__15) I believe that a person's deeds are stored in his or her 'karma.'

__16) People live more than one life, so that when they die they will be reborn after some time in another body ('reincarnation').

__17) Compared to most religious and nonreligious people, I am probably somewhat of a spiritual seeker with an unusually open mind.

__18) One's world around [sic] is mainly a mirror image of one's inner world, so that outer processes above all reflect one's inner processes.

__19) Tarot cards, horoscopes, or fortune telling can be good starting points from which to develop oneself and one's possibilities.

__20) Spirituality to me is above all about realizing my true nature or becoming one with [the] cosmos.

__21) I am a vegetarian/vegan for one/some of the following reasons: meat eating impedes the functioning of the astral plane, the individual's karma is impaired by meat eating, or all living creatures have a holy place in the cosmos.

__22) Several phenomena that are usually subsumed under the 'new age' label are personally valuable to me.

(Granqvist & Hagekull 2001: 541–2)

Donahue has also constructed a survey to measure New Age affiliation among Protestant Christians. Since it required 504 separate responses, it is not reproduced here in full. However, the analysis constructed a New Age 'ideology' which included the following factors:

a) Human nature is basically good . . .

b) I believe in reincarnation – that I have lived before and will experience other lives in the future . . .

c) I believe in astrology . . .

d) Through meditation and self-discipline I come to know that all spiritual truth and wisdom is within me . . .

e) I am in charge of my own life – I can be anything I want to be . . .

f) It is possible to communicate with people who have died . . .

g) An individual should arrive at his or her own religious beliefs independent of any church.

(Donahue 1993: 178)

Only when a number of statistical studies have used the same survey techniques will it be possible to compare profiles of New Age. Until this is done, all sociological comment on New Age is, at best, based on qualitative observation from fieldwork, and at worst, based on armchair theorising from secondary sources.

– SOCIOLOGICAL THEORIES –

Cult–Sect–Church Theory

Cult–sect–church theory is often known less helpfully as church–sect theory. Often attributed to Max Weber, it was in fact first substantially outlined by Ernst Troeltsch. Troeltsch defined established churches as conservative, universal, all-encompassing religious institutions which are an integral part of the social order. Bainbridge suggests (1997: 39) that the technical word 'ecclesia' might be used to avoid the ambiguities of the common word 'church'. People are usually born into an established church. Sects are defined as smaller than established churches with varying attitudes to secular society and often connected with lower social classes. People usually join sects voluntarily. Troeltsch also outlined a third category of religious groups, *die Mystik*, often later referred to as 'cults', in which the religious individual resolves the tensions between society and religion within him- or herself. 'Cult' is often used pejoratively, and for this reason many scholars prefer the term 'new religious movement' (NRM).

These three categories of religious groups – church, sect, cult – are difficult to locate in every society. For example, the United States has no established church; on the other hand it is difficult to call the Episcopal church (the Anglican Church in the USA) a sect. For reasons such as this, many modifications of Troeltsch's typology were proposed in the twentieth century.

H. Richard Niebuhr (1929) transformed cult–sect–church theory from a sterile tool of description and analysis into a dynamic theory of sociological development. In his conception, the sect is viewed as the church in waiting. However, York (1995: 241) criticises Niebuhr for being overly Christian in his concerns. Howard Becker (1932) created a fourfold typology of ecclesia, denomination, sect and cult. Yinger (1970) has a sixfold typology of universal church (e.g. the Roman Catholic Church), ecclesia (e.g. the Church of England), denomination or class church (e.g. the Baptists), established sect (e.g. Christian Science), transient sect (e.g. Pentecostalists) and cult (e.g. Scientology). Rodney Stark and William Sims Bainbridge (1979) sought to simplify rather than expand the typology by referring to the level of 'tension' between the religious group and the social environment.

It is difficult to locate New Age on a modified cult–sect–church continuum. Many scholars and protagonists suggest that New Age is a diffuse cultural phenomenon, so it should perhaps be akin to a universal church; but there are few of the structural artefacts traditionally manifested by such a church. Other scholars (see, for example, Bruce 2002) suggest that New Age is statistically insignificant, and this may indicate that it is more akin to cult phenomena; but, again, the structural attributes of New Age do not conform with those of groups usually considered as new religious movements.

It is clear that many New Age groups should be regarded as NRMs in their own right – for example, Neognostic churches, or followers of individual channellers such as J. Z. Knight. Conversely, New Age is clearly not a church, whether this be a universal church, ecclesia or denomination, in that its tension with established societal norms is too great and it lacks organisational focus. It is also problematical to typify New Age as a sect, even a transient sect, since again the level of organisation and hierarchy is lacking. If we were to have to locate New Age on the cult–sect–church matrix, it would currently be somewhere between cult and sect. However, there would be so many reservations to this categorisation that it is probably better to reject the application of traditional cult–sect–church theory to New Age altogether. New Age was not around when the theory was originated, and it does not fit the typology very conveniently.

NRM Theory

The cult–sect–church theory is not the only typology constructed by scholars of new religious movements. A sample of some other typologies available is considered below, with an attempt to apply each typology to New Age.

Bryan Wilson constructed a widely used typology of religious groups, based on the answer to the question 'What shall we do to be saved?' (Wilson 1970: 36–40). In one of its forms, this typology had eight divisions: conversionist, revolutionist, introversionist, manipulationist, thaumaturgical, reformist, utopian and acceptance of the world. While the adjectival divisions of the typology clearly relate to the examples Wilson gives, it is more difficult to decide which division properly describes New Age. It is perhaps more accurate to say that each division of the typology describes one aspect of New Age: a conversion is required by some New Age groups, especially the more defined NRMs within New Age; a revolution is required by other New Age groups, for example some of the Alice Bailey-inspired movements for world government; whereas many New Age groups are introversionist and call for little impact on world affairs. Similar examples of New Age instances for each of Wilson's divisions could be given, with the result that Wilson's typology does not pigeon-hole New Age into any one of his categories.

Roy Wallis greatly simplified Wilson's typology by concentrating on the attitude of the group to the world: rejection, affirmation or accommodation. Again, however, a New Age example of each of these categories may be given, thus putting into question their applicability to this spiritual movement. Many New Agers reject Cartesian philosophy, while at the same time attending prosperity workshops affirming the creation of wealth and also adapting or accommodating traditional religious rituals to this end.

Charles Glock and Rodney Stark designed a typology of religious movements which was organised according to the type of 'deprivation' suffered by its members (Glock & Stark 1965). Economic deprivation typically led to a sect-type structure; social deprivation to a church; organismic deprivation to a healing movement; ethical deprivation to a reform movement; and psychic deprivation to a cult. It can be seen that New Age again fits into each of these types of deprivation, and so no one structural result (whether sect, church, healing movement, reform movement or cult) applies to New Age. For example, New Age prosperity workshops may result from economic deprivation; rave masses may result from social deprivation; spiritual healers may result from organismic deprivation; environmental concern groups may result from ethical deprivation; and psychic fairs may result from psychic deprivation.

One sociological typology which does fit New Age quite well is that of Stark and William Bainbridge, as presented in Bainbridge (1997), which I quote here at length:

> *Private* New Age or occult phenomena are chiefly experiences that individuals and very small groups may have, without a leader or professional practitioner, and without any large-scale communication or organization. *Audience* phenomena display little or no formal organization, and their modern audiences typically partake of them through the media, including television programs, magazines, and books. Audiences typically are interested in several different such phenomena, although a given person selects to some degree among the ones available. *Client* services involve an exchange relationship between a practitioner and a customer, usually well defined and based on some special qualities or professional training possessed by the practitioner. Involvement with a particular practitioner generally prevents the individual client from simultaneously seeking the same service from other practitioners, but it does not prevent participation in audiences of all kinds, involvement with practitioners who offer distinctly different services, or even membership in a religious movement, so long as the movement itself does not reject the particular client service. (ibid.: 370–1)

The fourth category described is movement phenomena.

The reason this typology fits so well with New Age is that Bainbridge intends it to be used diachronically, that is with different parts of the typology applying at different points in an NRM's development. In the 1997 version of this theory, Bainbridge had New Age explicitly in mind. Therefore it is easy to describe New Age examples of each division of this typology: visualisation practitioners may be private; reading New Age books may be an audience phenomenon; healing centre attendees are client phenomena; and Ramtha's School of Enlightenment may be a movement phenomenon. This is not problematic, as it is in many other typologies, because of the diachronic nature of the model.

We have seen, then, that neither general theories of the cult–sect–church continuum nor specialised theories of NRMs are easily applicable to and useful in examination of New Age, perhaps with the exception of Bainbridge's typology, which explicitly accounts for New Age bridging the private, audience, client and movement types. New Age seems to cut across most of the categories that scholars have suggested are useful in categorising religious groups and NRMs in particular. Accordingly, some scholars have instead suggested the application of network theory, while others have suggested the application of new social movement theory.

SPIN Theory

Marilyn Ferguson's catalytic understanding of New Age as a 'conspiracy' or movement applied SPIN theory (segmented, polycentric, integrated network) to formerly disparate spiritual phenomena. Ferguson suggested that New Age or

> the Aquarian Conspiracy is, in effect, a SPIN of SPINs, a network of many networks aimed at social transformation. The Aquarian Conspiracy is indeed loose, segmented, evolutionary, redundant. Its centre is everywhere. Although many social movements and mutual-help groups are represented in its alliances, its life does not hinge on any of them. (Ferguson [1980] 1989: 236–7)

Preferring to emphasise his debt to the sociologists Luther Gerlach and Virginia Hine rather than the New Age populariser Ferguson, Michael York (1995) adopted the SPIN of SPINs model for academic analysis of New Age. York highlighted five types of 'linkages':

1. ties of kinship, friendship, social relationship . . .
2. intercell leadership exchange or personal, kinship and social ties among leaders and others in autonomous cells . . .

3. the activities of traveling evangelists, spokespeople, ecoevangelists, evangelist-organizers . . .
4. 'in-gatherings' and large-scale demonstrations . . .
5. the basic beliefs and ideological themes shared by traveling speakers, letters, word-of-mouth, discussions, lectures, workshops, individual and group interaction, publications, newsletters, books, and especially the increased communication system efficiency represented by desktop publishing.[2]

(ibid.: 326–7)

The notion of a SPIN was first outlined in a study of the Pentecostal movement, where Gerlach and Hine located 'Five factors crucial to the growth and spread of a modern religious movement' (1968). These were:

1. an acephalous, reticulate organizational structure,
2. face-to-face recruitment along lines of pre-existing significant social relationships,
3. commitment generated through an act or experience,
4. change-oriented ideology, and
5. real or perceived opposition.

(ibid.: 123)

Each of these five factors can be seen to be at work in New Age. Such organisational structure as exists is certainly acephalous and reticulate; Wood (1999) shows that recruitment is along kinship lines; Ferguson ([1980] 1989) emphasises the importance of personal transformation before social transformation occurs; New Age is eponymous of change; and there is real opposition from conservative Christians and sceptical rationalists (see Chapter 8).

Gerlach (1971) goes on to develop the model of organisational structure mentioned in the first of these five factors. Movements are described as:

a) *Segmentary:* a movement is composed of a range of diverse groups, or cells, which grow and die, divide and fuse, proliferate and contract.
b) *Polycephalous:* this movement organisation does not have a central command or decision-making structure; rather it has many leaders or rivals for leadership, not only within the movement as a whole, but within each movement cell.
c) *Reticulate:* these diverse groups do not constitute simply an amorphous collection; rather, they are organised into a network, or reticulate structure through cross-cutting links, 'traveling evangelists' or spokesmen, overlapping participation, joint activities, and the sharing of common objectives and opposition.

(ibid.: 817)

Again, New Age may be seen to fit well with this model. The constituent groups of the movement are myriad; there is no institutional centre; but they are nevertheless organised in some way into a network. Hine developed this analysis into the model of the SPIN. This is cell-like (segmented), many-centred and often duplicatory, without an organised hierarchy (polycentric), but nevertheless cohesive (integrated), a web-like structure or mechanism (network).

York developed Ferguson's idea that New Age is a SPIN of SPINs, extending it to define a 'contemporary "holistic movement"' that includes 'New Age, Neo-paganism, the ecology movement, feminism, the Goddess movement, the Human Potential movement, Eastern mysticism groups, liberal/liberation politics, the Aquarian Conspiracy, etc.' (York 1995: 330).

It may be questioned whether this list is over-inclusive and reminiscent of underground conspiracy theories (e.g. Shea & Wilson [1975] 1998). However, York does not expand on this concept, which appears in the last paragraph of his study, and perhaps all he is suggesting is that each of these groups individually may be analysed along SPIN lines.

SPIN theory provides a good description of New Age. Like any theory, it has its drawbacks. These include its use in the popular literature by Ferguson, which dulls its academic cut; and the description of the network as 'integrated', which is difficult to apply to New Age. An alternative sociological theory that may be applied to New Age is new social movement (NSM) theory.

NSM Theory

It is surprising that new social movement theory, a well-developed area of sociological theory (for an introduction, see della Porta & Diani 1999), has not been more often applied to New Age. To my knowledge, the only extended application of NSM theory to New Age is María Julia Carozzi's chapter in her own compendium of articles on New Age (Carozzi ed. 1999).[3]

Carozzi compares New Age to the 'socio-cultural macro-movement' in Western middle classes from the 1960s, which includes feminism, the gay movement and the civil rights movement. The particular macro-movement in which New Age is situated is described as autonomy, anti-authoritarianism and the concomitant rejection of the hierarchies of authority and institutional rules (Carozzi 1999: 149). In this way, NSM theory applied to New Age picks up on Michael York's 'conspiratorial' development of SPIN theory (see above).

Autonomy is located by Carozzi as the 'master frame' (Snow & Benford 1992) or key idea that unites New Age groups into a movement. The notion of 'frames' was developed by Erving Goffman (1974), and refers to the spectacles through which reality is seen by individuals, or more technically, describes 'schemata of interpretation' (Snow et al. 1986: 464). Carozzi suggests that the autonomy master frame has developed from roots in Human Potential in the USA in the 1960s, particularly at Esalen, and through the 1970s at post-Theosophical centres such as the Findhorn Community (see below), into the international New Age movement of today. New Age is described as a 'network of networks'.

A social movement has been defined as follows:

> Those sequences of contentious politics that are based on underlying social networks and resonant collective action frames, and which develop the capacity to maintain sustained challenges against powerful opponents. (Tarrow 1998: 2)

> A social movement is a collective actor constituted by individuals who understand themselves to have common interests and, for at least some significant part of their social existence, a common identity. Social movements are distinguished from other collective actors, such as political parties and pressure groups, in that they have mass mobilization, or the threat of mobilization, as their prime source of social sanction, and hence power. They are further distinguished from other collectivities, such as voluntary associations or clubs, in being chiefly concerned to defend or change society, or the relative position of the group in society. (Scott 1995: 6)

New social movements are said (ibid.: 30) to be locally based, organised around specific issues, oscillating between periods of high and low activity, with any organisations formed being fluid and loose, and with fluctuating membership. They are not related to traditional distinctions such class or gender, have no unifying ideology but show a plurality of ideas, are concerned with civil rather than political affairs, encourage previously weak forms of identity, involve personal aspects of life, employ radical mobilisation tactics, are related to a legitimation crisis in Western polities, and are decentralised (Johnston et al. 1994).

Alberto Melucci's first extended English exposition of his work on NSMs was given in *Nomads of the Present: Social Movements and Individual Needs in Contemporary Society* (1989). He rejects earlier treatments of collective phenomena as unified empirical data with an individual personage, epitomised in the notion of the working class, in favour of a constructivist view of collective action which sees it as a composite action system with a complex plurality of meanings. Melucci does not offer a new semantic term for this understanding of an NSM,[4] although he does define the process of constructing a collective action system as 'collective identity': 'Collective identity is an interactive and shared definition produced by several interacting individuals who are concerned with the orientations of their action as well as the field of opportunities and constraints in which their action takes place' (ibid.: 34, original emphasis removed).

According to Melucci, collective actors often claim a unity which is not apparent in reality – while those in power, opposed to the NSM, may dismiss it as pathological behaviour. NSMs involve solidarity, are engaged in conflict in opposition to an adversary and violate the boundaries or tolerance limits of a system. Melucci suggests the reason that self-identity has become a central issue in NSMs is an emerging awareness of our ability to work on our motivational and biological structures, whereas previous social movements were concerned only with acting on the world. This is reminiscent of Ferguson's ([1980] 1989) linkage of personal and social transformation. New social movements are thus engaged in self-reflexive action, which is not instrumental to a further end, but is the meaning or goal of the action in itself.

The title of Melucci's work, *Nomads of the Present*, comes from the fact that contemporary actors are said to be concerned with action in the present: as critics have pointed out, there is no programme or future plan of history in NSMs (Melucci 1989: 55). Melucci therefore asks what success or failure mean in relation to NSMs: 'Conflicts no longer have winners, but they may produce innovation, modernization, and reform' (ibid.: 78). He suggests that they initiate institutional change, select new social elites, and innovate new forms of culture. 'The movements no longer operate as characters but as signs, in the sense that they translate their action into symbolic challenges that overturn the dominant cultural codes' (ibid.: 75, original emphasis removed). This is achieved through 'prophecy' of alternative frameworks of meaning, the reversal of dominant social codes by the use of exaggeration and paradox, and 'representation', or the isolation of form from content to permit retransmission to the dominant system of its own contradictions.

Such a definition of NSMs seems *prima facie* to apply to New Age. New Age is formed around extant social networks, such as the kinship ties located by Wood (1999). It is not organised centrally, but around specific foci such as original teachers, texts or techniques. It has few fixed organisations, and those that do exist often change over time in form and substance. As is seen throughout this book, there is no overall New Age ideology, but a collection of New Age ideas and techniques. One criticism often levelled against New Age is that it is not concerned with worldly affairs. It develops individuals through alternative or complementary systems, which are often spiritual or 'self-help' in nature. It can sometimes employ 'radical mobilisation tactics', such as environmental direct action, is certainly related to the decline in confidence in traditional thought and hierarchies, and is a decentralised network.

Recent commentators on New Age have, however, denied that New Age is a movement.

> Movements are social systems with a minimum of structure, a recognisable hier-archy, points of reference in the territory and in the society in which they are located, in papers, activities which they follow – in a world more or less fixed – a precise programme and so on. (Introvigne 2000: 56, my translation)[5]

Massimo Introvigne prefers to describe New Age sociologically as a network or metanetwork.

Similarly, Steven Sutcliffe says that the phenomena he studies in his doctoral thesis do not constitute a movement, for

> they lack coordinating bodies, historical awareness, a plausible degree of stabil-ity and continuity, evidence of boundary and belonging, a realistic level of critical debate and mobilization (presupposing in turn the existence of an explicit level of ideological norm and practice) and, crucially, overt self-identity and concrete goals. (Sutcliffe 1998: 220)

Matthew Wood criticises scholars of New Age for using the concept of a movement, without properly considering what constitutes such a social organisation, and suggests usage of J. C. Mitchell's criteria for the notion of a corporate group:

> criteria of membership;
> acceptance of norms and rules;
> capability of joint action;
> common aims and interests;
> division of labour in terms of theses;
> persistence of such labour relations.
> (Mitchell 1973: 31–2, quoted in Wood 1999: 79)

Based on these criteria, Wood claims the spiritual network he studied is not a bounded entity, but may nevertheless be still be regarded as a distinguishable entity since the groups concerned brought together people from other groups and those who were practising alone.

Neither Introvigne, nor Sutcliffe, nor Wood, cite the extensive liter-ature on NSM theory explored above. This is surprising given their vocal rejection of such a concept. Of course, it remains possible that New Age does not conform to the definition of a movement as under-stood by Introvigne, Sutcliffe and Wood. However, as shown above,

New Age does conform in many ways to the definition of a movement given by NSM theorists.

NSRM Theory

Kemp (2003a) seeks to bring together cult–sect–church theory, SPIN theory and NSM theory in an analysis of Christian involvement in New Age. The model suggested is that of a new socio-religious movement (NSRM), the name emphasising the concept's similarities to theories both of NRMs and NSMs.

Colin Campbell described a 'cultic milieu' in which ephemeral groups arose and died without any coherence, but formed a continual subculture or backdrop (Campbell 1972). Geoffrey Nelson (1969a) calls these 'local cults', which may develop spontaneously or through the organisation of a charismatic leader. Charismatic cults are said to end with the demise of the charismatic leader. Spontaneous cults are said to end due to internal strife or simply lack of interest. Institutionalisation is seen as the key that enables local cults to survive (ibid.: 157). Nelson thought that charismatic cults typically develop by forming branch groups, and spontaneous cults establish links with similar spontaneous groups in other localities. Either way, institutionalisation and federation lead to assimilation with mainstream society.

In this way, we begin with a diffuse cultic milieu in which associations of cults form to produce a movement before, ultimately, the 'cultic' phenomena become mainstream. This model can be readily applied to New Age, but also fits with the other developmental models outlined above, as depicted in Table 6.1 below. (SPIN theory is not developmental, but static, and so is not included in this comparison. It fits best with the middle line of the comparison.)

Table 6.1   NRM, NSM and NSRM theory

NRM theory	NSM theory	NSRM theory
Cult	Friendship network	Cultic milieu
Sect	Activist network/ social movement organisation	Association of NRMs – broad movement
Church	Professional association	Mainstream assimilation

The developmental goal of a NSRM is mainstream assimilation in the sense of popularisation and acceptance. Even though some NSMs are not only reacting against the mainstream but also resisting adoption of traditional organisational structures, ironically their fundamental purpose (if they can be said to have a purpose) is evangelistic. New Age has not yet achieved assimilation across the board, although aspects of New Age already inform mainstream culture. New Age is currently typically in the middle developmental phase, where associations of separate NRMs form a broad socio-religious movement. Association with other NRMs in such a socio-religious movement has a centripetal normalising effect, so that the appeal of the broader movement becomes ever more mainstream. The final point of full integration with wider societal norms – however these are defined – may be regarded as the success point of a NSRM.

An example of this process is the Body Shop franchise, founded by Anita Roddick, which began with countercultural aims and appeal. As the franchise became more economically successful, it brought in more and more mainstream contributors to the project, including marketing professionals, lawyers and accountants, until the brand became a mainstay of the High Street and part of mainstream culture. To take another example, aromatherapy began (if we ignore its use in the ancient world) to be used more frequently in the Human Potential and early New Age milieu. It became a popular therapy and broadened its appeal to non-religious practitioners. Starting in the late 1980s and early 1990s aromatherapy was used as a marketing tool with, for example, bubble bath and shampoo being labelled as 'aromatherapy' brands. The technique is now used in mainstream medical practice.

It will be understood that an NSRM does not develop in a unitary way: some aspects of the NSRM are accommodated to the mainstream more quickly than others. So, while aromatherapy has been almost completely assimilated to mainstream culture, other New Age therapies, such as reflexology, have not. Neither is it inevitable that all manifestations of New Age will be assimilated in this way – the NSRM model is not teleological, merely descriptive of the integrating trend. Just as NSM theory emphasises that NSMs are volatile in their levels of activity, so NSRMs may decline and even disappear.

– SECULARISATION –

New Age is often proclaimed as a 're-enchantment' of the world (Berman 1981). This phrase harks back to traditional sociological theories of secularisation, which hold that society is becoming increasingly secular or 'dis-enchanted' with religion. Indeed, it has been claimed that the ancient Jews were the first to become dis-enchanted with religion, and began the process of secularisation. It is more common to point to recent history, the decline in church attendance and influence on mainstream society as proof of the theory of secularisation.

Proponents and observers of New Age often claim that here is a spirituality which flies in the face of this trend towards a more secular society. The reclamation of ancient spiritual traditions, such as Gnosticism and Wicca, and the adoption of native spiritual traditions such as American Indian or Celtic spirituality, may be seen as apparent confirmations of such a view of New Age.

Steve Bruce has examined the question of secularisation (Bruce 2000; see also Bruce 2002). He argues that modernisation makes the church form of religion, which was common in the pre-modern world, impossible, since such a structure requires either cultural homogeneity or a powerful elite. Modernisation introduced egalitarianism and increased contact with strangers. In the Reformation, the church form was challenged by the sect form of religion, with the result that both churches and sects tended to become denominations; that is to say, they accepted that other churches and sects held equally valid claims to truth.

New Age forms a cultic milieu, Bruce claims, which is both deviant in its external conception and pluralistically legitimate in its internal conception. He claims New Age is sociologically significant because many characteristics of New Age may be found in the mainstream churches, despite what Bruce claims is its statistical insignificance. New Age solves the problem of cultural pluralism, says Bruce, by adopting a perennialist view of reality which posits a single essence behind apparent diversity.

> But the idea of deviance presupposes a consensus. Obviously Methodism is still better thought of than Spiritualism, Theosophy or Wicca, but it is equally obvious that the distinction is being eroded. The decline of value consensus which is exemplified in the individualism and consumerism in the New Age means the distinction between the denomination and the cult will also decline. Rather than see the New Age as an antidote to secularisation, it makes more sense to see it as a style and form of religion well-suited to the secular world. (Bruce 2000: 234–5)

The debate over New Age and secularisation forms only a small and relatively recent part of the debate over the nature and existence of secularisation. Secularisation may briefly be described as the positing of a decrease in the influence of religion. It is to be distinguished from secularism, which is a quasi-religious belief that only non-religious concepts should govern the way we act in the world. In this way, a definition of secularisation depends on a definition of religion, which has yet to be agreed amongst scholars. It also depends on our interpretation of the history of the influence of religion, which again has not been entirely agreed amongst scholars. For example, religion may be defined along cognitive, social or expressive lines (Attfield 1978). That is to say, the decrease in the influence of religion, and thus the existence of secularisation, could be measured according to the level of religious belief among individuals, or the strength of the churches, or the practice of individuals in daily life and expression. These measures of secularisation are not necessarily consistent, and may be contradictory. When New Agers say they are 're-enchanting' the world, they do not usually mean they are returning to a more dogmatically orthodox state of religion, nor to an era when religious organisations held great sway over the population; usually New Agers mean that their way of life is now more spiritual. One problem with such an argument, however, is that it is not clear that humankind has ever been non-spiritual; what does it mean to be without a spirituality if, as we have suggested, even secularism may be regarded as quasi-religious?

Bruce (2002) claims that some scholars have moved the boundaries of what it means to be religious, in order to 'prove' that society remains as religious as it has been in the past. He claims that this argument, which would go against the secularisation paradigm, creates its own conclusion by its loose definition of religion. One of the problems with Bruce's comments on New Age is that they are generally based on secondary sources and surveys, with little original fieldwork or interviews with New Agers. Such armchair theorising makes it is easier to dismiss concepts of implicit religion or Self spirituality, which are in fact based on solid observational work. It is also difficult to see how Bruce's arguments apply to some of the concrete examples of New Age encountered in this book – which others might describe as implicit religion or Self spirituality. For example, meditation is quite obviously a religious practice; circle dancing is given explicit spiritual import by the dancers; New Age workshops are approached with the same interest and devotion as traditional religious retreats.

Of course, this does not mean that New Age will occupy the same space in modern society as the Christian churches occupied in Christendom. New Age is a different form of religion or spirituality compared to Christianity, just as Christianity is a different form of religion compared to Buddhism or other religions. Technical terms such as implicit religion, SPIN, NRM, NSM and NSRM attempt to highlight some of these differences. But they are only abstractions, drawn out from actual observation of the beliefs and practices of those involved. This is how sociology should be undertaken.

– VIGNETTES – NEW AGE GROUPS –

One of the most obvious artefacts of New Age is the large number of groups which are in some way related to it. As we have seen, individuals in these groups, and the groups as corporate bodies, may not necessarily identify themselves with New Age. However, as observers of these groups, we may note the similarities they have with our understanding of New Age. In the final section of this chapter, three New Age groups are described: Ramtha's School of Enlightenment, Alternatives, and the Findhorn Foundation. Other groups that could equally have been described include Damanhur, the once-secretive religious community in Italy, the many membership groups of specific NRMs, such as individual Wiccan covens, or extended New Age communities such as Sedona, Arizona or Glastonbury, England.

Ramtha's School of Enlightenment

Ramtha is channelled by J. Z. Knight (b. 1946), and lived in Lemuria in the north of Atlatia (Atlantis) 35,000 years ago. First reappearing in 1977, Ramtha was channelled by Knight from the following year in the usual New Age lecture circuits, but by 1988 had developed such a following that Ramtha's School of Enlightenment[6] was founded and public appearances declined. Constance Jones's statistical survey of the school (Jones forthcoming), confirms a typical picture of New Age students: mostly female and middle-aged, well educated, having respectable positions in the professions, technology or business, and often self-employed.

Melton (1998a) describes the curriculum for new students as consisting of: a two-day Level 1 Beginning C&E (Consciousness and Energy) Workshop; a one-week Level 2 Beginning C&E Retreat; and a three-day Level 3 Beginning C&E Follow-up. Each intake of students is named with titles such as Elohim, Akh Men Ra and Iaut Aleph. There are optional Assays, lasting a week to ten days, and group events for advanced students including Boktau, a summer retreat, and lectures by Ramtha.

C&E is described by Melton as 'concentrated dreaming combined with an intense breathing' (ibid.: 95) and is said to be the core practice upon which all other spiritual disciplines at the school are based. These include 'fieldwork', which could perhaps be described as a spiritual version of the child's party game 'pin the tail on the donkey': the student draws a wish or desire on two cards, which are collected and pinned face down to a fence around a large field. The students are then blindfolded, spun round and told to 'seek' their own cards along with other students in the field. Successful students shout out in joy, while others concentrate more clearly on their wish. Another spiritual discipline, the tank, is a large circular maze, 120 feet across, with mobile walls that are regularly shifted. Staff walk on top of the eight-foot walls while students attempt to find the centre, the 'void'. Throughout the maze there are obstacles to overcome, such as bridges and low entrances. Students are despatched in a crowd and are blindfolded – even before they are taken to the entrance of the maze. Other spiritual disciplines include 'tahumo', where students create internal body heat to overcome a cold environment; listing goals for manifesting in the daily C&E exercise; and healing through meditation on a large, blue painting of Shiva.

In the late 1980s, prior to the foundation of the school, Knight received media exposure of her expensive lifestyle and home, at a time when the Arabian horse-breeding ranch she encouraged many followers to invest in collapsed. Knight eventually agreed to reimburse investors, although no legal irregularities were confirmed, and media interest abated.

Ramtha's School of Enlightenment is a good example of a New Age group that has institutionalised into a fixed hierarchical organisation. It is not yet known whether this will prove to be a typical developmental pattern amongst New Age groups.

The Findhorn Foundation

The charitable Findhorn Foundation was created in 1972. Steven Sutcliffe (1998: 158) encapsulates Findhorn ideology and practice as 'experiential interiority'. The Findhorn Community consists of two sites, seven miles apart – Cluny Hill Hotel, bought in 1975, and Findhorn Bay Caravan Park, bought in 1983. In 1991 the Foundation had about 170 members, including children and dependants. The total community, including ex-members and associates, numbered 400–500. In 1989, almost two-thirds of adult residents were female, nearly three-quarters were aged between thirty and fifty, all were white-skinned. Sutcliffe (1997) conducted a small survey which confirmed this profile.

There is an international mailing list of 20,000, resulting in attendance of over 5,000 (in total) to at least one event per year.

Sutcliffe attended an 'Experience Week' at the Findhorn Community in 1995, joining an international group of ten women and four men in the initial training course of the Foundation.

On the Saturday Sutcliffe attended meditation in the Sanctuary. There were similar sessions twice a day, in the morning and at noon, although private use of the sanctuaries was more-or-less constant. 'Attunement' followed: joined hands in a seated circle, eyes closed. 'Sharing' followed that: self-expression to the group. Two hours of introductions to each other followed mastery of these skills. Food offered at Findhorn was vegetarian.

Sunday began with meditation in the Sanctuary at 8.30a.m., then 'sacred dancing' in the ballroom. A tour of Findhorn village and the caravan park ended at the nature sanctuary, where the attendees requested the quality they most wished for from the week, and drew an 'angel card' to select a quality to work with. Sutcliffe requested confidence and selected faith. After dinner, the group attuned for work placements, shared for half an hour and finished with a talk on 'inner life' and a visualisation exercise.

Sutcliffe had been assigned to the Community Centre in the Park, and arrived for work at 9a.m. on Monday morning – there is a strong work ethic at Findhorn. In the afternoon, the group played a mirroring game, imitating each others' movements; and then a driving game in which one closed their eyes and was 'driven' around the room by another. A game of tag followed, where the object was to hug the other people. Other games were also played.

After the morning's work on Tuesday there was a nature outing, where the group were encouraged to 'be in nature' – individually, alone. On Wednesday morning, Sutcliffe helped to spring clean the hotel lounge. In the afternoon they read David Spangler in a group, in a way that Sutcliffe describes as 'devotional reading'. Sharing again followed.

Cleaning the toilets was Sutcliffe's duty on Thursday morning. The afternoon was free, and there was a talk on 'Personal and Planetary Transformation' in the evening. Friday ended with a last session of sharing.

It is difficult to get a feel for a community in such a short description. Yet Findhorn is probably the best known New Age community worldwide, and it is important to describe the ways in which most visitors experience it. There may seem little that is markedly different from other spiritual communities. And indeed it is probably for his-

torical reasons that Findhorn is eponymous of New Age commr
in that Findhorn was, through the work of Spangler (b. 1945), one ot
the first 'Centres of Light' to become widely known. Differing perspectives on Findhorn can be obtained from Castro (1996), which is
highly critical, and Walker (ed. 1994), which is highly complimentary.

The Findhorn community thus shows some structural similarities to
the fixed organisation of Ramtha's School of Enlightenment, but is
more open to paying and transient visitors in the fashion of William
Sims Bainbridge's client phenomenon. Many visitors will still be at
Bainbridge's audience stage, as is more clearly shown in the next example
of a New Age group.

Alternatives

The Alternatives lecture series has been running at St James's church
in Piccadilly, central London, since 1989, when it took over from
the Turning Points lectures and meetings. William Bloom, Sabrina
Dearborn and Malcolm Stern were the founding directors, and the
ministry was encouraged by Revd Donald Reeves, rector from 1980 to
1998, and initially funded by the church.

The first programme included lectures on sexual politics, full
moons, Druidism, New Age and Neuro Linguistic Programming. There
were also workshops on inner music, meditation, painting and song,
and a series of New Age concerts. Together with the Creation Centered
Spirituality Ministry, also based until recently at St James's church,[7]
Alternatives also regularly celebrated the new and full moons, as well
as Wesak, Buddha's birthday.

The latest programmes of lectures still include some of the original
speakers, and the number of additional workshops has increased.
Speakers include Nick Williams, a trustee of Alternatives and founder
of the Heart at Work project; Robert Holden, founder of the
Happiness Project; and Vivianne Crowley, a Wiccan high priestess
and lecturer at Heythrop College, University of London. There are
workshops on Reiki healing, the Alexander Technique and the four
elements, among many others.

The weekly lectures are extremely popular, attracting around 300
people for each evening; a press release in October 1998 claimed an
audience of over 15,000 people per year; and according to a survey
conducted in 1999 (Kemp 2003a), fewer than one in three members of
the church electoral roll have not been to Alternatives. In the early
1990s, however, the ministry attracted hostile criticism, mainly from

the Evangelical wing of the Church of England, for its 'non-Christian' focus. Consequently, all Alternatives literature now includes a 'friendly disclaimer' written by Bloom: 'Although St James's Church, in its openness of heart and mind, includes Alternatives, the ideas in the programme are not representative of the church itself' (Alternatives brochure 2003). Some members of the church congregation and parochial church council now distance themselves from the Alternatives project.

The lecture evenings usually begin with a silent meditation. A candle is lit by a member of the audience, and the speaker chooses a spiritual quality to represent the evening. Sometimes the four directions are invoked. The lecture always finishes with an opportunity for questions. After the presentation, soup is often served and many of the audience stay to chat or buy New Age books from the bookstall.

The only published statistical survey of an Alternatives audience was conducted by Michael York in 1990 (York 1995: 179f.). Seventy-one per cent of respondents were female. The backgrounds of respondents were mixed: seventeen per cent worked in 'teaching, crafts, etc.', twelve per cent in therapy, eleven per cent in computers and eleven per cent were unemployed. Current religious preferences were described as follows: twenty-three per cent claimed no religious affiliation and eight per cent claimed New Age identity, with a similar number claiming a Christian identity.

Alternatives could perhaps be described as a client phenomenon (Bainbridge 1997) (see above). However, this definition most clearly applies to one-to-one relationships of clients with practitioners, and so Alternatives may be seen to be better characterised by Bainbridge's audience classification. Alternatives may be seen to be in the early stages of NSM development, having moved beyond a mere friendship network into an activist network or, with its involvement with other organised groups, into a social movement organisation. In NSRM theory, it is again in early development, having emerged from the cultic milieu to form associations with like-minded groups on the road to mainstream assimilation.

– CONCLUSION –

The three examples of New Age communities given in this chapter are noticeably different from each other – from an audience-based lecture series at Alternatives through a client-based open residential programme at Findhorn to a more closed community at Ramtha's School of

Enlightenment. A family resemblance mode of definition, as described in Chapter 1, is able to accommodate these differences while acknowledging the fundamental similarities that make each of the communities part of New Age.

There are a number of ways of looking at such communities sociologically, from traditional cult–sect–church theory, through NRM and SPIN to NSM and NSRM theories. Each sociological model will bring out different aspects of the communities under observation, and no one model gives the final, 'correct answer'; there are no answers in sociology, only points of view. Such a postmodern understanding of sociology applies equally to the discipline employed in the next chapter to study New Age, namely psychology.

– Notes –

1. A common questionnaire technique, Likert questions allow a range of responses from 'strongly agree' to 'strongly disagree'.
2. York would surely now add email and the Internet.
3. Excepting also, of course, Kemp (2003a) and Kemp (2001). Possamaï (1998) briefly mentions NSM theory but does not develop its application. See also Hetherington (2000) on NSM theory and New Age travellers. Carozzi's article was translated from Spanish to Portuguese for publication, before my attempt to understand the Portuguese. I apologise for any misunderstandings due to my inadequate language skills. The article was preceded by Carozzi (1996).
4. Melucci (1989: 29). Compare, however, Melucci's later usage of the term 'peace mobilization' in place of 'peace movement' (ibid.: 81f.).
5. 'I movimenti sono sistemi sociali con un minimo di struttura, una gerarchia riconoscibile, punti di riferimento sul territorio e nella società quali sedi, giornali, attività che seguono – in un modo più o meno rigido – un programma preciso e così via.' I am grateful to Nicole Purin for checking this translation.
6. According to Melton et al. (1991: 66), earlier organisations included the Church I Am and Sovereignty, Inc.
7. In December 2001, the administration of the Creation Sprituality Ministry, now known as GreenSpirit, was moved to a residential address in London, although links with St James's church are maintained. Many GreenSpirit members do not identify themselves as Christian.

CHAPTER 7

Psychology

Psychology is central to an understanding of New Age, both emically and etically.[1] On the one hand, schools of psychology such as Jungian, transpersonal and client-centred psychology were important influences on Human Potential and thus on New Age. On the other hand, attempts have been made to profile New Agers psychologically, both from a scientific perspective and from a critical (usually Christian) perspective. An oft-heard criticism of New Age is that it is over-concerned with the self. Using survey data from Kemp (2003a), Rose (1996), York (1995), Donahue (1993) and Roof et al. (1993), I will attempt a portrayal of a typical New Ager. We will see that the figure which emerges from these statistics is very different from the common media portrayal of a young, unemployed, dope-smoking New Age traveller. Psychological theory also has an input into conversion theory, which is another aspect of New Age studies and the study of new religious movements more generally. Another vignette on the application of psychology to New Age is given in the example of the relation between New Age and mental health.

– HISTORICAL –

The history of New Age psychology starts with Carl Gustav Jung (1875–1961), who was at first a disciple of Sigmund Freud (1856–1939), departing from him shortly before the outbreak of the First World War. Jung's later psychology was deeply marked by his wide readings in astrology, Gnosticism, alchemy, the I Ching and other esoteric traditions. He believed these traditions revealed the archetypes or patterns of human behaviour that are engrained in humanity's collective unconscious.[2] These influences also surface in dreams, and perhaps in what he called 'synchronicity', an 'acausal connecting principle' which links seeming coincidences through deeper meanings.

Another of Jung's influential theories is the idea of the 'shadow' personality, which we typically try to subvert. New Age has also taken to heart the idea of an *anima* or *animus* residing within and complementing each male and female respectively. Jung was among the first established scientists to take flying-saucer phenomena seriously. Perhaps the most widely read Jungian text among New Agers, the autobiographical compendium edited by Aniela Jaffé, *Memories, Dreams, Reflections* (Jung 1962), has been questioned by some as to the integrity of its authorship (Noll 1997: xii–xiv). Jungian psychology is today not mainstream science, but enjoys a huge currency on the bookshelves of the general public, not just those of New Agers.

Unlike Freud, Jung and other psychoanalysts, Abraham Maslow (1908–70) did not study neurotics; he was interested in what he called 'self-actualised' people – successful, healthy, fulfilled individuals – and the 'peak experiences' that they attained. He taught that human motives may be represented in a pyramid, with lower levels requiring satisfaction before higher levels can be attained. Bottom up, these psychological sources are sex, hunger, thirst; security, comfort; belongingness, love; self-respect, success; and lastly, self-actualisation.

Fritz Perls (1893–1970) met Maslow and had a great influence on Human Potential and humanistic psychology, developing Gestalt Therapy. Gestalt means 'whole', with the nuance that the whole is greater than the sum of its parts. Perls integrated bodily, emotional and mental aspects of the human situation in his work, for example using psychodrama. Perls emphasised the 'here and now'. Gestalt psychotherapy assumes that, left alone, humans spontaneously regulate themselves, although the fulfilment of needs is an active process for which each individual must assume responsibility.

Carl Rogers (1902–87) taught that there is one single human motive, 'the actualising tendency', which aims towards the fulfilment of potential. Our feelings of self-worth are dependent on the positive regard shown to us by others, especially in the formative years. Rogers outlined several rules for 'client-centred therapy'. Firstly, the therapist is 'genuine' and does not hide behind his professional role. Secondly, the client – Rogers initiated the turn from the word 'patient' – must receive positive regard or acceptance from the therapist. Thirdly, the therapist must have empathy with the client.

Maslow, Perls and Rogers were central to the development of Human Potential, one of the precursors of New Age. One of the most accessible studies of Human Potential is Nevill Drury's *The Elements of Human Potential* (1989). Drury suggests that Holistic Health emerged 'in the early 1970s in part as a non-drug response to the psychedelic exploration undertaken in the 1960s' (ibid.: 2). He further suggests that Human Potential is the 'more academic counterpart' of New Age (ibid.: 14), and traces the roots of both to William James, Freud, Jung, Alfred Adler and Wilhelm Reich. Human Potential's theoretical wing, transpersonal psychology, deals with states of consciousness beyond the ego.

The Esalen Institute in Big Sur, California, played an important part in the development of transpersonal psychology. Big Sur Hot Springs was begun in 1962 by Michael Murphy and Richard Price as a forum for diverse religious traditions and the exploration of consciousness. Alan Watts, Aldous Huxley, Ken Kesey, Carlos Castaneda, Paul Tillich, Perls and Maslow were among the early lecturers at Esalen. By 1967, Esalen was well known enough to feature in a *Time* magazine article. Although illicit drugs had been used by some of the early lecturers and attendees at Esalen, a ban on drugs was later introduced. Esalen continues to be influential today, and its programme includes T'ai Chi, Zen, shamanism, Taoism, Feldenkrais, lectures on Findhorn and feminist spirituality.

− PSYCHOLOGICAL PROFILES OF NEW AGERS −

There have been a number of attempts at psychological profiles of New Agers. These include Granqvist and Hagekull (2001), DeMarinis (1998), Heelas (1996a), Faber (1996), Lasch (1979, 1987), Vitz (1994), Green (1992) and Dubrow-Eichel and Dubrow-Eichel (1988), and are considered in this section in order of my perception of relative clinical and statistical authority.

Pehr Granqvist and Berit Hagekull (2001) have tested whether an emotional compensation hypothesis is applicable to New Age orientation (see Chapter 6). In a small sample of 193 participants from Swedish schools, Christian youth organisations and New Age venues, they found that New Age orientation was directly linked to attachment insecurity and emotionally based religiosity, and inversely related to socially based religiosity. Attachment insecurity was also linked to the experience of spiritual change. Granqvist and Hagekull suggest that attachment theory may highlight predisposing factors for New Age orientation, measuring one part of the emotional compensation profile.

Valerie DeMarinis (1998) reports on a clinical case-study investigation of New Age participants in Berkeley, California. She uses Paul Pruyser's 'Three-World Model' theory, which categorises the effects of a religious system into three worlds: autistic (inner), realistic (outer) and illusionistic (balancing). In the autistic world, the universe is self-centred, resulting in fantastical, omnipotent thinking. In the realistic world, the universe is tested according to logical consequences, factual needs, rules and work. The illusionistic world links these two worlds, meets cultural needs, domesticates fantasy, orders imagination and represents mature religion. DeMarinis' study was limited to twenty-three psychotherapeutic clients who had described their beliefs as New Age, and who had consciously rejected childhood Christian traditions; none had long-term psychiatric problems or psychoses. The data presented six patterns of religious development.

DeMarinis claims that the timing of the break from the Christian religious system of early childhood is crucial to understanding its psychological impact – the earlier in the development cycle the break begins, the more extensive the psychological consequences. Each subject explained their participation in New Age as due to a conscious critique of Christian religion. The majority of subjects experienced an interval of on average two years between the final break with Christianity and the exposure to New Age.

A two-stage process in involvement with New Age is identified, from the autistic to the illusionistic world. Initial involvement has little social context and addresses the deep ritual loss from early childhood on an individual basis. Stage two fulfils the need for community. The interval between the two stages varied from two months to two years. A number of hypotheses are made at the conclusion of the study, including: New Age participation can assist the self-development process; New Age participation can restore the religious function if the community dimension is present; and there can be a psychological need for religious ritual in individuals who have experienced it in childhood.

Paul Heelas's *The New Age Movement* (1996a) is usually considered as employing a sociological rather than a psychological approach, essentially developing an earlier article on 'Self-Religions' (Heelas 1982). This article described (ibid.: 74–5) secondary institutions providing a middle way between the unstructured subjectivity of anomie and the systematised bureaucracy of public institutions. 'The New Age shows what "religion" looks like when it is organized in terms of what is taken to be the authority of the Self' (Heelas 1996a: 221).

The notion of Self-Religions (Heelas 1982) modifies through Self spirituality (Heelas 1996a) to expressive spirituality (Heelas 2000), perhaps in response to emic criticism first about the notion of religion and later about overemphasis of the notion of self.

> This is the spirituality which has to do with that which lies 'within' rather than that which lies over-and-above the self or whatever the world might have to offer. This is the spirituality which is integral to what it is to be truly oneself; which is integral to the natural order as a whole. This is the spirituality which serves as the font of wisdom and judgement, rejecting authoritative sources emanating from some transcendent, tradition-articulated, source. This is the spirituality which informs ('expressive') authenticity, creativity, love, vitality. This is the spirituality which interconnects. (ibid.: 243)

However, all three terms appear to be largely synonymous, in addition to the term New Age.

> The term 'New Age' can usefully be deployed to characterise all those, belonging to the realm of the 'alternative', who hold that contact with inner spirituality – the spirituality which can be experienced from within the person and, for many, the natural order as a whole – serves as the basis for a new, transformed way of being. (Heelas 1998: 257)

Heelas claims that Self spirituality is the *lingua franca* of New Age. He also reproduces (Heelas 1996a: 227–8) a psychological analysis based on the California Psychological Inventory questionnaire returns of fifty people who took the Exegesis seminar in 1994. Before the seminar, participants were said to be confused and unhappy, rebellious and resentful of authority, highly self-centred and lacking commitment, impulsive and willing to take risks, and not very aware of the impression they create on others. After the seminar, the respondents were found to have increased their social poise and confidence, be less apathetic and more enthusiastic, have a better sense of self-worth, were better able to use social skills to achieve their aims, had exaggerated tendencies to be reckless, rebellious and impulsive, with lowered integrity, and were more manipulative, wanting more attention.

The notion of Self spirituality has been criticised by Adrian Ivakhiv (2003) with reference to his fieldwork on New Age pilgrimage. Ivakhiv suggests that at least three different kinds of New Age 'self' can be identified. Firstly, a bounded, essential self which guards against the threat of depletion or impurity is suggested by an emphasis on self-development, personal growth and clearing auras. Secondly, a multiple self is suggested by notions of an inner child, wild man, animal teacher, spirit guide, past incarnation and ancestral figures. Thirdly, a cosmic self is suggested in references to a higher self (or, in Earth spirituality, this is presented as a depth self).

An extended examination of New Age psychology is found in M. D. Faber's *New Age Thinking: a Psychoanalytic Critique* (1996), building on his earlier *Modern Witchcraft and Psychoanalysis* (1993). Faber explains psychoanalytic theory in some detail, especially the importance of the conflict between separation and merger of the child and parent (usually mother). The earliest stage of development is said to be an 'autistic' state where the needs of the baby are fulfilled by the mother, as if magically. Increasingly, the child becomes aware of its separation and differentiation from the mother until it is able to function as an autonomous individual. Faber's understanding of New Age thinking is that it regresses the adult to the infantile stage of magical wish fulfilment and merger with an imagined mother figure. At times, he goes so far as to suggest that New Agers are delusive and insane (e.g. Faber 1996: 159). Faber explores his thesis in depth using the examples of crystals, shamanism, channelling, witchcraft and healing. The bulk of the text is based on an analysis of written works, but there is also a chapter of interviews illustrating his critique.

Ken Wilber describes the type of argument employed by Faber as the 'pre/trans fallacy' – namely, pre-conscious material tends to be thought of by such critics as uniformly worthless, even if dealing meaningfully with transcendental themes; while to New Agers, pre-conscious material tends to be thought of as uniformly meaningful, even if devoid of insight that transcends the self. Wilber estimates four-fifths of New Age is prepersonal, and only one fifth is transpersonal (Wilber 1991: 268, quoted in Hanegraaff 1996: 250).

Christopher Lasch's *The Culture of Narcissism* (1979) described the narcissistic personality from a psychological and cultural–historical viewpoint. While the personality type is incisively recognisable (if a little overdone), Lasch did not yet in this earlier work relate it to New Age. Lasch later wrote a magazine article about New Age (Lasch 1987), which builds on *The Culture of Narcissism*, and claims that

> the question is not whether New Age therapies really work but whether religion ought to be reduced to therapy. If it offers nothing more than a spiritual high, religion becomes another drug in a drug-ridden society . . . The only corrective to the ersatz religions of the New Age is a return to the real thing. (Lasch 1987: 180)

Lasch contends that religious experience can be equated with enlightenment, arguing that this was the point of argument between Christianity and Gnosticism – the difference between faith and knowledge. Another article by Lasch, reprinted in the paperback edition of *The Culture of Narcissism*, states that New Age is rooted in what Freud called primary narcissism, which posited a state of consciousness prior to awareness of a reality distinct from the self. New Age, Lasch claims, seeks to restore this illusion of symbiosis and oneness with the world by denying the reality of the material world.

In a similar way, Paul Vitz reissued his popular *Psychology as Religion: The Cult of Self-Worship* (1977) with an additional chapter on New Age in 1994. The original work was a critique of 'selfism', with an emphasis on traditional family values and educational discipline, as against youth culture, the language of victimisation and non-Christian idolatry. The arguments were based on a scientific and philosophical refutation of the assumptions of 'psychology', with few theological arguments from Christian scripture. Vitz's chapter on New Age, based on an earlier article with Deidre Modesti (1993), defines New Age as characterised by 'the notion of a psychological or spiritual process or activity as the goal' (Vitz 1994: 112), and uses Douglas Groothuis's list of the basic tenets of New Age (see Chapter 4). Vitz points out that the social heterogeneity of American culture supports the pluralism of New Age, the 'international mentality' of many Americans supports the development of a global village, and the collapse of 'mainline' Protestantism has left a spiritual vacuum. Other 'supports' include the drug culture, America's rootlessness and the consumer-society approach.

Vitz suggests that 'psychology was one of the major intellectual and social forces that brought today's [New Age] movement into cultural prominence' (ibid.: 117). In particular, he concentrates on humanistic and transpersonal psychology, especially the work of Abraham Maslow and Carl Rogers. This psychology is said to be 'fundamentally narcissistic' (ibid.: 124) and focused on the individual's glorification of his or her own self, creating a form of self-worship. According to Vitz, self-actualisation led to two disappointments: the breakdown of interpersonal relations (e.g. divorce) and the realisation as people aged that they would not attain self-actualisation in their lifetimes. Traditional religion restrains narcissism in a way that New Age spirituality does not, he says.

Martin Green, basing his theories on historical and not psychological research, identifies three temperaments: the voice of triumph and authority that seeks power and possession; the systematic academic temperaments; and the 'naïve and enthusiastic mind that comes to expression in New Ages. People of this type (and we are all of this type part of the time) have a different sense of limits, and try things the others wouldn't dare. They affirm absolutes and realize ideals' (Green 1992: 3). Green illustrates this thesis with historical evidence from the eighteenth century onwards, including people such as Mahatma Ghandi, Thomas Paine, Percy Bysshe Shelley, Gary Snyder and Shirley MacLaine.

Steve Dubrow-Eichel and Linda Dubrow-Eichel, psychotherapists at RETIRN, the Re-Entry Therapy, Information and Referral Network, detail from a Christian fundamentalist perspective the 'impact of manipulative aspects of the New Age movement on the psychological well-being' of their clients (Dubrow-Eichel & Dubrow-Eichel 1988: 177). With the caveat that 'New Ager' is a self-described grouping rather than a new diagnostic category, the authors make the following 'clinical' observations about New Agers:

> New Agers generally place unusually great value on subjective experience . . .
> New Agers tend to be impatient sensation seekers . . .
> New Agers . . . appear to have unusual difficulty in making long-term emotional commitments or the sacrifices common to relationships (e.g. marital fidelity) . . .
> New Agers frequently protest therapist–client boundaries . . .
> There often appears to have been one alienating event, or even trauma, that moved the client toward an acceptance of New Age beliefs and techniques . . .
> New Agers often have become familiar, even comfortable, with dissociative states.
> (ibid.: 179–82)

Identifying three categories of New Agers – dabblers, hoppers and cultists – according to their level of commitment to New Age, the authors suggest varying levels of intervention required for a 'cure' of a New Ager, ranging from traditional psychotherapy through education on the process of 'systematic manipulation of experience' through to full-blown exit counselling and re-entry therapy.

None of these psychological profiles of New Agers is particularly complimentary. They range from the obviously biased accusations of hostile Christians, through armchair psychoanalysis to more serious clinical and statistical studies, but all locate psychological deficiencies with New Agers. Such analyses are in direct contrast to the common emic New Age theme that alternative therapies and spiritual practices contribute to psychological and physical well-being. However, the emic claims are rarely backed by statistical or clinical evidence. In the next section, statistical data will be presented with the aim of describing a 'typical' New Ager.

– A Typical New Ager –

New Agers may be said to be part of the new middle class described in new social movement theory (see Chapter 6) which forms the backbone of most NSMs. The new middle class is better educated than the traditional middle classes, is employed mainly in the tertiary service sector, but does not consist of typical managers or professionals and is pitted against bureaucrats of the military–industrial complex (Della Porta & Diani 1999: 47–8, 259).[3] Alberto Melucci reports that members of the new middle class include new elites challenging established elites, and 'human capital' professionals. They are involved in contemporary social structures – households, communities, and political, social and voluntary organisations – are relatively well educated and usually young (Melucci 1989: 53).

Respondents in the largest extant survey of New Agers were nearly four in five from the middle-class social groups B and C1, compared to a national average of just over two in five (Rose 1996: 373). They found various reasons given for adopting New Age ideas and practices, including self-development, seeking wisdom, dissatisfaction with traditional norms, 'because they made sense', unconscious guidance, and influence by teachers or teachings (ibid.: 369). Of thirty-two New Age activities investigated by Rose, creative visualisation was the most common practice – eighty per cent of respondents had visualised – closely followed by recycling, aromatherapy and massage. Over eight in ten respondents had practised ten or more of the thirty-two activities, with over half reporting current practice of more than five of the listed activities (ibid.: 367). Nearly three-quarters had read more than twenty-five books on New Age (ibid.: 371).

Wade Clark Roof et al. (1993) portray typical New Agers as follows:

> Compared with others of their generation, they are older [sic], more of them are white collar and professionals, and they are better educated. However, they earn less in their jobs and careers. More are female. Fewer are married. They are more liberal in political views. As we would expect, these seekers have low levels of institutional religious involvement. (Roof et al. 1993: 80)

This portrayal is based on the statistics tabulated below (Table 7.1), and although there may be some problems with the significance of the inferences,[4] the characteristics identified as typical are confirmed in York (1995), Rose (1996) and Kemp (2003a).

I conducted a number of simple sociological enquiries on three Christian New Age groups, and compared them with data from an Evangelical Christian congregation, Michael York's survey of an

Alternatives lecture evening and Stuart Rose's survey of New Age magazine *Kindred Spirit* readers (Kemp 2003a). Some of the tabulated results are reproduced below, with additional statistics from later studies where relevant.

Table 7.1   *Roof et al.'s highly active seekers*

	Highly active seekers (N=50) %	All others (N=486) %
Over 35 years of age	62	54
Some college	72	53
White collar	67	60
Professionals	31	28
Earns $40,000+ annually	37	45
Married	54	66
Female	54	50
Liberal political views	44	26
No religious affiliation	24	7

(Roof et al. 1993: 81)

Table 7.2   *Key to tables*

Survey Population	Abbreviation
Alternatives lecture evening (York 1995)	Alt
Three Christaquarian populations (Kemp 2003a)	CQ
Two Evangelical Anglican churches, electoral rolls (Kemp 2003a)	Ev
Kindred Spirit magazine (Rose 1996)	KS
National statistics (National Statistics 2003)	Nat
Psychology of Vision and *The Spark*, South West England (Corrywright 2001)	SW

Sample size and return:

Alt	CQ	Ev	KS	SW
48/121=40%	339/601=56%	53/114=46%	908/5350=17%	60/?ᵃ=50–59%

a. Corrywright (SW) does not reveal the exact number of surveys distributed to each group, but reports a total return of 65 surveys, 60 of which were analysed, with response rates at 50% for *The Spark*, 58.7% for participants of three Psychology of Vision workshops, and 56% from the 'Unveiling the Goddess' seminar with Roger Woolger.

Table 7.3 *What is your age?*

Age range	CQ %	Ev %	KS %	Nat %	SW %
0–18	0	4	0	2	25
19–24	0	6	3	4	6[a]
25–34	5	13	16	13	14
35–44	9	13	30	38	15
45–54	18	19	27	26	13
55–64	25	15	14	6	11
65+	42	25	10	11	16
No answer	1	6	1	-	-

a. The 2001 census used the far more logical age range of 0–19 and 20–24.
These data are reproduced histographically in Figure 7.1 below.
Columns do not necessarily total 100% owing to rounding of figures.
The Alternatives survey produced incomparable results.

Figure 7.1 *What is your age?*

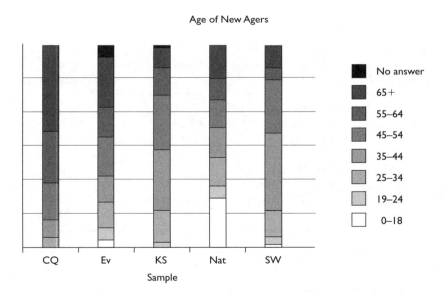

Table 7.4 *Are you male or female?*

Sex	Alt %	CQ %	Ev %	KS %	SW %	Nat %
Male	29	28	26	30	40	51
Female	71	71	72	70	60	49
No answer	-	1	2	-	-	0

These data are reproduced histographically in Figure 7.2 below.

Figure 7.2 *Are you male or female?*

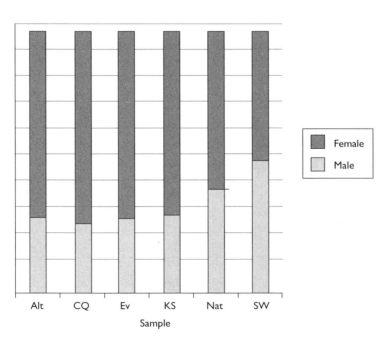

Gender of New Agers

'No answer' responses ignored.

Table 7.5   What is your approximate annual income?

Income	Alt %	CQ %	Ev %	KS %	Nat[a] %	SW %
£0–4,999	21	36	9	19	17	20
£5,000–9,999	23	9	17	21	33	15
£10,000–14,999	35	9	20	18	23	8
£15,000–19,999	13	6	18	16	13	7
£20,000–24,999	} 4	6	14	} 21	} 14	} 32
£25,000–34,999		11	5			
£35,000+		4	11			
No answer	4	19	7	5	0	25

a. Inland Revenue figures cited in Rose (1996: 373).
Columns do not necessarily total 100% owing to rounding of figures.

Table 7.6   What is/was your occupation?

Occupation	CQ %	Ev %	KS %
Therapist	8	0	20
Retired	0	-	13
Student/teacher/library	22	11	12
Managerial/sales	0	0	12
Nurse/carer/social work	12	4	7
Housewife/parent	4	25	6
Creative	8	2	5
Secretarial/clerical	6	0	5
Professional	14	9	-
Unskilled/skilled labour	2	2	-
Religious	5	0	-
NA/other/unclassified	21	30	20

Data for other groups not available.
Columns do not necessarily total 100% owing to rounding of figures.

Table 7.7   *What is your employment status?*

Status	CQ %	Ev %	Nat %
Employed/self-employed	35	-	60
Retired	48	36	13
Student	1	9	5
Unemployed	2	4	4
No answer[a]	14	51	-
Other	-	-	15

a. Due to an oversight, there was no category on Evangelical and one sub-group of Christ-aquarian questionnaires for employed/self-employed.
Data for other groups not available.
Columns do not necessarily total 100% owing to rounding of figures.

Table 7.8   *Highest level of education*

Qualifications	CQ %	Ev %	Nat %
None	7	11	}60
O-level	11	25	
A-level	10	11	
BA, BSc	24	17	}40
Masters	15	0	
PhD	1	0	
Professional	30	26	
No answer	3	9	-

Data for other groups not available.
Columns do not necessarily total 100% owing to rounding of figures.

Table 7.9   *Have you ever participated in or used any of the following?*

Practice	CQ %	Ev %	KS %
Acupuncture/shiatsu	52	9	57
Alexander Technique	33	2	32
Aromatherapy	50	17	73
Buddhism	42	0	50
Channelling	14	0	49
Colour therapy	24	2	48
Creative visualisation	53	0	80
Crystals	21	0	71
Dance therapy	33	0	30
Earth mysteries	12	0	43
Ethical investing	33	4	18
Flower remedies	45	8	70
Green politics	38	8	45
Healing workshops	54	13	67
Herbalism	39	9	57
Homeopathy	61	21	39
Hypnotherapy	17	6	39
Massage	63	15	73
NLP	9	2	18
Past-life therapy	8	2	39
Psychotherapy	48	8	42
Rebirthing	12	0	18
Reflexology	47	11	64
Recycling	63	55	74
Shaman/Pagan rituals	15	0	35
Sound Therapy	15	0	34
Spiritualism	13	6	55
T'ai Chi Ch'uan/Yoga	56	4	67
Transactional analysis	19	8	21
Veganism	4	0	14
Vegetarianism	47	11	71
Women's Studies groups	24	11	20
Average of above	33	7	47

Data for other groups not available.

Table 7.10   Number of practices listed in Table 7.9 ever practised by each individual[a]

Number practised	CQ %	Ev %
0–4	20	85
5–9	26	15
10–14	25	0
15–32	28	0

a. Kindred Spirit figures not available from Rose (1996).
Data for other groups not available.
Columns do not necessarily total 100% owing to rounding of figures.

Although the data from Kemp (2003a) primarily concern New Agers who belong to Christian-oriented groups, the correspondences with York's data from Alternatives attendees and Rose's data from *Kindred Spirit* readers in general demonstrate that they may be representative of New Age more widely. From these surveys, the following picture emerges.

The typical New Ager is at least thirty-five years old, and may be well into retirement. She is twice as likely to be female as male. She is better off in financial terms than average, and typical careers include therapists, teachers, managerial/sales, nursing or social work. It is more likely than not that she will have at least one degree or a professional qualification. She has probably participated in ten or more of the New Age practices listed in Rose (1996).

– VIGNETTE – CONVERSION –

How does one become a New Ager? Hostile accounts of many new religious movements attribute conversion to 'brainwashing', 'love-bombing' and other surreptitious techniques employed by believers to entice converts. Though still common,[5] such accounts are generally rejected by scholars of new religious movements (Zablocki 1998). The conventional model of conversion attributes much importance to spiritual experience, as in Saul's conversion experience on the road to Damascus.

Charles Tart described 'altered states of consciousness' (ASCs) in the introduction to the well-known collection of essays he edited under that title, as follows: 'An altered state of consciousness for a given individual is one in which he clearly feels a *qualitative* shift in his pattern of mental functioning, that is, he feels not just a quantitative shift (more or less alert, more or less visual imagery, sharper or duller, etc.), but also some quality or qualities of his mental processes are *different*' (Tart ed. 1990: 1–2, *original emphasis*). Tart was writing in a period when drug-induced ASCs would have been familiar to many of his readers (see Chapter 3). He was also building on Thomas Kuhn's notion of a 'paradigm shift', outlined in *The Structure of Scientific Revolutions* (1962), which described new ways of thinking about new problems, such as the shift between Ptolemaic and Copernican thought about the solar system.

While not explicitly referring to Tart, Marilyn Ferguson's *Aquarian Conspiracy* ([1980] 1989) thesis is based on the same notion: that a personal change in values will be effected through a mystical experience. Indeed, the book was originally subtitled 'Personal and Social Transformation in the 1980s', bringing out her claim that global reform can only be achieved through starting change at the level of individual consciousness.

However, the conversion-through-experience model is also difficult to apply in many cases to New Age. Tanya Luhrmann points to 'the slow, often unacknowledged shift in someone's manner of interpreting events as they become involved with a particular activity' (Luhrmann 1989: 12; see also ibid.: 312, 322) and dubbed this 'interpretive drift'. Starhawk, a witch, describes her own conversion in terms which fit the notion of interpretive drift:

> Over all these years of practising ritual and magic . . . I have actually come to believe it. When I started I was really a rationalist, and it was all very wonderful but it was all very psychological, and I could have a lot of good explanations of the Goddess as, you know, this archetype or that energy. I think in some ways I was a more effective speaker at that point because I could talk to people rationally about it, it would make sense and it would be not threatening. But over the years I have really come to, not so much believe, but my experience has been that if you work with the Goddess in a particular aspect something happens. (Starhawk, public lecture, 30 April 1996, London)

Similarly, Sir George Trevelyan claims:

> This is not doctrine you've got to believe . . . the New Age is not a proselytising religious movement. We're talking spiritual ideas and you are free to accept or reject them. If you don't like the ideas I've talked tonight . . . forget 'em! I'm not going to argue . . . it doesn't matter. But if you do like them, well I can't prove – you can't prove – the things I've been saying. But what you can do is to take the idea, put it in your thinking – put it in your heart – and choose to live for a month as if you believed it. Look at the world in the light of it. And if it's true, it draws an inner certainty to itself. And if it's not true, it fades away. (Trevelyan 1983)

The process through which interpretive drift occurs can be defined more clearly. First contact with new religious movements, including New Age, is usually through people known to the convert (Wood 1999; Kemp 2003a). This is despite the fact that New Age groups are often quite active in advertising, especially when they charge for their services, lectures and literature. Studies with other networks, such as carried out by Diani (1995) and Snow et al. (1980), have found that often over seventy-five per cent of recruits to new social movements were first contacted through pre-existing social networks, in accordance with NSM and SPIN theories of social movements (see Chapter 6) which highlight the crucial factor of pre-movement networks.

Frederick Lynch (1977) divides the process of conversion to the occult into four phases (see Figure 7.3). In phase one, intellectual curiosity leads to lone occultism, what Rae Beth (1990) called being a 'hedge witch'. This creates tension and stress within the individual (phase two), which in turn can create spiritual experiences and emotional conviction, as in the traditional theory of conversion. In phase three, the lone occultist meets like-minded individuals or a charismatic leader. This allows social support in an occult community, collective rituals and the sense of growth, development and achievement which comes with it (phase four).

Lynch's model was constructed before the concepts of New Age seekership and interpretive drift were floated – and possibly also before they were a reality in the field. Nevertheless, his description of the process remains credible, especially when it is noted that the phases are inter-related, and not necessarily totally linear in their action.

It remains to consider emic denials of conversion. In my fieldwork with Christian New Agers, I often encountered the notion that the subject had 'come home' to their true, original spirituality and thus had not changed their beliefs – they were in effect saying that they belonged to 'a religion without converts'. Margot Adler claims, 'no one *converts* to Paganism or Wicca' (Adler 1986: x, quoted in Gallagher 1994: 851). According to Eugene Gallagher, the traditional notion of conversion is rejected in Paganism because it implies a passive understanding of the self, whereas Pagans (like New Agers) believe in the divinity of the self. Gallagher suggests Pagans (and by extension, this could apply to New Agers) distance themselves from the conversion model because of its association with new religious movements or 'cults'. Rather than distinguishing conversion to Paganism from conversion to other new religious movements, Gallagher suggests acknowledging that conversion includes both gradual conversion (what Luhrmann called 'interpretive

Figure 7.3   Conversion to the occult

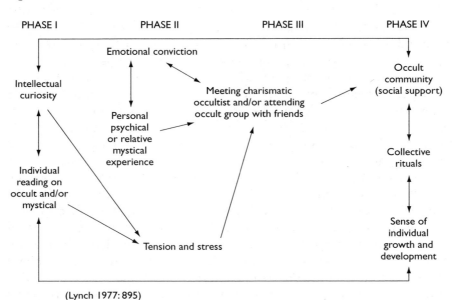

(Lynch 1977: 895)

drift') as well as sudden conversion (the traditional model, based on spiritual experiences).

– VIGNETTE – CHANNELLING AND MENTAL HEALTH –

Psychological profiles of New Agers, as seen above, often describe New Age beliefs and practices in terms of pathology usually reserved for the mentally ill. This is a common occurrence in hostile critiques of new religious movements, and more generally in psychological studies of religion – and there is a large body of literature on the subject (see e.g. Schumaker 1992). In this section, channelling is explored to illustrate the relevance of mental health issues to New Age studies.

In Kemp (2000), I discussed the commonly encountered identification of psychosis and mysticism, arguing that there is a tradition of such an identification in Western thought that goes back at least to Plato's idea of divine madness. In particular, contemporary psychological and psychiatric models and descriptors of mental illness are in many ways close to the traditional worldview of the mystic, and thus by extension to the contemporary New Ager. A comparison can be made between the healthy, mystic and psychotic person as understood in contemporary clinical practice (see Table 7.11).

Table 7.11   A comparison between the healthy, mystic and psychotic person

Healthy	Mystic	Psychotic
Independent	Dependent on God	Dependent on a 'controlling force'; thought insertion
Conforms to social roles and position	Only conforms if it is 'right'	Conforms to their own interpretation of the world. Adoption of messiah/saint stance
Communication through speech	Communication with God through prayer	Communication with others through telepathy; broadcasting of thoughts
'Self-assertive': i.e. neither introverted nor extroverted	Oscillates between being meek and humble, and claiming to be a child of God	Delusions of grandeur, e.g. claims to be Christ, coupled with intense feeling of shame or guilt
Imaginative and creative	Believes in supernatural phenomena; receives visions or signs	Visual or auditory hallucinations
Not compulsive; spontaneous	Follows divine rules	Obsessive about apparently mundane matters
Mood equilibrium	Sinner/saved polarity	Intense polarity of moods: overjoyed/damned
Able to adapt to new situations	Adapts new situations to unchanging laws	Mission to change the world
Reason as source of knowledge	Revelation	Voices
Stability between life-(eros) and death-(thanatos) libido	Claims to be born again, be dead to the old life and have eternal life	Wants to die/ believes to be already dead
In control of thoughts at all times	Seeks to gradually lose control of thoughts through following God's will	Sudden, passive experience of loss of control of thoughts
Sociable	Loves strangers and enemies	Everyone knows them and is plotting against them

(Kemp 2000: 162)[a]
a. Slightly modified. See also Tart (1992) and Chadwick (1992, 1997).

Jon Klimo (1998: 261–76) makes a more focused comparison between the characteristics of one aspect of New Age, namely channelling, and mental disorders as set out in the *Diagnostic and Statistical Manual of Mental Disorders* (American Psychiatric Association 1994) (DSM IV), which is used by psychiatrists in diagnosis. DSM IV describes a 'delusion of being controlled in which feelings, impulses, thoughts, or actions are experienced as being under the control of some external force rather than being under one's own control'.[6] Grandiose delusions are defined as those 'whose content involves inflated worth, power, knowledge, identity, or special relationship to a deity or famous person', particularly 'when the central theme of the delusion is the conviction of having some great (but unrecognized) talent or insight or having made some important discovery'. Hallucination is 'a sensory perception that has the compelling sense of resulting from a true perception but that occurs without external stimulation of the relevant sensory organ'.

Channelling is the New Age term for mediumship, which in recent history is associated with the Spiritualist movement, starting in the mid-nineteenth century (see Chapter 3). As Jon Klimo reminds us, however, spiritual possession has been practised throughout history, from ancient shamans to the oracles of the Greeks and even Jesus, Paul the Apostle and the author of Revelation. Klimo defines channelling as 'the communication of information to or through a physically embodied human being from a source that is said to exist on some other level or dimension of reality than the physical as we know it, and that is not from the normal mind (or self) of the channel' (ibid.: 2, original emphasis removed). In this definition, channelling takes many forms, including simple intuition, inspiration and creativity, but ranging also through non-verbal 'inner dictation' (such as experienced by Helen Schucman in 'scribing' *A Course in Miracles*, see Chapter 2), speaking with the dead (as in traditional Spiritualist séances), automatic writing from extraterrestrials, to full-blown trance channelling, where the channeller is not conscious of what they are saying throughout the performance (as with J. Z. Knight's channelling of Ramtha).

Klimo concludes:

> Many of the features of Schizophrenia certainly seem to parallel various channels' experiences with telepathy, voices in the head, automatic writing, and the informing presence of invisible 'others' in general. However, while some of the descriptions may sound the same, the strong presence of overall mental health and adaptedness, and the pronounced lack of underlying dysfunction or problematic ongoing or recurring disconnection from ego and surrounding public reality, makes it inappropriate to diagnose the great majority of channels as psychotic, schizophrenic, or in terms of other DSM disorders. (ibid.: 266)

It is perhaps naïve to think that non-clinicians can give a useful answer to the relation between mental health and New Age, or indeed between mental health and spirituality or religion more generally. Further doctoral research is currently being conducted on the precise relationship (see Farias & Lalljee 2003).

– CONCLUSION –

The discipline of psychology impacts on New Age studies in a number of ways. In this chapter, we have seen the influence of psychological theories on understandings of a central New Age practice, chanelling, and on the process of becoming a New Ager, or conversion. The chapter started by sketching the historical input of psychological theory on the development of New Age, before attempting a profile of a typical New Ager from statistical survey results. Despite the availability of some literature on the psychology of New Age, this discipline remains relatively undeveloped in its application to New Age, especially compared to other disciplines considered in this book. This is perhaps surprising given the centrality of psychological theories to New Age at an emic level.

– NOTES –

1. For an explanation of these technical terms, see Chapter 1.
2. Earlier described by Jung as the 'racial' unconscious.
3. See the references in Della Porta & Diani (1999) for further details of research in this area. They point out that it is not clear whether the new middle class is structurally responsible for the emergence of NSMs, or whether NSMs are simply the result of the typical tendency of intellectual middle classes to engage in conflict.
4. That seekers are 'older': sixty-two per cent of these fifty are over thirty-five years of age; fifty-four per cent of the 486 'all others' were over that age. The difference between sixty-two and fifty-four per cent of respondents is eight per cent of fifty, or four people. These four people, who may be aged thirty-four, are the people of whom Roof confusingly says 'Compared with others of their generation, they are older . . .' This statistic, resting on four responses, is hardly significant in a boomer population of seventy-six million. In a sample of 536, these percentages show nothing more than that fifty-five of the sample were over thirty-five. Similar difficulties apply to Roof's other conclusions.
5. See for example Richardson and Introvigne (2001).
6. All quotations from DSM IV are taken from Klimo (1998).

CHAPTER 8

Non-Academic Approaches to New Age

There has been a huge variety of approaches to New Age, employing the scholarly disciplines covered in earlier chapters of this book plus insights from other areas of study and other walks of life. Apart from existing academic studies of New Age, which are considered at length in the next chapter, the following approaches are considered here: those given by New Agers themselves, media approaches, Christian, rationalist, Native American, feminist, Jewish, Sufi and local community approaches. Such perspectives on New Age deserve separate attention, distinct from the disciplinary perspectives considered earlier in this book, because the popular understanding of New Age is probably influenced more by these perspectives than by the scholarly perspectives.

Both popular and scholarly perceptions colour what it means to be New Age. A definition of such a fluid category as New Age works best when it is always subject to refinement based on feedback from current research. No single approach – even that given by New Agers themselves – has the final, objective definition of New Age, which should always be tantalisingly just beyond our grasp.

– NEW AGE –

New Age definitions of New Age abound. Many scholars argue that we should prioritise self-definitions, and thus accord such New Age definitions of New Age prime place in any description of the phenomenon. 'Let us never forget that there exists no other religious reality than the faith of the believer' (Kristensen 1954: 17, quoted in Morgan 1996). Other scholars, however, have 'argued that the adherents of a religion do not necessarily understand their religion, and a person who disagrees with a religion does not necessarily misunderstand it' (Burke 1984: 631).

With this debate in mind, we may review approaches to New Age from New Agers themselves. Some brief definitions of New Age given by New Agers were mentioned in Chapter 1. Rather than quote further literary definitions of New Age by believers, which are readily available, I will give a sample of responses given to a questionnaire by members of Christians Awakening to a New Awareness (CANA), a British New Age Christian network:

In a few words please describe what you think the New Age is.
- An awakening to subtler levels of consciousness that leads to an awareness of the one-ness of all life.
- Not sure!
- A non-dogmatic, non-theological search for a spiritual path with lots of 'fringe activities'.
- An evolution of human consciousness towards spiritual development and away from orthodox religion.
- A contemporary worldview which emphasises the inter-connectedness of all being, including spiritual and material dimensions.
- A spiritual movement searching for the reality and inter-connectedness of all being through awareness of the natural world, the elements, the Cosmos, as we approach the Aquarian Age.
- A dawning of a re-emergence of spiritual values and an interest in alternatives – in all aspects of life.

A further question in the questionnaire asked for typical examples of New Age phenomena. The results given below are the combined average results from three Christian New Age groups.

Table 8.1   Please give five examples of groups, individuals, books or practices that you think are most typically New Age[1]

Example	Average %
Findhorn, Spangler, Caddy	8
Healing	8
Green issues	5
Creation Spirituality	5
The Omega Order[2]	4
Alternatives	4
Crystals	3
Eastern religion, etc.	2
Astrology, tarot, occult	2
Theosophy, Bailey, Steiner, Gurdjieff, Trevelyan	2
De Chardin, Happold, Carey, Wilber, Huxley	1

These answers demonstrate the range of understandings of New Age even among people very familiar with it. No shared definition emerges. If we are to locate trends in the definitions given, we may say that there is an emphasis on a change in era, possibly due to astrological influences, which indicates a pluralistic approach to spirituality and especially awareness of oneness, ancient traditions and alternative possibilities. The only examples given of New Age that achieve anything remotely statistically significant are the Findhorn Foundation and its leaders, healing and green issues (combined with Creation Spirituality), and even these examples give very low returns. Given that healing and green issues are such wide-ranging categories, the Findhorn Foundation is probably the only concrete example of New Age in this survey that can be said to be agreed upon by New Agers themselves.

– Media –

A knowledge of media portrayal of New Age is central to an understanding of popular conceptions of it. In general, we may say that the mass media were first ambivalent to New Age, becoming more hostile when many New Age groups tried to capitalise on their exposure by exploiting the opportunities for marketing spiritual techniques and merchandise, and especially hostile in Britain with the advent of New Age travellers (see Chapter 3). Mass media approaches to New Age are related to and influence the approaches of book publishers, magazine publishers and the lecturing and book-signing circuit.

The similarity between television culture and New Age has often been noted. Jay Rosen argues that both television and New Age promote the destabilisation of self necessary for the functioning of modern capitalism: 'the scarcity of meaningful work, the strain the economy places on marriage and childbearing, the emptiness at the heart of a culture that values movement and change often for their own sakes' (Rosen 1988: 288). He suggests that New Age should be seen as a business effort to sell merchandise – books, tapes, seminars, crystals or other commodities. 'Both [television and New Age] seek to dissolve the boundary between the self and the world, because both treasure the sort of self that results – fluid, formless, open to any incoming message' (ibid.: 271).

Both television and New Age, Rosen claims, aim to feed back 'redundant' messages that we already have within us. Television aims for higher audience figures by striking a chord with people's fears and desires, repackaging it to look fresh and maintaining links with what people have watched before. Similarly, New Age offers no new ideas, but recycles views we already hold, describing them in new language, and relating them to previous traditions, says Rosen.

Shirley MacLaine (b. 1934), the actress, did much to popularise New Age in the mass media with her five-hour ABC-TV film, *Out on a Limb*, broadcast in January 1987, which tells the story of her conversion to New Age. TV critics tended to be derogatory – a *Far Side* cartoon pictured a desert with two gila monsters, one saying, 'There it is again . . . a feeling that in a past life I was someone named Shirley MacLaine'[3] – but New Age had reached an unprecedented mainstream audience. MacLaine wrote a number of books describing her New Age life, including *Out on a Limb* (1983), *Dancing in the Light* (1985), *It's All in the Playing* (1987b) and *Going Within: A Guide for Inner Transformation* (1989). The last mentioned is less biographical than the earlier works, constituting a kind of popular New Age manual. While the media could therefore be positive about New Age, Caryl Matrisciana's *Gods of the New Age* (1985), a hostile Christian book on New Age, was also the subject of a feature-length film.

The first major exposé of New Age on British television was commissioned by Channel 4 in 1990 and centred around a conference held by William Bloom. A publication, *The New Age: an Anthology of Essential Writings* (Bloom ed. 1991) accompanied the series, including excerpts from writers such as Alice Bailey, Eileen Caddy, Fritjof Capra, Marilyn Ferguson, Louise Hay, Carl Jung, Abram Maslow, Peter Russell and Sir George Trevelyan. Peter Donebauer, the executive producer of the series, says in the preface that 'the New Age is neither a movement nor a religion set apart from others. It is not something one can choose or not to join. It is essentially a view of the time we live in and the world we are creating' (ibid.: xiii). Bloom acknowledges that 'some who are identified as New Agers actively reject the label for fear of being associated with seemingly incompatible elements' (ibid.: xvi). Across the English Channel, French television presents such core New Age material, including *The X-Files*, that Marie-Jeanne Ferreux in her anthropological study *Le New-Age* (2000) devotes an entire chapter to the presentation of the New Age image on television.

Publishers have long produced occult or esoteric lists. Steven Sutcliffe (1998: 38) cites one catalogue issued by Rider in the late 1930s, with a quarter of its contents categorised under 'Spiritualism' and around a fifth under 'Occult' and 'Psychology', and another Rider catalogue prior to the First World War which advertised 'Mind and Body Handbooks'. He describes an 'armchair religiosity' (ibid.: 38) which was only made possible by the wider print culture that made this kind of alternative religiosity public.

Henry Gordon was among the first to argue in print that the creation of the New Age category helped market books. 'If I were asked to name one particular reason why the New Age philosophy has spread so rapidly in the 1980s, I would attribute it to book publishers, major and minor' (Gordon 1988). Christoph Bochinger (1995) has explored in fine detail a similar thesis with regard to New Age in Germany.

Newspaper reports on New Age have followed discernible trends. Early accounts, starting in the *Los Angeles Times* in the mid-1980s, put the term in inverted commas – 'New Age' – or qualified it with terms such as 'so-called' or '(Human Potential)' (e.g. Smith 1986; Sipchen 1987; Dart 1987; Lindsey 1987). As the reports were taken up in other regions, they tended to describe it in terms of its growing popularity: 'the New Age is upon us' (Donato 1987), 'rapidly becoming a fashionable buzzword' (Saunders 1989), 'having an increasing impact' (Harpur 1990) or 'now mainstream ... considered fairly respectable' (Reed 1990).

Of course, newspaper headlines are driven by sensationalism, and the subjects that have generated interest in New Age include MacLaine, Deepak Chopra, Marianne Williamson, Ramtha, harmonic convergence, the Solar Temple, and the turn of the millennium. Journalists also write in a style which tends to reify New Age in terms already known to readers, but which because of New Age's sociology (see Chapter 6) may not be appropriate. Thus we find various cities located as the 'capital', 'Mecca' or 'Athens' of New Age, various people described as 'founder', 'shepherdess', 'leader', or 'the Billy Graham of the New Age movement'.[4]

Media portrayal of New Age travellers in Britain inevitably took the side of the majority who were inconvenienced by the illegal occupation of fields for rave festivals and by the queues of dilapidated vans that clogged country lanes, and who were horrified by pictures of police intervention at Stonehenge and elsewhere. Rave culture was associated in the media with the dangers of drug culture, particularly following the introduction of Ecstasy and a number of well-publicised teenage deaths. As discussed in Chapter 3, although it is not clear why so-called New Age travellers and New Age spirituality share the same sobriquet, the emblem was tarnished in the popular mind.

By the early 1990s, publishers and bookshops were beginning to react to a shift away from the popularity of the New Age category. Thorson's Aquarian Press imprint was disbanded. Waterstone's, one of the major British bookselling chains, renamed its New Age s‹ 'Mind, Body, Spirit' in many branches in the mid-1990s. *Publ Weekly* as early as 1990 (issue 237 D 7) wrote about 'The flight from "New Age": The old label, once useful, is being phased out by many publishers.' In 1993 (issue 240 D 6), *Publishers' Weekly* again commented: 'Publishing for "Spiritual Seekers": The New Age handle is long gone, but there's still a burgeoning market for books with a new kind of awareness.'

In the early 1990s, the small British Christian network Christians Awakening to a New Age changed their name to Christians Awakening to a New Awareness, preserving their acronym CANA but distancing themselves from the excesses portrayed on television and the bad taste that the term 'New Age' was acquiring. The Omega Order, another British New Age Christian group, having published *A Christian in the New Age* (Spink 1991), had explicitly distanced itself from the term 'New Age' by 1996 when I commenced my fieldwork there. British television became cynical about New Age: *Desperately Seeking Something* (1996) took a light-hearted tour of New Age across Britain, exploring Wicca including Vivianne Crowley, Druids, alternative healing and the Church Universal and Triumphant.

The religion writer for the *Los Angeles Times*, Russell Chandler, took an eight-month sabbatical from the newspaper to research and write *Understanding the New Age* (1989). Chandler's investigation into New Age is among the most wide ranging and original for the time at which he was writing. However, he tends towards a conservative Christian conspiracy conception of New Age, and relies too heavily on the earlier writings of such Christians. It is perhaps unfortunate that he chose to set out his own Christian beliefs in a section at the end of the book.

— CHRISTIAN APPROACHES —

Christians were among the first to recognise the existence of a New Age movement.[5] In fact, it could be argued that Christian critiques of New Age did much to disseminate knowledge among the general public about what was, in the late 1970s, still an obscure underground movement. The most obvious Christian response to New Age has been hostile. This response has been put forward generally by Evangelical and conservative Christians. However, it cannot be overemphasised that there is no one, authoritative Christian response to New Age. In fact, some Christians have responded positively to New Age (see Kemp

2003a). Many mainstream churches have issued formal documents with a cautionary approach to New Age which is not as extreme as those of Evangelical and conservative Christian churches.

John Saliba has examined hostile Christian approaches to New Age in some detail, dividing them into three groups: Evangelical/fundamentalist, Protestant/Orthodox and Catholic. Evangelical and fundamentalist approaches to New Age are categorised as:

(1) confrontational, in which the New Age is resisted;
(2) apologetical, where Christian doctrine is clearly expressed and New Age teachings evaluated from a biblical standpoint; and
(3) pastoral, where advice is given to Christians to prepare themselves to counteract the movement's influence or to New Agers to draw them back into the Christian fold. (Saliba 1999: 63)

Protestant and Orthodox approaches (although it is unclear why these should be considered together) are categorised as:

(1) an exclusive theology that maintains that only Christianity is the true religion . . .;
(2) an inclusive theology which, while taking Christianity as the normative faith, allows for some truth and goodness in other religions . . .; and
(3) a pluralistic theology that argues that all religions are equally valid paths to revelation and salvation. (ibid.: 124)

Catholic approaches to New Age are categorised as:

(1) traditional, concentrating on dogmatic issues;
(2) also traditional, but open to the positive side of New Age;
(3) the official Catholic approach incorporating materials from the first two methods; and
(4) an innovative approach harmonising New Age and Catholic worldviews. (from Saliba 1999: 141–90)

One of the earliest books to bring knowledge of New Age to a wider Christian audience was Constance Cumbey's *The Hidden Dangers of the Rainbow* (1983). Cumbey is a Christian lawyer from Detroit who brings together a number of conspiracy theories around New Age, without apparently much first-hand knowledge of the field. New Age is presented as an organised movement with a plan for one world government written by Alice Bailey, the theosophist who split to create her own Arcane School (see Chapter 3). New Age is linked to the Third Reich.[6]

Cumbey's book had a wide circulation. In the United Kingdom, Roy Livesey made a similar contribution to Christian critiques of New Age. He began circulating prayer letters against New Age among Christian groups in 1984, and these were regularised into a bi-monthly *New Age Bulletin* by 1988. Livesey is a self-professing conspiracy theorist, and his attack on New Age is wide-ranging enough to include Catholicism, bankers and Jews – who he believes are all conspiring for a New World Order.

President Bush Sr's call for a New World Order following the first Gulf crisis and the dismantling of the Soviet Union was heralded by many Christians, like Livesey, as proof of how widespread New Age ideology had become. Former First Lady Nancy Reagan's consultation of astrologers and her influence on President Reagan were also cited by Christians in the New Age debate, along with criticisms of Prince Charles' apparent New Age leaning.

Dave Hunt and T. A. McMahon wrote best-sellers entitled *The Seduction of Christianity* (1985) and *The New Spirituality* (1988) (first published as *America: The Sorcerer's New Apprentice*). They are mainly concerned with the infiltration of New Age into the church, but the 1988 volume described itself on its front cover as a broader-based 'consumer's guide to the exploding New Age movement'. In the extreme final chapters, New Age is linked to Satanism and Anton LaVey's First Church of Satan in San Francisco, which is said to perform human sacrifices in the form of curses and hexes. The well-worn Christian critique of rock music as an instrument of evil is rehearsed. Again, links between occultism and Nazism are recited. Earlier chapters link New Age to naturalism, scientism and supernaturalism, nature religion, Freud, Jung and the occult.

By the early 1990s, there was a myriad of Christian critiques of New Age. New Age had replaced 'secular humanism' as the enemy of traditional Christians. Other Christian anti-New Age works include Douglas Groothuis's three-part series beginning with *Unmasking the New Age* (1986) and Walter Martin's *The New Age Cult* (1989).

The mainstream churches have tended to be less overtly hostile in their official responses to New Age than some of the smaller Evangelical denominations, acknowledging that there is some value in the innovative approach to spirituality. However, their knowledge of New Age is often based on works by Evangelical or fundamentalist Christians and is strongly coloured by them.

The Pontifical Council for Culture and the Pontifical Council for Interreligious Dialogue issued *Jesus Christ: The Bearer of the Water of Life – A Christian reflection on the "New Age"* in February 2003. There is a very good description of New Age, referencing important scholarly works, unlike some other church documents which rely on Evangelical tracts for their information. It is acknowledged that there are 'rapidly-growing numbers of people who claim that it is possible to blend Christianity and New Age, by taking what strikes them as the best of both'. But it is suggested that fundamentally the two are irreconcilable. 'It is impossible to reconcile these two visions [of the life and significance of Jesus Christ] . . . The gnostic nature of this movement calls us to judge it in its entirety. From the point of view of Christian faith, it is not possible to isolate some elements of New Age religiosity as acceptable to Christians, while rejecting others' (Pontifical Council for Culture & Pontifical Council for Interreligious Dialogue 2003).

The Irish Theological Commission's *A New Age of the Spirit? A Catholic Response to the New Age Phenomenon* (1994) lists a number of positive aspects of New Age, but generally follows a sensationalist approach, writing of:

> The reconstruction of a new World Order . . .
> Part of this plan is also a One World Church, which these writers refer to as the New World Religion . . .
> What would happen to the Church is she resisted this take-over? There are subtle hints in these NAM books that resistence [sic] will be crushed.
> (ibid.: 50–2)

The Church of England's report, *The Search for Faith and the Witness of the Church* (Mission Theological Advisory Group 1996) has one chapter on New Age, 'The world is my oyster' (ibid.: 74–109). It acknowledges that there are elements of New Age in Christianity. New Age may be approached through: services meeting people's experiences; artwork; the metaphor of pilgrimage; praise of the Creator God; community; celebrating the wholeness of creation; and reclaiming 'spiritual' language, for example 'angels'. New Age is essentially seen as an opportunity for Christian mission.

The Methodist Faith and Order Committee's *Report to Conference 1994* fears New Age concepts 'are becoming all-pervasive' (Faith and Order Committee 1994: 3). Typical features are said to be: emphasis on spiritual rather than material, especially reincarnation; ideas of harmony, unity and wholeness, including pantheism; emphasis on individuals and free choice of religion; and hope at the beginning of a New Age (ibid.: 5). The report retains the hostility of its secondary sources on New Age, but calls for 'critical dialogue' (ibid.: 17), beginning with the ideas of: the Spirit as an expression of the divine life; the process of continuous spiritual development towards self-transcendence; and the presence of the Spirit in people throughout history (although retaining the uniqueness of Christ) (ibid.: 26–7).

I have examined positive Christian responses to New Age in my doctoral thesis, *The Christaquarians? A Sociology of Christians in the New*

Age (Kemp 2003a). 'Christaquarian' is a neologism used to describe what I perceived as the possibility of a nascent movement of New Age Christians. The central case studies for this thesis were: CANA – Christians Awakening to a New Awareness – a 150-strong mailing list of Christians across Britain who are sympathetic to New Age; The Omega Order, near Bristol, a residential community now known as Winford Manor Retreat; and St James's church, Piccadilly, London, home to the Alternatives lecture series discussed in Chapter 6.

There are a wealth of other Christians who respond positively to New Age. These include the Brazilian author Paulo Coelho (b. 1947), whose best-selling novel *The Alchemist* (1988) established his popularity among New Age readers (in fact Coelho denies that he is New Age, and instead professes Catholicism). Fr Anthony de Mello (1931–87) is also popular among New Age Christians, despite the Catholic Church's Congregation of the Doctrine of the Faith's notification (1998) against his writings. Thomas Merton (1915–68) is another Christian whose writings are popular in New Age circles. Fr Bede Griffiths (1906–93) entered an Indian ashram in 1958, and continued to receive spiritual seekers from all over the world until his death. Revd Adrian Smith (b. 1930) gives seminars in Britain and has written a number of works on Christianity and New Age, including *God and the Aquarian Age* (1990). Fr Diarmuid Ó' Murchú (b. 1952) lectures in Britain and North America, and has also written a number of books on the spiritual life under the banners of Creation Spirituality and Goddess Spirituality rather than New Age *per se*.

Christian approaches to New Age are among the most significant in shaping both popular and scholarly understandings of the phenomena, perhaps even more influential than the media considered above. Compared to these two non-scholarly approaches, the other approaches considered below in this chapter are relatively insignificant.

– RATIONALIST APPROACHES –

Introvigne ([1994] 2001) describes hostile responses to New Age as either anti-New Age or counter-New Age. Massimo Introvigne's distinction refers to the motivation of the group responding to New Age: anti-New Age responses tend to come from the scientific and sceptical communities, which Introvigne seems to suggest do not have a religious bias; whereas counter-New Age responses tend to come from groups with a strong religious bias, and see New Age as a threat which must be countered. The former I describe here as rationalist responses, and the latter have been considered under Christian responses, which they almost always are – I know of no Islamic counter-New Age responses, for example. Many books mentioned in this section are published by Prometheus Books, which despite promoting a rationalist stance is also publishing an important collection of academic essays on New Age with some primary source material (Lewis ed. forthcoming) (see Chapter 9).

Not Necessarily the New Age: Critical Essays (Basil ed. 1988) brings together essays from a number of well-known critics of New Age, including J. Gordon Melton, James Webb, Martin Gardner, Carl Raschke and Carl Sagan. Webb's contribution, despite being billed on the dust cover as tracing the origins of the movement to the 1960s, is in fact an adaptation of his book *The Occult Establishment* (1976) and so does not explicitly relate to New Age. Sagan's advocacy of scepticism is similarly adapted from an address which did not directly refer to New Age. There are rationalist critiques of past-life regression, karma and reincarnation, out-of-the-body experiences, Shirley MacLaine, UFO abductions and New Age music. The general tone of the book is popular rather than scholarly, and tends to scoff despite claiming to be the first book to offer a 'thorough, rigorous, and fair analysis of the movement as a whole' (Basil ed. 1988: 9).

Channeling into the New Age: The 'Teachings' of Shirley MacLaine and Other Such Gurus (Gordon 1988) was, like Basil's anthology, published by Prometheus Books – and in the same year. Henry Gordon, a magician and Fellow of the Committee for the Scientific Investigation of Claims of the Paranormal (CSICOP), takes a lively and jovial, sceptical approach to New Age. He quotes and dismisses selected New Age 'teachings' in three chapters: philosophical, metaphysical and scientific, having concentrated in the first part of the book on channelling and MacLaine.

In *Science in the New Age: The Paranormal, Its Defenders and Debunkers, and American Culture* (1993), David Hess describes three cultures – New Age, parapsychology and scepticism – which he argues are interrelated in their approach to the paranormal. There is no fieldwork, all examples being drawn from literary sources, with New Age exemplars being Lynn Andrews, José Argüelles, MacLaine, Ruth Montgomery, Katrina Raphaell and Diane Stein. Despite this drawback, Hess isolates a number of themes that continue to tax New Age scholars, including the nature of New Age as a cohesive social movement (ibid.: 5); New Age as 'the graying of the greening' (ibid.: 5), that is to say, a movement of the baby-boom generation; and New Age as a reaction to political defeats in the 1960s (ibid.: 171). A final chapter gives Hess's personal critique of each of the three cultures, concluding with New Age, which he describes as following traditional patterns of hege-mony and legitimation in holistic medicine, and having been appropri-ated by traditional political parties. The aim of the book seems to be to enable New Agers, parapsychologists and sceptics to find a common language, bracket questions of the relative scientificity of their truth claims, and instead discuss the cultural meanings of their paradigms.

Martin Gardner (1988, 1996) has reprinted a number of his essays from his 'Notes of a Fringe Watcher' column in *Skeptical Inquirer* mag-azine and elsewhere. This column was originally headed 'Notes of a Psi-Watcher', covering only psychic research, but its remit was subse-quently widened to include not only New Age but other 'fringe' reli-gions and science. Gardner has written on MacLaine (Gardner 1988: 32–7), Rupert Sheldrake (ibid.: 109–14), channelling (ibid.: 202–8) and Marianne Williamson and *A Course in Miracles* (1996: 29–37), but his essays also debunk a wide range of other scientific, anthropological and mathematical phenomena.

Another work that takes a rationalist or scientific approach to refut-ing New Age is Ernest Lucas' *Science and the New Age Challenge* (1996). Although Lucas comes from a conservative Christian bias, this book does not generally employ theological arguments, but discusses the theories of Pierre Teilhard de Chardin, Fritjof Capra, Sheldrake, James Lovelock and others in a scientific manner.

Overall, rationalist critiques of New Age have far less exposure than media or Christian approaches, but are nevertheless an important strand in non-academic understandings of New Age.

– OTHER NON-ACADEMIC APPROACHES –

Any number of other interest groups may have their own individual approach to New Age. To give a flavour of the approaches available, in this section I briefly outline Native American, Jewish, feminist, Sufi and local-community approaches to New Age. These are non-academic approaches that have been documented; others exist, of course, that remain to be expressed (or at least discovered by New Age scholars) in print. Possibilities include approaches to New Age from lesbian and gay, environmentalist, Muslim, Buddhist, conservative, socialist viewpoints – indeed from any interest group.

It is well known that New Age appropriates Native American tra-ditions such as sweat lodges, sun dances and traditional medicine.

However, Native Americans often accuse New Agers of being insincere, trivialising and desecrating their traditional life in a weekend search for a 'quick fix' (Pazola 1994). Native Americans have emphasised that their tradition is part of a lifelong process, and should not be commercialised (Aldred 2000). 'Shake and bake shamans', as pseudo-Native American medicine men and women are known by some Native American activists, include Lynn Andrews, mentored by Canadian Cree medicine women Agnes Whistling Elk and Ruby Plenty Chiefs, and Mary Summer Rain, mentored by No-Eyes. Aldred asks, 'Why would New Agers continue to consume Native American spirituality when so many Indian people have expressed their reprehension of this commercialization?' (ibid.), reporting that the most frequent answer given by New Agers was related to the First Amendment right to religious freedom. Philip Deloria (1998) traces the notion of 'playing Indian' from the first days of the United States, but suggests that New Age appropriation is qualitatively different in that it focuses on individual freedom rather than social justice:

> The tendency of New Age devotees to find in Indianness personal solutions to the question of living the good life meant that Indian Others were imagined in almost exclusively positive terms – communitarian, environmentally wise, spiritually insightful. This happy multiculturalism blunted the edge of earlier calls for social change by focusing on pleasant cultural exchanges that erased the complex history of Indians and others. (ibid.: 174, quoted in Aldred 2000)

Catharine Albanese (1990) takes a slightly different perspective, comparing the original 'nature religion' of the Algonkian Indians of southern New England with modern-day manifestations in Sun Bear (Vincent La Duke, b. 1929) and other New Age figures. Adam Possamaï (2002) suggests not only that New Age appropriates North American Indian, Australian Aborigine and other indigenous cultures, but that this is part of a larger phenomenon, of cultural consumption of parts of history, including contemporary popular culture.

It is sometimes remarked that there is a large presence of former Jews in New Age (e.g. York 1995: 192; Goldstein 1996). As Michael York points out, both Malcolm Stern and William Bloom, early directors of the New Age Alternatives lecture series, have Jewish backgrounds. Other prominent examples include Danah Zohar, Marianne Williamson and the early community around Helen Schucman and *A Course in Miracles* (see Chapter 2). There is an obvious overlap with Qabbalah and New Age – for example Laibl Wolf, an Australian rabbi, has recorded a tape entitled '*The Celestine Prophecy* and Kabbala' (Goldstein 1996). New Age in Israel has been described as a 'dual revolt

– against the Judaism of the Orthodox establishment and the secularism of the Zionist founders' (Halevi 2001). Alternative festivals are said to take place on most Jewish holidays, such as the Boombamela (apparently named after an Indian religious festival, the Kumbh Mela), a gathering of former Jewish visitors to India who wear dreadlocks, dance and promote peace. Melton et al. trace (1991: 300–33) 'New Age Judaism' to the work of Zalman Schachter-Shalomi, Shlomo Carlebach and Joseph H. Gelberman from the 1960s, and also emphasise the importance of the *havurots* (Jewish communal groups) of that period.

In *New Age and Armageddon: the Goddess or the Gurus? Towards a Feminist Vision of the Future* (1992), Monica Sjöö rails against patriarchal aspects of New Age she encountered in attempts to heal her terminally ill son in the 1980s. Sjöö is a Swedish expatriate living in Britain, a 'radical Goddess feminist and artist' (although she has not been initiated into a coven (ibid.: 223)) and co-author of *The Great Cosmic Mother: Rediscovering the Religion of the Earth* (Sjöö and Mor 1987). When Sjöö gave a paper at a conference entitled Nature Religion Today, hosted by Lancaster University in 1996, she first prayed that evil spirits not influence her lecture. Interestingly, patriarchal elements in New Age are likened to patriarchal elements in Christianity, especially fundamentalist Christianity (e.g. Sjöö 1992: 184, 192, 199), because 'New Age men grew up in societies with Christian notions of contempt for the body and for nature and its spirits' (ibid.: 278). However, Sjöö reclaims the New Age label for her own style of thought:

> I do believe that the Goddess is re-emerging, that Persephone is returning to Her mother Demeter/Gaia at last, and that the Earth will rejoice and that She will green again.
> The New Age is the Second Coming of the Goddess and only then will there be true peace and another Golden Age as experienced in ancient Atlantis. (ibid.: 289)

Mustafa Draper (forthcoming) has investigated two Sufi brotherhoods, the Qadiri-Shadhiliyya of the Qadiri-Budshishiyya and the Naqshbandiyya of Haqqaniyya of Sheikh Nazim, which are engaging with contemporary alternative spirituality in Glastonbury, England. Though raising questions about the representativeness of such Sufi engagement with New Age, Draper makes interesting points about the differing foci of the two *tariqas*, the former with the more Pagan-aligned Glastonbury Tor, the latter with the Christian abbey. In both cases, there was a conscious decision to focus on Glastonbury as a spiritual centre in Britain, although both also seem very low key and the first real engagement is still relatively recent, having occurred in 1998.

One approach to New Age that may be easy for readers to relate to is the approach of local communities to New Age when New Agers appear *en masse* in their home town. Such approaches have been examined by Hexham (1972) and Prince (1992; see also Prince & Riches 2000) at Glastonbury and by Ivakhiv (2001) at Glastonbury and Sedona, Arizona. It is interesting to see the change in attitudes to New Age over time at Glastonbury – from the 'freaks' observed by Irving Hexham in the early 1970s, through the 'Glastafarians' in the 1980s by Ruth Prince, to the 'alternative community' studied by Adrian Ivakhiv in the 1990s. It is possible that the softening in these descriptions represents a softening of the boundary maintenance of regular Glastonbury residents, or Glastonians as they are known. It is also useful to be able to compare approaches at Glastonbury with approaches at Sedona. Both are important New Age centres in their respective countries.

– Conclusion –

This chapter has scratched the surface of non-academic approaches to New Age, including those given by New Agers themselves, media approaches, Christian, rationalist, Native American, Jewish, feminist, Sufi and local community approaches. Of course, there are as many approaches to New Age as there are people who give any thought to the phenomena. The point of including such approaches in this book is so that purely academic approaches are not prioritised to the exclusion of equally important approaches by others. While earlier chapters have explored New Age from the point of view of various academic disciplines, the next chapter pulls together extant academic studies of New Age in a detailed literature survey.

– Notes –

1. Average percentages calculated from responses from three groups (The Omega Order; St James's church, Piccadilly; and CANA surveyed in Kemp (2003a). Total response rate to combined surveys: 48%. Total population surveyed: 601. The calculation of percentages ignored blank entries.
2. The Omega Order is a small, originally New Age-focused residential community in Bristol, England, now known as Winford Manor Retreat.
3. United Press Syndicate, 1987, quoted in Chandler (1989: 53). See also the *New Yorker* cartoon, 30 March 1987 (quoted in Gardner 1988: 188), which shows a television weather forecast, with the caption: 'Rain in the

Northeast, clear skies to the South, while large portions of the Midwest continue to be blanketed by Shirley MacLaine's aura.'

4. E.g. Bordewich (1988), Bremner (1990), Phelan (1992), White (1993).

5. Although Melton et al. (1991: 312) state: 'Evangelical Christians were slow to turn their attention to the New Age Movement.' Nevertheless, the auhors agree that Cumbey (1983) thrust the New Age onto the counter-cult agenda. Perhaps their point is that the Christian counter-cult movement attacked the cultic milieu before it was known as New Age, and so far as this analysis goes it is of course correct.

6. Cumbey's arguments are less convicing than Nicholas Goodrick-Clarke's *The Occult Roots of Nazism* (1992), which provides a more scholarly case for the existence of crossovers between occultism and Nazism. See also Kalman and Murray (1995) on possible links between David Icke, a well-known British New Ager, and Nazism.

CHAPTER 9

Academic Literature Survey

New Age studies have sometimes contained a caveat that is now dated: that the scholarly literature on New Age is limited.[1] Furthermore, many studies of New Age inadequately review existing literature, making a scholarly consensus about New Age elusive. This chapter seeks to address such caveats and inadequacies by providing a survey of scholarly literature on New Age. The material is so abundant that non-English language studies of New Age are not fully considered here (see Kemp 2003c). The presentation in this chapter is not ordered according to the disciplinary approach taken in previous chapters, but rather reverse chronologically, in order to get some sense of the historical progress of New Age studies; and according to the format of publication. Prominence is given in this review to unpublished academic theses, some of which have not had the exposure they deserve. Some theses on New Age have been published, and join a growing number of book-length objective considerations and academic journal articles on New Age. While a number of critics have highlighted the role of publishers in promoting New Age *per se* (see Chapter 8), there has been little comment on the similar role of publishers in promoting academic studies of New Age.

Due to normal market pressures, publishers shy away from complex studies based on thorough fieldwork (such as Kemp 2003a, which was self-published) in favour of wide-ranging overviews that appeal to broader sections of the market (such as this very volume). Indeed, when impressively detailed studies have been published (e.g. Bochinger 1995, Hammer 2001b), these have sometimes been exorbitantly expensive – up to six times the cost of a regular textbook – and hence less accessible. A number of prospective publishers have also commented to me and colleagues on the need to appeal to a trans-Atlantic audience, that is both British and North American readers, as well as to other English-speaking readers across the world. The effect of such market forces is perhaps to slant published New Age studies towards overemphasising the globalising and populist tendencies of New Age.

Original book-length scholarly considerations of New Age include Lewis (ed. forthcoming a), Rothstein (ed. 2001), Sutcliffe and Bowman (eds 2000), Introvigne (2000), Heelas (1996a), Steyn (1994), Lewis and Melton (eds 1992), Melton et al. (1991), Albanese (1990) and Bednarowski (1989). Many published books devoted to New Age derive from doctoral and masters theses, including Sutcliffe (2002), Hammer (2001b), Ivakhiv (2001), Prince and Riches (2000), Ferreux (2000), Amaral (2000), Guilane-Nachez (1999), Weidner Maluf (1996), Hanegraaff (1996), York (1995), Bochinger (1995), English-Lueck (1990) and Scott (1980). It is hoped that further theses on New Age will also be published, including Corrywright (2001), Wood (1999), Possamaï (1998) and Rose (1996), while others such as Greer (1994), Roberts (1989) and Brown-Keister (1982) are now probably already too dated for this to occur.

– ORIGINAL PUBLICATIONS –

James R. Lewis's *Encyclopedic Sourcebook of New Age Religions* (forthcoming a) sets out to be the definitive reference work on New Age, including both primary and secondary material in one large volume. A large number of the articles are reprints of classic essays on New Age, including Bowman (1995 and 1999), Hill (1987 and 1993), Shimazono (1993) and Walter (1993), and it is useful to have them collected together in one place. The majority of the papers examine individual New Age groups, including Edgar Cayce, Findhorn, Kashi, the Solar Temple, Lazaris, Damanhur and the Church Universal and Triumphant. There is a précis of my own doctoral thesis (Kemp forthcoming b) together with other materials on Christianity and New Age by John Saliba, Reender Kranenborg and Gillian Paschkes-Bell. Further themes include spiritual commodification and ethical issues, and the sociology of New Age. As an up-to-date and comprehensive starting point for study of New Age, this must be the place to go, although it is relatively expensive.

Mikael Rothstein edited a volume of papers (Rothstein ed. 2001) presented at a conference at Copenhagen in November 1999. The volume is entitled *New Age Religion and Globalization*, and it is not surprising that Wouter Hanegraaff, who popularised the term 'New Age religion', tops the bill with 'Prospects for the Globalization of New Age' (Hanegraaff 2001), a paper in which he argues that the central New Age idea of a perennial philosophy rejects the concept of relativity and thus New Age spirituality falls back into the very religious authoritarianism that it claims to overcome. Liselotte Frisk, Olav Hammer and Massimo Introvigne provide further introductory theoretical papers. The volume then considers particular cases of New Age globalisation – Reiki (J. Gordon Melton); prosperity consciousness (Lisbeth Mikaelsson); Gnostic and Goddess spiritualities (Invild Sælid Gilhus); UFO spirituality (Rothstein); and workplace spirituality (Karen Salamon).

The rationale for the title of Steven Sutcliffe and Marion Bowman's compendium of articles, *Beyond New Age* (2000) is to point 'to the historical dimension of the field in question, which both predates and will survive the term or emblem "New Age"' (ibid.: 1); the term 'alternative spirituality' is preferred for the subject matter of the essays. These include essays by well-known authorities such as Martin Green, Robert Segal, Graham Harvey, James Beckford, Malcolm Hamilton and Steve Bruce, among others, on (variously) spiritual centres at the turn of the twentieth century, Jung, vernacular religion, Pagan spirituality, holism and healing, the Festival for Mind-Body-Spirit and secularisation. Michael York's comparative contribution on alternative spirituality in Europe repeats much of the discussion in his article for *Social Compass* (York 1999), and it is fair to say that as a whole the volume is more useful as a summary of current knowledge rather than breaking new ground. Given Sutcliffe's aversion to the notion of a substantive movement of New Age (see below), it is surprising that this is not brought out more clearly in the compendium. This peculiarity is exacerbated by the very nature of the work as a collection of essays, which lacks an overall theoretical stance on the nature of New Age despite the introductory remarks of the editors.

New Age & Next Age (Introvigne 2000) is a revised edition of *Storia del New Age 1962–1992* (Introvigne 1994) with a lengthy new introduction. In many ways, it is the new introduction that is the most valuable part of the book, and discussion of this will take place in Chapter 10. The body of the text traces the history of New Age from 1962. This date is chosen largely because of the founding of the New Age communities of both Esalen and Findhorn in that year (Introvigne 2000: 53).[2] Rather than giving a definition of New Age, Introvigne gives a description: from a psychological point of view, it is the conviction of having entered – or being on the point of entering – into a new era (ibid.: 54); from a sociological point of view, New Age can be described as a network or meta-network.

Introvigne divides the history of New Age into three 'mountains': alternative spirituality, alternative therapies, and alternative social organisations. The first includes interest in non-Christian religions, the metaphysical tradition and Christian esotericism, Spiritualism, occultism, Paganism, UFOs and extraterrestrials, and astrology. The second includes holistic medicine, the vegetarian movement, alternative psychology, and the recovery movement. The third includes the commune movement, deep ecology and the new science, and the new politics. Introvigne then analyses the philosophy of New Age under the headings of relativism, pluralism, God and the world, man, the Christ and Jesus Christ, and morals and politics. A final chapter explores the relationship between New Age and Catholicism.

Paul Heelas's *The New Age Movement* (1996a) is probably the most widely cited academic text on New Age. His portrayal of New Age, however, relies on dated examples and fieldwork – Bhagwan Shree Rajneesh and Exegesis are two of the most frequently cited examples, but these are now rarely encountered among contemporary New Agers.

As seen in Chapter 1, Heelas suggests there are three elements of the essential *lingua franca* of Self spirituality: 'Your lives do not work', 'You are Gods and Goddesses in exile' and 'Let go/drop it'. Joanne Pearson has shown difficulties in application of these elements to Paganism, but it is also sometimes hard to distinguish all these elements in New Age as separate from the common currency of Western spirituality. For example, the notion that we must change our thinking to make our lives work was first popularised by the New Thought and Christian Science tradition (see Chapter 3), and later by the positive-thinking tradition. Heelas himself cites Gurdjieff (see Chapter 3), but Gurdjieff is perhaps better seen as a historical influence on New Age rather than an instance of it. Similarly, the notion that we are spiritual people in a material world is hardly unique to New Age. And the solution of 'letting go' is more typically associated with 1960s culture and psychotherapy rather than New Age.

Other central characteristics for Self spirituality suggested by Heelas are that of unmediated individualism – the idea that you are your own authority; the Self-ethic that valorises intuition and the inner voice; belief in responsibility for our own lives and the Earth, including through the use of magical power; liberation from the past, the traditional and the ego; and perennialism. Again, these suggested characteristics may be common in much Western spirituality, and indeed, as we have seen in Chapter 4, Heelas acknowledges the similarities of Self spirituality with late modern culture. While Heelas' portrayal is insightful and interesting, it is perhaps rather a portrayal of a more generalised Self spirituality instead of New Age *per se*.

Chrissie Steyn defines New Age as not necessarily identifying with a movement, but acceptance of the idea of humanity being at a turning point in its history, and belief in evidence of a transformation of consciousness (Steyn 1994: 11). *Worldviews in Transition* (Steyn 1994) is based on thirty interviews held in Southern Africa in 1990, plus a small amount of participant observation. The New Age 'grid' is as described as follows:

> The four tributaries (the alternative tradition, the Eastern philosophies, humanistic and transpersonal psychology, and the new physics) that have converged in the mainstream of the New Age movement give us a vertical distinction, while the four levels identified by Spangler (the commercial, the New Age as glamour, personal and social transformation, and the New Age as the incarnation of the sacred) . . . provide us with a horizontal distinction, which together form a framework or grid in which each individual phenomenon within the movement can be situated and the spectrum of beliefs plotted. (ibid.:125)

Useful articles in Lewis and Melton (eds 1992) include international papers on New Age in Nigeria (Hackett 1992), Japan (Mullins 1992), South Africa (Oosthuizen 1992) and Italy (Poggi 1992). These studies belie the often-made comment that New Age is a purely English-speaking or purely Western phenomenon. Alexander (1992) studies the historical roots of New Age; Diem and Lewis (1992) trace the influence of Hinduism on New Age; and Ellwood (1992) asks whether New Age can really be seen as new. Various aspects of New Age are considered, including the baby-boomer character of New Agers (Brown 1992); channelling (Riordan 1992); training seminars (Rupert 1992); witchcraft (Kelly 1992); the Evangelical response (Hexham 1992); feminism (Bednarowski 1992); and a comparison of New Age with the pentecostal or charismatic revival (Lucas 1992).

Melton, Jerome Clark and Aidan Kelly's *New Age Almanac* (1991) remains an extremely useful reference work, compiling detailed information on the whole range of New Age phenomena including historical groups, altered states, mysteries, yoga, health and healing, astrology, metaphysics and community life. Its major drawback is that these subject divisions are in practice a little idiosyncratic when the work is consulted on a particular group or individual, especially since it is nearly 500 pages long and has no index. Each entry provides in a scholarly fashion the basic facts such as dates, membership numbers and publications. Another criticism of the nature of the book is that there is no commentary on this basic compilation of facts.

Catherine Albanese's *Nature Religion in America from the Algonkian Indians to the New Age* (1990) constructs the etic category of 'nature religion' as the way of organising reality for which nature is the central referent. In fact, although the term is widely cited in New Age studies, only one chapter of the book is devoted to New Age, since nature religion is a far wider category than New Age as such. This chapter describes Sun Bear, Annie Dillard, Charlene Spretnak, Starhawk, Virginia Samdahl and Michio Kushi as speaking a similar language of centring and connection, energy vibration and flow.

New Religions and the Theological Imagination in America (1989), Mary Farrell Bednarowski's study of New Age theology, is an easy-to-read discussion of central theological questions such as 'who or what is God like?' (ibid.: 19f). Bednarowski returned to New Age in an article (1991) which discusses fourteen primary and secondary works on New Age.

The best sources of published articles on New Age are three journal volumes: *Culture and Religion*, volume 4: 1; *Social Compass*, volume 46: 2; and *Religion*, volume 23. There are also of course an endless number of individual journal articles on subjects related to New Age, which are not discussed here.

Culture and Religion 4: 1 is entitled 'Formation and the History of "New Age"', and guest edited by Sutcliffe. Sutcliffe (2003b) himself gives another presentation on the history of New Age as a category, while Adam Possamaï (2003a) relates alternative spiritualities to the cultural logic of late capitalism. Douglas Ezzy (2003) explores what he tentatively describes as 'New Age witchcraft', Christina Steyn (2003) gives a case study in South Africa and Adrian Ivakhiv (2003) explores New Age pilgrimage. David Riches (2003) compares New Age and 'alternative' communities, I myself (Kemp 2003b) explore New Age from a legal studies approach, and Matthew Wood (2003) discusses possession in relation to New Age.

Social Compass also devotes an entire issue (volume 46.2) to New Age, under the editorial of Hildegard van Hove. Van Hove's own contribution to the journal (van Hove 1999) describes the emergence of a 'spiritual marketplace' at the fringe of religion, but not organized as a religion. Bowman (1999) explores similar areas in 'Healing in the Spiritual Marketplace'. A number of examples of Holistic Healing are detailed, and it is suggested that the new healing industry is now a well-developed facet of late-twentieth-century spirituality. York (1999) likewise employs the image of a religious supermarket.

Hanegraaff's contribution to *Social Compass* (Hanegraaff 1999) gives 'a Historian's Perspective' on New Age spiritualities. It is based on a theoretical distinction between religion, religions and spiritualities, which views New Age as a form of 'secular religion', much as in Hanegraaff (1996). It also discusses in relation to the self the private symbolism of New Age as distinct from the private interpretations of existing collective symbolisms found in traditional spiritualities. Meanwhile, Susumu Shimazono (1999; see also Shimazono 1993) gives an unusual perspective on New Age in that he writes from the Japanese situation, which is not averse to adherence to multiple spiritual traditions and does not see New Age as 'alternative' to the mainstream. Nevertheless, he sees many similarities with the situation in other industrialised countries. His main input is the substitution of the phrase 'New Spirituality Movements and Culture' for the term 'New Age movement', which he thinks is unsuitable for academic usage. His articles also contain interesting comparative material on contemporary 'alternative' spirituality in Japan. For international comparison, Tadeusz Doktór (1999) presents what he describes as the New Age worldview of Polish students, based on a questionnaire survey of 183 students in Warsaw, and Anneke van Otterloo (1999) describes a number of New Age centres in the Netherlands.

This volume of journal articles relays much more hard fieldwork, rather than theoretical speculation, than an earlier volume, *Religion* (volume 23), and also presents this in an international perspective, which was previously lacking. Heelas edited the volume of *Religion* devoted to New Age. Articles in this volume have already been discussed earlier in this book, including Lyon (1993) and Heelas (1993) on New Age and postmodernism, Bowman (1993) on Celtic traditions in New Age, Walter (1993) on understandings of death in New Age and Kent (1993) on the relation between the demise of anti-Vietnam War radicalism and the rise of New Age.

Journal articles have a number of advantages over book-length studies of New Age. Particularly important is that they tend to go to press much more quickly, and so can be much more up-to-date. Also, there is perhaps less of the market pressure (mentioned above) in a scholarly journal for a broad market appeal, and so articles can concentrate on and more fully explore closely defined problem areas. This second advantage of journal articles is also apparent in contrasting the detail available in original book-length studies of New Age with that in published theses.

– PUBLISHED THESES –

In general, the original book-length studies of New Age considered in the first section above are good introductory works but lack the depth and detail of understanding provided in book-length studies that are based on doctoral research. Such works will now be discussed.

The historical analysis of the term 'New Age' put forward by Steven Sutcliffe has been partly covered in Chapter 3. Sutcliffe concentrates on Alice Bailey's work in the inter-war period, the pre-history of the Findhorn Community in the 1950s, and New Age networks in the 1960s and after. Sutcliffe acknowledges that activists like Peter Caddy and Anthony Brooke 'saw an opportunity in the mid-to-late 1960s to convert this kind of low-key, privatistic religiosity into a genuine movement' (Sutcliffe 1998: 95). However, he argues that the resultant 'movement' was insufficiently distinguished to achieve this: it embraced both socially privileged figures as well as the unemployed; it had grassroots structures of maintenance and reproduction; it displayed loose and shifting patterns of association around different charismatic teachers; it was indistinguishable from secular norms and fashions; and it was ideologically tolerant.

Sutcliffe concludes his thesis with the acknowledgement that although a 'collective world of sorts exists' (ibid.: 100), within which a cluster of ideas and techniques is associated with a New Age, this alternative religious world consists of 'seekers, gathered in groups, within wider networks of common interest and association' (ibid.: 100). The published version of the thesis is even slightly more pessimistic as to the existence of a New Age movement, 'for its reflexive biographies, its loose collectivities and its one potentially explosive emblem – 'New Age' – lack a viable level of collective focus and mobilisation effectively to deliver its challenge' (Sutcliffe 2002: 225).

Sutcliffe's fieldwork was conducted with a 'unit of service' in the Bailey tradition, founded in 1984 (see Chapter 3). Sutcliffe participated semi-regularly in full-moon meditations for two years, meeting seventeen different individuals, with a core of three Arcane School students also involved in Triangles, a meditation network. Perhaps Sutcliffe's most detailed and interesting fieldwork was conducted at the Findhorn Community. This material has already been discussed in Chapter 6 and earlier by Sutcliffe himself (1995a, 1995b).

An alternative health fair in Glasgow, attended in October 1994, is also profiled by Sutcliffe. Around seventy different groups attended, including the Bates Method of eyesight improvement, the Alexander Technique, acupuncture, T'ai Chi and the NFSH. Some new religious movements were present, including the Brahma Kumaris, the Glasgow Buddhist Centre and the Gnostic Movement. Around thirty free talks and demonstrations took place over a weekend. Sutcliffe reports that the expression 'New Age' was scarcely in evidence. Finally, a firewalking workshop was attended in 1996 at the Westbank Natural Health Centre which was established in 1959 and had been part of the '1960s matrix', according to Sutcliffe.

Sutcliffe's attack against New Age is based on both emic and etic reasons (see Chapter 1). Firstly, emic affiliation to the New Age emblem is not necessarily central to alternative spirituality that is commonly described as New Age – it is an optional idiom. Historically, 'New Age' self-identification has been limited, he argues, to a relatively small number of specific groups and individuals. Even where 'New Age' is acknowledged by participants, this has been tentative and circumscribed with qualifications, according to Sutcliffe.

Secondly, and etically, Sutcliffe compares the idea of a New Age 'movement' with loose types of collective behaviours, for example the 'crowd', 'fads' and 'crazes' differentiated by Turner and Killian (1972).

> Several sociostructural formulations of 'movement' have been advanced historically – new religious, social, cultural, etcetera – and certainly part of the problem is that scholars on New Age have not always specified their usage. But the phenomena in question are deficient in most features of these formulations: for example, they lack coordinating bodies, historical awareness, a plausible degree of stability and continuity, evidence of boundary and belonging, a realistic level of critical debate and mobilization (presupposing in turn the existence of an explicit level of ideological norm and practice) and, crucially, overt self-identity and concrete goals. (Sutcliffe 1998: 220)

Sutcliffe comments that 'New Age' is an 'emblem' which has been invoked in various fads and crazes, especially before the 1980s, but should not be used to demarcate these networks. Today, he suggests, New Age is an even looser 'idiom' available to spiritual seekers. Ultimately, he writes, the networks depend on seekers. Sutcliffe originally differentiated seekers according to three role models: singular, serial and multiple (Sutcliffe 1997, 1998; see also Balch & Taylor 1978). The singular seeker zealously pursues a particular religion, and is sensibly dropped from the typology in Sutcliffe (2002). The serial seeker has changed allegiance more than once. Multiple seeking proceeds multidirectionally and synchronically. Sutcliffe continues:

> I have argued that a New Age movement does not exist. The phenomenon in question is actually an assemblage of seekers, which persists irrespective of the extent to which it finds temporary common cause in the expression 'New Age'. Thus seekers are the constant in this alternative culture. (1998: 234)

He now asks to what extent seekership is religious, citing the absence or weak presence of empirical features usually associated with traditional or world religions, or even new religions, such as buildings for worship, leader figures or foundational texts. Furthermore, organised religion is positively attacked by seekers, in favour of 'spirituality'. This notion is discussed by Sutcliffe, with a history of its usage. Sutcliffe argues that spirituality associated with New Age is a particular instance of contemporary spirituality, namely alternative spirituality. Other 'irrigating currents' include 'denominational spiritualities, "interfaith" and ecumenical endeavours, Humanistic psychology and psychotherapy, health and healing practices, and sport and physical fitness techniques' (ibid.: 242).

The summary of Sutcliffe's argument above has been largely drawn from the original text of his thesis (ibid.). Although the presentation has been refined in the published version (Sutcliffe 2002) and supplemented with further historical detail, particularly from the Findhorn archives, this refinement, while easier to read, tends to obscure the underlying arguments without modifying them to any great extent. For a complete understanding of Sutcliffe's latest and more nuanced thought, *Children of the New Age* should obviously be consulted further.

Olav Hammer's *Claiming Knowledge: Strategies of Epistemology from Theosophy to the New Age* (2001b) is a weighty historico-philosophical examination of Western esotericism, much in the line of Hanegraaff (1996), with many new and insightful examples of the adaptation of religious creativity to Western modernity. First, theoretical terms and concepts are explained, with a brief historical overview of esotericism. The second, largest section of the book delineates three typical discursive strategies used by late modern esotericists: the claims of ancient authority, of confirmation by modern science, and of validation by personal experience. The final section brings these suggestions together in a case study, namely reincarnation.

Adrian Ivakhiv's *Claiming Sacred Ground: Pilgrims and Politics at Glastonbury and Sedona* (2001) employs an unusual methodology in

New Age studies: that of environmental cultural studies, exploring the New Age communities and the reactions of other residents at Glastonbury, England and Sedona, Arizona. Thus Ivakhiv is interested in questions not raised by other scholars of New Age trained in disciplines such as sociology and philosophy, for example, why do certain landscapes attract New Agers?

'New Age culture', a term wider than 'New Age spirituality' and assuming less than 'subculture', is split by Ivakhiv into ecospirituality (or Earth spirituality) and New Age millenarianism or ascensionism. Earth spirituality is said to overlap New Age but remain distinct, including women's spirituality, ecopaganism, pantheistic nature mysticism, whole-Earth beliefs, and feminist and environmentalist versions of mainstream religious traditions, as well as native traditions such as Wicca and Celtic and Druidic Paganism. 'New Age millenarianism' is described as including channelled traditions and dualist or neognostic cosmologies. Together, Earth spirituality and ascensionism are described as 'two sides of a loosely unified spiritual-cultural movement . . . within the amorphous culture of New Age and alternative spirituality' (ibid.: 8).

Ivakhiv's understanding of New Age millenarianism is different from Wouter Hanegraaff's understanding of New Age *sensu stricto* (with an emphasis on an imminent apocalypse) (Hanegraaff 1996: 98–103) and is in fact more akin to Hanegraaff's understanding of New Age *sensu lato* (where this literal apocalypticism has been lost). This can be seen by Ivakhiv's alternative term for 'New Age millenarianism': ascensionism – although not discussed in depth by Ivakhiv, ascensionism is perhaps better understood as a movement within the wider, popular New Age culture (New Age *sensu lato*) (see e.g. Cooper 2001).

A useful pictorial representation of the relationships between traditional/mainstream religious culture, popular culture, scientific/academic culture, New Age culture, the New Paradigm movement and other new religious movements is redrawn from Ivakhiv below, in Figure 9.1, slightly amended to allow for an overlap between scientific/academic culture and traditional/mainstream religious culture.

The most interesting parts of Ivakhiv's study, for scholars of New Age, are the extended ethnographies at Glastonbury and Sedona, which form the bulk of the book. Particularly interesting within those detailed accounts are the approaches of non-New Age residents to the New Age communities in their midst – little other academic work has been done on this important topic. However, it is unfortunate that

Figure 9.1   *Relationships between cultures*

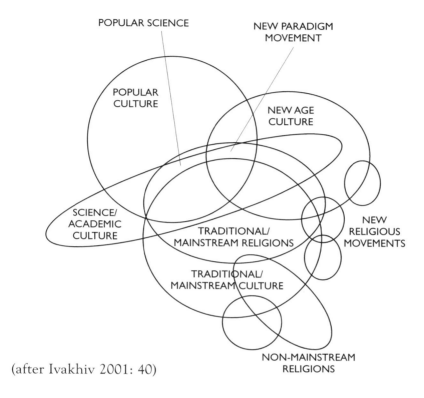

POPULAR SCIENCE

NEW PARADIGM
MOVEMENT

POPULAR
CULTURE

NEW AGE
CULTURE

SCIENCE/
ACADEMIC
CULTURE

TRADITIONAL/
MAINSTREAM RELIGIONS

NEW
RELIGIOUS
MOVEMENTS

TRADITIONAL/
MAINSTREAM CULTURE

NON-MAINSTREAM
RELIGIONS

(after Ivakhiv 2001: 40)

Ivakhiv did not have sight of Ruth Prince and David Riches' manuscript on Glastonbury before it was published (2000), although he does refer to Prince's thesis (1992).

Prince and Riches' study *The New Age in Glastonbury* (2000; see also Riches 2003) is based on Prince's research as a postgraduate student in Glastonbury in 1987 and from 1989 to 1990. Despite using a tape recorder only twice (Prince & Riches 2000: xi), Prince's field notes are amazingly rich and precise: the book contains a wealth of detail and examples, including many sections of quotations from New Agers which are quoted as if from transcriptions. The material has been much worked over since the presentation of Prince's thesis, although the themes of holism and individualism remain.

A new theoretical setting for the fieldwork is introduced: that of mainstream versus non-mainstream. Prince and Riches acknowledge that the non-mainstream may have values in common with the mainstream, and thus that the notions may be misleading, but assert instead that 'with respect to the local level the experience of a mainstream/ non-mainstream divide is fundamental' (ibid.: 27). Perhaps the most insightful section of the work is contained in the last chapter, although unfortunately there is no reported fieldwork outside of Glastonbury to support the wider-ranging theoretical observations made. All religious movements are plotted in relation to eight variables, as follows:

aggregation *spatially discontinuous* with the mainstream (e.g. Hutterites)	vs	aggregation *spatially continuous* with the mainstream (e.g. Glastonbury New Agers)
nomadic aggregation (e.g. New Age Travellers)	vs	*sedentary* aggregation (e.g. Findhorners [farming communards])
high density aggregation (e.g. Hare Krishna)	vs	*low density* aggregation (e.g. Glastonbury New Agers)
non-episodic aggregation [long-term/life-long association with the aggregate] (e.g. Hutterites)	vs	*episodic* aggregation [short-term association with the aggregate] (e.g. Rainbow people)
aggregation is *non-natal in respect of members* (e.g. Glastonbury New Agers)	vs	aggregation is *natal in respect of members* (e.g. Hutterites)
total aggregation [aggregation pertains to all life's affairs] (e.g. Hare Krishna)	vs	*partial* aggregation [aggregation pertains to only some of life's affairs] (e.g. many Glasonbury New Agers)
experiential involvement in social aggregation (e.g. Shakers)	vs	*vicarious involvement* in social aggregation (e.g. Hare Krishna people who live outside the Temple)

(from Prince & Riches 2000: 283–5)

Published in the same year as Prince and Riches' study is *Le New-Age: Ritualités et Mythologies Contemporaines* (Ferreux 2000). It has a serious methodological flaw, in that participant research was conducted covertly (ibid.: 38), without the knowledge of the subjects. However, perhaps the work's greatest contributions to the study of New Age are theoretical, especially in its examination of *la représentation imagée* (ibid.: 109–60). The importance of visual media to New Agers is often mentioned in New Age studies, but seldom examined in such depth. Chapters on the origin of New Age and the political dimension of New Age are not groundbreaking, omitting nearly all reference to standard scholarly works on New Age; for instance the chapter on death and New Age omits reference to the important study by Tony Walter (1993). Nevertheless, this work is one of the few published French scholarly works to go beyond the Christian analysis of Jean Vernette (1990) and the popular critiques of Michel Lacroix (1995) and Jean-Luc Porquet (1994).

Other French works that achieve such scholarship are also published doctoral theses. Erica Guilane-Nachez, in *Sources, Mythes et Pratiques du New Age de ses Origines à Nos Jours* (1999), presents an ethnography of twenty-six informants, with substantial extracts from the interviews. The presentation begins with a long list of motivating themes in New Age, including for example Eastern religion, paradigm theory and a multi-dimensional vision of the universe. These themes are then illustrated with more specific examples, such as rejection of religions of the Book (Judaeo-Christian and Islamic), espousal of syncretism/eclecticism and belief in the existence of God. The themes and specifics are then contrasted with Western cultural ideas, in a table of 'soft' and 'hard' ideas which is admitted to be a caricature. This stark presentation of New Age is then backed up with historical, philosophical, sociocultural, artistic and scientific notes, emphasising French influences. Reference to the large body of English literature on New Age is, as with other French works, almost completely absent.

Sônia Weidner Maluf (1996) examines (also in French) alternative spirituality and therapy in the south of Brazil, and although the New Age Aquarian motif figures only in her title, it is obvious to the reader that the phenomena she studies are at least connected with New Age. Again, though, there is a paucity of references to the established English literature. Interesting anomalies between the Brazilian and French alternative spirituality scene are noted, such as the fact that psychoanalysis is more an acceptable part of Brazilian culture, not as 'alternative' or socially embarrassing as it can be in France – and other

Western countries. The fieldwork centres on Porto Alegre, the capital
of the Rio Grande do Sul region at the far south of Brazil. In one
respect, this choice of location is unfortunate, since it seems to overemphasise the presence of *Saniases* – disciples of Osho Rajneesh – who
held a number of courses in the city. The core of the ethnography is a
detailed account from one informant, which raises questions of
representativeness.

Another doctoral thesis that looks at New Age in Brazil is Leila
Amaral's *Carnaval da Alma: Comunidade, Essência e Sincretismo na
Nova Era* (2000), although Weidner Maluf (1996) is not discussed.
Again, there is an emphasis on healing, but other areas of New Age are
also covered, including occultism (psi, magic, Feng Shui, chi, ley lines),
the sacred power of sound and spirituality as a market place. Fieldwork
is more wide-ranging than in Weidner Maluf, and includes a chapter on
a week spent in 1993 at a national gathering of 'Alternative Aquarian
Communities' (17th ENCA – *Encontro Nacional de Communidades
Alternativas Aquarianas*). The final chapter broadens the outlook to
the global perspective, examining how an alternative religious tradition relates to globalisation. Amaral's thesis is summarised (at some
length) in Carozzi (ed. 1999: 47–79); and see also Heelas & Amaral
(1994).

As seen in Chapter 1, Hanegraaff defines New Age as follows:

> The New Age movement is the cultic milieu having become conscious of itself,
> in the later 1970s, as constituting a more or less unified 'movement'. All mani-
> festations of this movement are characterized by a popular western culture crit-
> icism expressed in terms of a secularized esotericism. (Hanegraaff 1996: 522,
> original emphasis removed)

Hanegraaff's argument is usefully summarised and updated in
Hanegraaff (1998 and 2002). Hanegraaff's philosophical approach is
entirely literary, without contextualising fieldwork, and even more
worryingly was limited to works available in European continental
bookshops (Hanegraaff 1996: 13). Despite these serious limitations,
Hanegraaff's work is impressively detailed and there is no comparable
study of the philosophy of New Age. New Age religion is divided into
four major trends: channelling, healing and personal growth, New Age
Science and Neopaganism. Thematic approaches to New Age discuss
holism and evolution, meta-empirical and human beings, the philosophy of mind, death and survival, good and evil, visions of the past, and
the idea of a New Age. The third part of the work, described as an
'interpretation', gives a historical perspective on New Age religion
from the modern Hermeticist revival and the emergence of Western

Esotericism, through the Renaissance, Enlightenment, Counter-Enlightenment, Romanticism, occultisim, Theosophy, the theory of evolution, and the 'psychologization of Esotericism' with Mesmerism, New Thought and Jung.

Some of Hanegraaff's central insights had been achieved earlier by David Spangler (1993). In particular, Hanegraaff's concept of New Age *sensu stricto* and *sensu lato* (see above) is foreshadowed by Spangler's idea of the prophetic movement based on an astrological interpretation of history which was something to await rather than in which to participate: 'One did not create a New Age; one waited for its predestined arrival' (ibid.: 86). Spangler describes how this fringe idea 'piggybacked' on other movements in the 1960s and 1970s, including the civil rights movement, the drug culture and the hippie counterculture, such that the New Age idea was 'liberated' from its 'prophetic context'. Spangler's explanations of this transformation of New Age also go far in explaining the dichotomy Sutcliffe locates between the apocalyptic New Age 'emblem' prior to the 1960s and the diffuse cultural 'idiom' after that era.

A second theme in which Spangler pre-empts Hanegraaff is the 'psychologizing of spirituality' (ibid.: 94), in which spirituality is seen as a kind of psychological or therapeutic process. Hanegraaff develops this critique in a section on 'the psychologization of religion and sacralization of psychology' (Hanegraaff 1996: 224–9). However, it is clear that Hanegraaff has not lifted these notions directly from Spangler, even though his wide reading of Spangler's texts may have influenced his interpretation. For Spangler makes it quite plain that the term Hanegraaff would later popularise to refer to these spiritualities, 'New Age religion', is not appropriate: 'It is quite erroneous and misleading to say that someone who chooses one of these paths as his or her primary route into the divine is following a "New Age religion" or worse, the "religion of the New Age."' (Spangler 1993: 84)

In complete contrast to Hanegraaff's thesis on New Age, Michael York's thesis, completed in 1991 and published as *The Emerging Network: A Sociology of the New Age and Neo-Pagan Movements* (1995), is based on extensive fieldwork and first-hand knowledge of the New Age scene. The methodology is explicitly sociological rather than philosophical or literary. York is concerned even in the title of his study to highlight the distinction made by participants between New Age and Neo-Pagan, and this is a constant theme throughout the work. In-depth fieldwork was carried out at the Alternatives lecture series at St James's church, Piccadilly, London and Shan's House of the Goddess. Nevertheless, although a large amount of fieldwork and participant contact is evident in the text, there is little extended presentation of participant observation (ibid.: 223–32). The 'statistical surveys' undertaken are likewise insubstantial, in one case consisting of just seventeen replies (House of the Goddess), with incongruous 'control groups' being a centre for people with AIDS, and two groups of York's friends. York's analysis of New Age as a SPIN – segmented, polycentric, integrated network – has been discussed in Chapter 6.

Christoph Bochinger began his doctorate in New Age in 1987, around the same time as York started his in London, and published it also at a similar time. Bochinger's thesis (1995), submitted in 1993, looks at New Age as one facet of the 'new religious scenery' in relation to modern religion. His main argument is that German New Age is a publishing phenomenon, initiated by public calls for translations of popular English-language New Age works. Bochinger makes a number of important sociological suggestions, in particular discussing the application of Ernst Troeltsch's category of *die Mystik* (ibid.: 57f), looking at the new descriptive category of 'social movement' (ibid.: 193f), and presenting New Age as a result of wider cultural and technological shifts (ibid.: 27f).

Bochinger decries the definition of New Age as 'non-Christian religion' and 'alternative theology' (ibid.: 531). An example he gives of this is the false equation of New Age reincarnation teachings as an alternative to Christian eschatology, which equation he rightly considers logically contradictory. The real question, Bochinger says, is how in the modern world one can think of the existence of the soul after death. Yet it is not clear how 'alternative theology' differs from Bochinger's preferred sociological term, 'the flipside of the Enlightenment' (ibid.: 523), the 'secular religion' (ibid.: 523) of Swedenborg, Blake, Spiritualism, Transcendentalism, New Thought and others which Bochinger says seek to synthesise science and religion. Irving Hexham (1999) calls for the translation of Bochinger's thesis into English, and with this I must concur.

Prior to these studies of New Age, I have not located any published doctoral theses on New Age *per se*. If we widen the net, there are of course many works on subjects related to New Age, such as Holistic Health and witchcraft. Two such publications are briefly mentioned here.

A Place for Healing: an Ethnography of Holistic Health Practitioners (1985), June Anne English's doctoral thesis, was published in 1990 (English-Lueck 1990). English's fieldwork was no doubt carried out before the term 'New Age' was commonly used to describe the 'Holistic Health practitioners' she studies, and so this is an interesting work on the early days of New Age. English predicted that practitioners could cooperate with orthodox medics, introducing reforms into the medical establishment though losing some esoteric aspects; emerge as a distinct profession of 'empirical medicine', competing with rationalist medicine; or continue in 'decentralized, egalitarian, informal networks' (English 1985: 329). The life cycle of the Holistic Health movement is described (ibid.: 21). The cycle starts with a 'problem' which has no solution in the *status quo*. A 'catalytic analysis' is made and then confirmed in a crisis situation. Members gather around this analysis, before a secondary analysis becomes the basis for professional groups to coalesce in a more institutionalised and formal way. English hopes that holistic healers will professionalise before they are absorbed or destroyed by orthodox medicine. Alternatively, Holistic Health groups continue informally *sub rosa*.

Cult and Countercult: a Study of a Spiritual Growth Group and a Witchcraft Order (Scott 1980) is based on Gini Graham Scott's doctoral research between 1974 and 1976 with the Inner Peace Movement, with approximately 20,000 members meeting in workshops, and the Aquarian Age Order (a pseudonym for a Pagan group in the San Francisco Bay area) with about 150 members. It is therefore one of the earliest academic studies of New Age. The groups are not compared, nor are they contextualised as part of a general cultural trend; Scott's thesis is that mainstream groups help members function better in the mainstream, while countercultural groups seek alternative meanings (ibid.: 8).

The doctoral theses which have been considered in this section provide some of the best accounts of New Age that have been published. Any serious scholar of New Age must be familiar with them.

– As Yet Unpublished Theses –

The most up-to-date and original work on New Age is generally found in academic theses which are as yet unpublished. The more recent theses on New Age that remain unpublished have appeared in Britain (Corrywright 2001[3]; Wood 1999; Rose 1996; Greer 1994) with Possamaï (1998) from Australia. The earliest theses on New Age that remain unpublished, however, appeared in the United States (Roberts 1989; Brown-Keister 1982). This mirrors a similar distribution pattern between the UK and the US as for published theses, which were considered above. The final section of this chapter describes in depth some unpublished theses on New Age.

Dominic Corrywright's doctoral thesis, *Theoretical and Empirical Investigations into New Age Spiritualities with Special Reference to the South West of England* (2001; see also Corrywright (2000)), is a sympathetic portrayal of New Age. Corrywright criticises existing academic research for inaccuracies (2001: 1) and instead describes a new framework for organising the research data: 'the idea of webs, in which the threads are created by individuals' activities and beliefs' (ibid.: 2). Throughout, New Age is described as consisting of 'spiritualities' rather than as a New Age movement or New Age religion.

However, despite promising to present a 'thorough theoretical analysis of both scholarly critical studies and insider expressions of the religiosity of New Age spiritualities' (ibid.: 7), Corrywright does not undertake an extended critique of existing literature on New Age (other than works by Paul Heelas and Michael York), and omits reference to important sources such as the 1999 issue of *Religion* devoted to New Age, and doctoral theses by Steven Sutcliffe and Matthew Wood. Corrywright's over-simplistic and underdeveloped methodology is to be 'accurate and useful'.

The thesis is divided into four sections: theoretical, methodological, empirical and evaluative. The theoretical foundations consist of Michel Foucault's critique of power and the structure of discourse; Thomas Kuhn's notion of paradigm shifts; and feminist criticisms of patriarchal forms in the history of religions. Corrywright describes his approach as '*post*-postmodern' (ibid.: 46, *original emphasis*), apparently on the basis that New Age holds paradigm shifts to be 'the result of the multiple confluences of the mundane and the cosmic, a web-like form of interactions' (ibid.: 46).

The empirical section of the research was conducted between 1997 and 2000 with a free newspaper in South-West England, *The Spark*, and a local group of Chuck Spezzano's Psychology of Vision. A 'survey of spirituality' was undertaken, yielding sixty analysable responses.[4] From these responses, a further five individuals from each group were selected for extended interviews. A survey of the primary literature of these two groups was also undertaken, although this is not related in any great detail. Corrywright's thesis does not claim to present extensive new empirical data – indeed, he plays down the value of phenomenological fieldwork (ibid.: 110) and he should perhaps therefore not be criticised for this apparent paucity of fieldwork – but it is difficult to evaluate his lengthy theoretical, methodological and evaluative comments on such a small body of empirical research.

Corrywright uses the image of a web to inform both his model of New Age and his methodology. 'Methodologically the web describes the scholar's use of a multiplicity of methods to define phenomena' (ibid.: 91). His critique of family resemblance theory in New Age studies replaces the assumption of similarity or identity of beliefs by the notion of a web of relationships: 'the underlying familial resemblances are to be found in the *modes of connection* between individuals, organisations and the wider network' (ibid.: 104, *original emphasis*).

Corrywright's brief mention of SPIN theory (see Chapter 6) fails to distinguish it from his own web theory. It is not clear why Corrywright did not adopt existing terminology for New Age pioneered by York (1995) and Ferguson ([1980] 1989). Perhaps the only differences between a SPIN and a web are that a web has a central node (Corrywright 2001: 105) and is usually two-dimensional. Corrywright acknowledges the limitations of two dimensions in a model for New Age and describes a three-dimensional web, but apparently concurs that New Age does have a central node (which is not identified).

The Spark is a free newspaper aimed at New Age, with a print run of 25,000, distributed through voluntary placement in shops and other public sites within a twenty-mile radius of Bristol. Corrywright discusses the distribution of the newspaper at length (ibid.: 190–7). The newspaper is paid for by advertising and hence consists largely of listings of events, courses and services, together with a small amount of editorial comment. However, Corrywright does not provide an analysis of these listings or the editorial, and apart from the combined results of his statistical surveys (see Chapter 7), analysis of *The Spark* is confined to comments on his interviews of five readers.

Psychology of Vision was founded by Chuck and Lencay Spezzano, and is based in Hawaii with a number of national subsidiaries including Psychology of Vision United Kingdom Ltd, with offices in Pewsey, Wiltshire, England. Psychology of Vision disseminates its model of psychology and spirituality through workshops, seminars and books written by the founders. Corrywright describes Psychology of Vision using Ferguson's ([1980] 1989) term 'psychotechnology'. Corrywright conducted an undisclosed amount of participant observation with the group, and five formal interviews. The central method Psychology of Vision uses for promoting its processes is the course, according to Corrywright. There are one- or two-day courses promising radical life changes, as well as further courses for the initiated and for training trainers of Psychology of Vision, for which the fees are prohibitive (for example, US$5,500 for a twenty-day workshop in Hawaii in November 1999). The second method Psychology of Vision uses for promoting its processes is distribution of what Corrywright calls 'products', mainly texts by Chuck Spezzano, and audio and video tapes of Psychology of Vision courses.

Chapter 8 of Corrywright's thesis, 'Re-evaluation of spiritualities in the New Age', begins with a discussion of J. Gordon Melton's explanation (1988) of the decline of the New Age Movement, ignoring his subsequent pronouncement of its death (Melton 1998b). The New Age as movement is usefully described as a '*synthetic* category' (Corrywright 2001: 263), a 'fluctuating polymorphic collection of identities and networks' (ibid.: 262). It is suggested that internal instability within New Age spiritualities will bring about not collapse, but higher-order structures along the lines of Ilya Prigogine's theory of dissipative structures. Corrywright suggests that the term 'New Age' 'has a distinct life-span . . . But that which it once described may not be so circumscribed by historical terminology' (ibid.: 264).

The criticisms of narcissism and consumerism as essential elements of New Age are rejected by Corrywright, as are further criticisms of trivialisation, simplification and popularisation of scientific concepts. In this section of the thesis, Corrywright tellingly uses the first person plural: 'How might we respond to the criticisms . . .' (ibid.: 278).

Corrywright next reviews the notions of 'web thinking' and 'web methodology' as tools for the study of New Age. This is more than a simple claim that New Age is structured like a web; Corrywright invokes the motif of a web to describe his whole approach in the thesis. Such an approach is indeed, as Corrywright points out, more akin to the subject of his study than the discipline of his study. He suggests the web model could be used to study traditional religions. Finally, Corrywright briefly defends his usage of the term 'New Age spiritualities'.

Matthew Wood describes his doctoral thesis as 'a challenge to New Age Movement studies' (Wood 1999: 2). It is a study of a religious network in Nottinghamshire, England, which would normally be described as part of New Age. Fieldwork was conducted between 1992 and 1994, and for six months in 1996. Up to twenty people regularly attended the groups studied, but 'only a handful' were selected for (informal) interview. While Wood comments that this raises questions as to the validity of conclusions derived from fieldwork, in fact his fieldwork is among the most extensive on New Age available at the time of his writing.

The first chapter sets the theoretical scene in which the New Age fieldwork is to be analysed, concentrating on anthropological and sociological debates concerning the body, performance and power. It is argued that social authority is derived from personal relations, which are partly controlled by the method of use of the body, in contrast to the common sociological emphasis on discourse and meaning. The chapter is a highly theoretical critique of Steven Lukes, Abner Cohen, Alfred Schutz, Peter Berger, Thomas Luckmann, Gerardus van der Leeuw, Emile Durkheim, Anthony Giddens and others. Its purpose is apparently to provide a grounding for the fieldwork, which is said to show that knowledge is not the primary actor in social life but is open to ongoing reinterpretation with the shift of power relations.

Wood claims the Nottinghamshire Network is not a bounded entity, but may nevertheless be still be regarded as distinguishable since the groups concerned brought together people from other groups and those who were practising alone. Wood seeks to explore this by attention to the power relations within and between the network's groups, using the concept of nonformativeness. This exploration is drawn from observation of the Essene Meditation, an evening meditation group of around two dozen people which met fortnightly, and the Spiritual Fair, held monthly, attracting up to 100 visitors. Wood's analysis centres on four key practices: Holistic Healing, meditation, divination and spirit possession or channelling. Spirit possession is singled out as 'super-structural' to the other practices, since it is said to be the ground and origin of many of the groups in the network. Wood writes, 'Although this Thesis contends that a New Age Movement does not exist, the social phenomena that are considered part of that clearly do; the widespread presence of the four sorts of practice described above is not in doubt' (ibid.: 93).

It is suggested by Wood that the reason for the categorisation of these phenomena as New Age is polemical, a 'hegemonic construction by political authorities' used to oppress people who practise that which is so labelled. Four academic portrayals of New Age are considered to illustrate Wood's thesis. He briefly considers Melton, York and Hanegraaff before concentrating on Heelas. Wood criticises such New Age studies for assuming that a movement of ideas entails a social movement.

Wood then introduces his notion of 'nonformative spirituality', which refers to the relative absence of formal social structures in participants' attitude and the organisation of groups and events and of the network as a whole, united by the four main practices of channelling, meditation, divination and holistic healing (ibid.: 110–14).

The notion of seekership as used in Wood (1999) is derived from Sutcliffe (1997), and the multiple seeker is seen as particularly apposite to Wood's network. Multiple seekers are people who 'quest' for religious meaning in more than one tradition simultaneously. Wood's discussion of dissonance, however, does not concentrate on the traditional cognitive elements examined in Festinger et al. (1956), but calls for greater emphasis on issues of bodily dissonance expressed in the notions of existential shock or anxiety.

What Wood calls the Essene Meditation was a group he studied over eighteen months in Nottinghamshire, which met every other Friday evening. The Meditation was led by one couple, who were practising therapists (in Bach flower essences, astrology and counselling), in the home of another couple, who healed through biorhythms. Around fifteen people attended each evening, evenly distributed between the sexes and with ages ranging from mid-twenties to mid-fifties. Wood emphasises the social importance of the meetings as much as the meditation, and discusses notions of the sacred, ritual and the liminal before moving on to consider meaning and symbols. The key symbol in the meditation was white light, but this had different meanings for different people. Wood claims that direct group leadership was lacking in the Essene Meditation, although he does examine the issues of power and authority among the hosts.

The career of the channeller is then compared to Ioan Lewis' (1971) anthropological analysis of spirit possession, which describes a shift from uncontrolled involuntary possession to controlled, voluntary possession. Wood is, however, aware of the differences between shamanism and channelling, which include the social context and purpose – healing in shamanism, communication in channelling.

Fieldwork at a spiritual fair took place during the summer and autumn of 1996, when the fair was over a year old. It had previously been known as a psychic fair, then Earthlights Festival, then Mind, Body and Spirit Festival. 'Spiritual Fair' appears to be Wood's own name for it. The fair took place in a small city-centre hotel, attracting about 150 people each Sunday it was held, with around twenty stalls selling goods and offering healing or clairvoyance sessions, as well as ten speakers throughout the day.

Wood reports that although there was a distinction between stall-holders and consumers, this was fluid, as producers also acted as consumers, paying interest in the other stalls. He divides the producers into spiritualists, other healers and cosmologists. The organiser of the fair, Michael, was a Spiritualist and the Spiritualist lectures were the best attended. Cosmologists comprised the smallest of the three groups of producers. Some producers promoted local businesses, including a flotation tank centre, courses in practical philosophy, Feng Shui consultations and a reflexology clinic. However, the spiritualists tended not to promote businesses, and Wood reports that the majority of consumers did not follow up their experiences at the fair by patronising the local businesses. The significance of the fair lay for Wood in providing people with the means to orient their current spiritual practices.

Wood argues that

> performances by producers at the Fair were used to unite social authority with spiritual authority. Explanations of spiritual authority through the presentation of biography helped establish social authority. And enactments of social authority by occupying prominent positions, as speakers and stall holders, helped establish spiritual authority. (1999: 231)

He suggests that deriving authority from biographies of spiritual experiences, rather than from membership within a group, demonstrates the nonformativeness of the fair.

Wood questions the relevance of Max Weber's analysis of charismatic authority, suggesting that charisma in channelling, meditation, divination and healing in the Nottinghamshire Network was curtailed by the charismatics themselves, through their continued seekership, and their audiences, through their varied allegiances. This is said to be 'another way of describing nonformativeness.' He goes on to describe the attitude of producers and consumers at the Spiritual Fair as a reaction against both formative groups and the formativeness of groups. The Spiritual Fair is then compared with the London Festival for Mind-Body-Spirit, which Wood attended in 1993 and 1994, and which has been given a more extended analysis by Malcolm Hamilton (2000). Wood comments in particular on the absence of traditional Spiritualism at the Festival, in contrast with the Fair, which he explains by the non-business attitude of Spiritualists.

A discussion of theories about healing and Holistic Health follows, in an attempt to show the importance of Holistic Health therapies in the lives of nonformative spiritualists. A crystal healing workshop held by Michael, the organiser of the Spiritual Fair, is described, where he led eight people in a visualisation and explained how to use crystals. Wood acknowledges that Michael's leadership was clearly established. Next a number of therapies practised by three friends who first met at the Essene Meditation are described. These include Reiki, aromatherapy, reflexology and silent meditation. The friends were associated, variously, with ISKCON (International Society for Krishna Consciousness) and White Eagle teachings, and their spiritual biographies are presented as examples of seekership.

Wood places the Nottinghamshire Network within a wider British context by examining the related traditions of Spiritualism, the Anthroposophical Society and an occult study group. There is some overlap in membership of these groups and of groups within what Wood calls the Nottinghamshire Network.

The final part of the thesis examines the relationship between formative and nonformative group structures. The formative/nonformative distinction is said to be partly about the process of institutionalisation, but also about the dynamic structures of social power. Having taken us through Roy Wallis' analysis (1975) of Scientology's institutionalisation, Wood considers Colin Campbell's notion of the cultic milieu (1972). Wood distinguishes the Nottinghamshire Network from the cultic milieu in that: deviance was not a distinguishing characteristic; seekership itself was varied, with people sometimes engaged with religious institutions; and different parts of the Network consisted of a structure of practices focused around channelling, whereas the cultic milieu has no structure. Wood suggests that the Nottinghamshire Network drew its members from more established religious groups of cults and sects. He concludes, 'The cultic milieu, despite initial appearances, therefore cannot be equated with nonformative spirituality, which, despite its characteristic of lack of enduring structures of social power, can be distinguished on its own terms from other phenomena' (Wood 1999: 326).

It is argued that even concerted efforts to establish formal groups fails in the nonformative context. The examples of the Meditation group hosts failing to maintain the Essene lifestyle, and Michael's lack of bureaucracy in organising the spiritual fair, are given. These groups are contrasted with the Anthroposophical Society, which maintains more control over its social boundaries. The occult study group is described as 'ambiguous' as regards formative/nonformative structures. Wood argues that his informants showed 'no evidence of a New Age identity. Although some people would at times talk of the new age, even when pressed in interview they would not class themselves as New Agers. Such a term held no meaning for them' (ibid.: 331). It is suggested by Wood that Paganism is more closely integrated than nonformative networks, as exemplified in the occult study group.

Wood's conclusion is that nonformativeness tends to exclude formativeness, although formativeness often includes nonformativeness. He suggests this explains why the Nottinghamshire Network endured, since it drew upon formative traditions in order to maintain its own lack of organisation. He argues that this appears to be contrary to conventional models of religious transformation, from cultic milieu to cult to sect, in that nonformative spirituality appears to arise from cults and sects.

The main suggestions of Adam Possamaï's thesis *In Search of New Age Spirituality: toward a Sociology of Perennism* (1998) are summarised in Possamaï (2003). Possamaï's starting point is that his interviewees were negatively disposed to the term 'New Age', which also lacks a clear academic definition. He sets out to find a common descriptor for the phenomena he studies, and coins the ideal-type concept of 'perennism': 'Perennism is a syncretic spirituality which interprets the world as monistic, whose teleology for its actos is the Integral Self, and whose soteriology is sought through gnosis' (Possamaï 1998:132). This concept is distinguished from the more familiar 'perennialism', which is said to contain the sociologically unacceptable notion that the perennial philosophy is the common core of all religions. Three sub-types are then located: Aquarian perennism, neo-paganism and presentist perennism.

It is suggested that the term 'New Age' was introduced as a synonym for the astrological concept of the 'Age of Aquarius' by Alice Bailey in the 1930s, and that New Age (or perennism) is a corresponding innovative development in esotericism. This innovation is described as the shift, initiated by contact with modernity, to democratise esoteric knowledge, removing the centrality of secrecy, and transferring from a preference for universal knowledge to a knowledge of the self. Aquarian perennists are said to focus on the future.

Neo-pagan perennists are said to focus on the past, and have little concern for a New Age or interest in theories of critical mass. Possamaï's evidence for this sub-type is five interviewees who performed rituals. This is flimsy evidence, and indeed I have encountered self-describing Pagans who do also expect a New Age; conversely, there are self-describing New Agers who perform rituals. Nevertheless, we have seen in Chapter 1 that Paganism is often distinguished from New Age proper.

The third sub-type, presentist perennism, is described as a new discovery by Possamaï, and is used for those who focus their spirituality on the present, denying the relevance of objective time and substituting a subjective time experienced by mystics. As Possamaï points out, such informants did not reject the Aquarian eschatology, but devalued it from the final end to one change among many. It is not clear why, therefore, presentist perennists are not a sub-type of Aquarian perennists. Furthermore, I have also encountered self-describing Pagans who have such a subjective notion of time.

As Possamaï acknowledges, the concept of perennism and its sub-types are ideal types which are fuzzy and overlap. Possamaï also suggests that there may be other sub-types of perennism, and further that the concept could be extended from the New Age field to describe other spiritualities or even esotericism.

It is difficult to see what has been achieved by the introduction of these new terms. Is there increased clarity? Or would the current terms 'New Age' and 'Pagan' have sufficed? So-called presentist perennists are not claimed to form a sociological grouping or to identify with each other, and it is not clear why this similarity in conception of time is considered sufficient to separate them out as a distinct category. Ultimately, the suspicion is that Possamaï's main contribution to New Age studies is, like Wood's, merely semantic. This suspicion is partly borne out by Possamaï's own ability to use the terms 'New Age' and 'New Age Spiritualities' (NAS) (a term and acronym which is not widely used) throughout the first half of his thesis without problem.

This having been said, the thesis is packed with a host of other insights into the nature of New Age which together make this one of the most highly theorised and conceptually structured accounts of New Age. The characteristics that make up perennism, namely monism, the Integral Self and gnosis, are each described in detail. Universal Gnosis, a universal knowledge gained from sources external to the self, is distinguished from Auto Gnosis, knowledge of the self gained in individual experience. Those who work for a Critical Mass by Meditation – believing that external energy may be harnessed by a certain number of people meditating – are distinguished from those who work for Critical Mass through Social Action.

The main drawback of the thesis is its sampling technique and the consequent significance of the evidence. Thirty-five interviewees were selected by distributing leaflets asking people to contact Possamaï, and successful contacts were asked to name further possible interviewees. While these are commonly used techniques for generating a population, they can bias the selection of volunteers. Possamaï reports one instance where an informant was reticent in interview about the notions outlined to him in some detail prior to the interview, but a similar biasing effect is undoubtedly present in all interviewees who responded to Possamaï's leaflet. It would have been interesting for the text of the leaflet to be appended to the thesis. Possamaï even acknowledges that he had to change the wording of the leaflet to clarify its terms, when he noticed that respondents were misinterpreting his meaning. These problems are most evident in a chapter where Possamaï attempts to calculate statistical trends in his 'population' – but as he repeatedly points out, such calculations lack any statistical significance.

Despite these criticisms, Possamaï's thesis is a highly original and well-thought out consideration of New Age, and certainly deserves publication. It is a shame that his work has not yet been taken up in mainstream New Age studies, although with the publication of Possamaï (2003) and Possamaï (forthcoming), this may be set to change.

Possamaï was not referenced in Kemp (2003a), Corrywright (2001) or Wood (1999). Wood also fails to discuss in detail the questions raised by Stuart Rose (1996) over the notion of New Age. Rose discerns several movements within New Age – including ecology, spirituality and psychotherapy. His analysis of New Age uses William Bloom's definition of 'four major fields: New Paradigm/New Science, Ecology, New Psychology, Spiritual Dynamics' (Bloom ed. 1991: xvi), and the text concentrates on two of these four domains: spiritual empowerment and healing.

Spiritual empowerment is described as 'a total transformation of an individual not only in terms of her or his way of thinking but in a complete change with regard to the way they lead their lives' (Rose 1996: 46), and is related to making contact with the higher self. In fact, the description of spiritual empowerment then concentrates on the psychotechnologies of the Human Potential movement, which I think are more correctly considered under the domain of healing practices, especially given Rose's articulation that

> the difference between the two is, primarily, that ideas and activities in the healing domain are predominantly to do with health, whereas the nature of spiritual empowerment is more to do with individuals seeking to change or develop themselves in terms of spiritual growth through an educative or experiential process. (ibid.: 53)

There is evidently some overlap where psychotechnologies are concerned as to whether they are undertaken for psychological health or improved spiritual well-being, and if these domains – spiritual and healing – are indeed fundamental, Rose ought to have considered this overlap. The boundary of the healing domain is further blurred when Rose declares that 'many such practices are not necessarily specific to the New Age and can be used simply as alternative or complementary to allopathic forms of medicine' (ibid.: 54). Again, this qualification is so great an inroad to his consideration of New Age healing that it deserves more attention.

Rose attempts to define key words in New Age such as transformation, connectedness, love and compassion, higher self and God. He also considers what he calls 'access to the New Age': intuition is held to be the prime guide for people in the New Age, networking the means by which these intuitions are fulfilled.

Rose conducted a large survey of readers of *Kindred Spirit* magazine, a popular New Age magazine in the United Kingdom, receiving 908 responses. Unfortunately, the survey used pre-defined New Age: 'For our purposes, 'New Age' covers any activity or idea in our culture – for example, including healing, self-development, ecology, etc – whose value can be considered new or alternative to the traditional Western mainstream' (ibid.: 362). Only after this pre-definition is the question asked of readers, 'In a few words please describe what you think the New Age is' (ibid.: 362). Rose divides the responses into five themed clusters:

1. Greater awareness
2. Growth in spirituality
3. Recurrence and renewal of aspects of life which have become distorted
4. Reaction against materialism
5. More holistic outlook on life.
(ibid.: 153–5)

Fieldwork is conspicuously absent from inclusion in the thesis. Rose mentions a lecture by Jonathon Porritt, a sermon by Revd Donald Reeves and a five-day workshop. Not one interview – however informal – is mentioned. Rose must surely have conducted more fieldwork than this; why not mention it in the text?

The final chapter details 'fundamental problems' with New Age:

1. Efficacy of healing practices and spiritual empowerment
2. Trivialization of New Age
3. Narcissism
4. Consumerism and profiteering
5. Self-centredness, lack of concern for community
(from ibid.: 302–51)

Finally, consistencies and inconsistencies between the survey and earlier discussion of New Age are considered, with a self-congratulatory conclusion that the survey bore out other commentators' views.

A very different British thesis from those in the tradition of Sutcliffe, Wood and Rose was presented by Paul Greer in 1994. 'The aims of this thesis are to provide a general overview of New Age spirituality/theology, and to organize this overview within a framework which highlights and explains many of the fundamental contradictions of the movement' (Greer 1994: ii). Greer's stated research plan is thus structured along Christian lines of thought, which, while readily highlighting problems of categorisation, cannot adequately explain or systematise New Age. This underlying Christian thought structure in effect creates the very 'contradictions' Greer's thesis seeks to explain.

The starting point of Greer's thesis is to note that, despite agreeing that New Age is difficult to characterise, most 'researchers' (see below) describe 'common values' and a 'common vision'. Greer's stated aim is to show that in fact 'some New Agers are just inherently contradictory!' (ibid.: 38) and to provide a framework for highlighting this. It is hardly exaggerating to quip that Greer's research aim is therefore to provide a self-contradictory model of New Age.

Greer's published summary of his thesis (1995) delineates well the main new idea of the thesis: a sliding typology of New Age between two conflicting 'poles' or 'tendencies' of patriarchal and ecological spirituality. The examples used in this article – respectively Lectorium Rosicrucianum, Trevelyan, Ramtha, Creation Spirituality and Wicca – are also the central examples in the thesis. This patriarchal–ecological continuum may be compared with Adrian Ivakhiv's distinction between New Age millenarianism/ascensionism and ecospirituality/Earth spirituality (see above).

The 'researchers' of New Age upon whom Greer so relies for his understanding of the movement are Russell Chandler, Elliot Miller, Ted Peters, Melton et al. and Bloom (Greer 1994: 18). Only Melton among these has any claim to academic objectivity, but Greer's discussion of his works is limited. Bloom is a key figure on the British New Age scene, but again Greer's consideration of Bloom is inadequate. Greer expresses his preference for the explicitly Christian considerations of New Age given by Chandler, Miller and Peters (ibid.: 2).

The two spiritual dynamics are defined in terms of belief. 'The "ecological" rubric is employed in a . . . sense, indicating: 1) the belief that the earth and the cosmos are home to the human; 2) the belief that all things are interrelated and interdependent; 3) a high regard for "diversity"' (ibid.: ii). Greer is describing here not ecological spirituality as a New Ager would understand it, but a belief system as a conservative Christian would understand it. A further acute logical problem with the thesis is that Greer's 'definition of "patriarchal spirituality" is derived from ecofeminist theory' (ibid.: ii). 'Patriarchal spirituality' is thus by definition the opposite of 'ecological spirituality' (of which ecofeminism is cited as a main example and central root), and by definition there are 'fundamental contradictions' between the two spiritualities. One also suspects that, despite ecofeminism's alleged centrality to ecological spirituality, the more natural-style 'matriarchal spirituality' (to contrast with patriarchal spirituality) is not used because it does not accord with Greer's Christian tendencies.

Greer's concluding remarks could more fruitfully have been the starting point of his research:

> If the New Age does indeed embrace such antithetical types of spirituality/ theology, why, it must be asked, do many researchers continue to present and preserve the image of the New Age as something distinguished by, as Chandler puts it, 'a common vision'. (ibid.: 433)

Consideration of the answers to this question deserves fuller exploration in the main body of the thesis. As it is, eight reasons are suggested without prior discussion of their evidence or subsequent indication of their relative importance:

(1) New Age is a publishing phenomenon that needs a marketing name;
(2) 'many interpretations of the New Age are founded on partial and distorted images of what the movement actually is' because some New Agers do not use the term;
(3) to keep up a 'conspiratorial' image of the New Age;
(4) the antagonism between the fundamentalist/evangelical pole of Christianity and the dualistic New Age denotes, as Palmer observes, not fundamental opposition, but 'sibling rivalry';
(5) spiritual disciplines associated with the ecological New Age dynamic can easily be tailored to fit the separatist assumptions of the patriarchal dynamic;
(6) some New Agers are just contradictory;
(7) the patriarchal dynamic advances such thoroughgoing relativism that it can, in a sense, embrace everything. Both spiritual dynamics of the New Age are relativistic to a degree;
(8) New Age researchers are guilty of focussing upon 'universal' New Age ideas (like monism, gnosis, and self-realization) and not upon the frameworks (patriarchal and ecological) within which these ideas are structured. (ibid.: 433ff)

Two earlier US unpublished theses on New Age and Holistic Health deserve brief mention to conclude this survey.

Susan Roberts's *Consciousness Shifts to Psychic Perception: the Strange World of New Age Services and Their Providers* (1989) is a thesis for which thirty-six taped interviews were conducted in the California area. Three groups of New Agers are identified: psychics, those converted after a traumatic experience, and purposeful seekers. The thesis is, however, largely a reproduction of excerpts from transcripts of the interviews, and in this sense presents invaluable primary source material.

Katherine Brown-Keister's *Legitimation Strategies of an Alternative Health Occupation: the Lay Holistic Health Practitioner in the Bay Area* (1982) is another early thesis on New Age-related phenomena, although the term is used only once (ibid.: 139). 'Lay Holistic Health practitioners' are distinguished from 'licensed Holistic Health practitioners'. Brown-Keister identifies two strategies in the process of legitimation: 'carving out a territory', where practitioners claim a distinct area for their work unclaimed by any other professional group; and 'cultivating a clientele' (ibid.: i–ii). Four techniques of legitimation are outlined. Firstly, care is taken over the use of language to avoid encroachment upon orthodox medicine. Secondly, the practitioner–client relationship is outlined in contract form. Thirdly, clients are often referred to orthodox medical practitioners. Fourthly, legitimation is borrowed from established sources of legitimacy such as religion, a general business licence, and working in association with orthodox medics.

In a brief conclusion, three possible end-game scenarios for lay Holistic Health are sketched: Holistic Health practitioners will not attain autonomous professional status due to domination by existing medical professionals, the insurance industry and government; Holistic Health will be legitimated but control of access to resources remains with more established practitioners; or groups of Holistic Health practitioners will break away from Holistic Health and build separate rationales for their individual therapies for which professional autonomy will be sought (ibid.: 175–6). Brown-Keister's scenarios, theorised in 1982, are compared with the historical legitimation process of New Age in Kemp (2003b).

– CONCLUSION –

We have now surveyed a huge variety of approaches to New Age. These range from impressively detailed but unpublished academic theses, through published academic theses, original book-length studies and journal articles by academics, the approaches of other religionists, rationalists, Christians (hostile, cautionary and positive), the media and finally the approaches of New Agers themselves to New Age. These approaches employ the methodologies of disciplines considered earlier in this book, including the history of ideas, philosophy, anthropology, sociology and psychology, along with other academic disciplines and some non-academic approaches. Again I will emphasise that none of these approaches is to be privileged above any other if we are to gain a full understanding of what it means to be New Age. All that remains in this extended guide to New Age is to point towards an evaluation of these many approaches, and suggest possible directions for future research and studies of New Age.

– NOTES –

1. E.g. York (1995: 3).
2. Introvigne refers to 1962 as the date the Caddys took up residence at the Findhorn Bay Caravan Park. As mentioned in Chapter 3, the Findhorn Foundation was established in 1967.
3. Published as this text went to press (Corrywright 2003).
4. It is not clear from the text whether these responses include surveys returned from a third group, a seminar by Roger Woolger on 'Unveiling the Goddess'. Corrywright reports (2001: 134) a 56% return from this seminar, but says that further research was abandoned for interpersonal reasons. A further curiosity is that Corrywright explains in some depth the analysis he undertook on the data using the Statistical Package for the Social Sciences (ibid.: 136–7; 140–1), yet does not reproduce any results from this analysis other than bare percentages indicating male:female split, the age profile, an income analysis and the results of several non-consequential idiosyncratic questions reproduced from Rose (1996). The results given are those of the combined population of the two groups, which are not separated out. Corrywright describes the database as a 'useful resource for further analysis' (Corrywright 2001: 141).

CHAPTER 10

Future

Is the term 'New Age' useful? It is a common perception that fewer individuals now explicitly identify themselves as New Age than did in the early 1980s. Indeed, many people in the field are now actively hostile to the term New Age. Perhaps more importantly, the term has also recently come under criticism from scholars, for various reasons.

Already in 1988, J. Gordon Melton believed the days of New Age 'as a movement' to be 'numbered' (Melton 1988: 51). One of the reasons he gave for this analysis was New Age's reliance on contemporary science, which would continue to change. Indeed, this is a plausible analysis, but Melton does not give a timescale to the development of a post-New Age science, and in fact this has not yet occurred – at least not in popular writings on science. Melton's second cited reason for the demise of a New Age movement was the fragmentation of the new religious market that had opened up in the 1970s. He argued that some elements of New Age had been more successful in attracting long-term support than others, and that these elements were

> taking the primary religious commitments of large segments of the movement away from the movement as a whole. People will eventually find means to search for realization of the inherently religious ideals of the New Age Movement in very definite structured patterns. Those groups that supply those patterns will survive to become long-term religious institutions. Other, more-limited organizations will fall by the wayside. (ibid.: 51)

Again, in itself this analysis rings true – but the fact is that there are now so many successful elements of New Age that a vibrant market still remains; success has not stifled competition.

The third reason Melton gave for the probable decline of New Age was the incompatibility of New Age entrepreneurs (alternative health practitioners, publishers, writers, store owners, etc.) with the ideal of a co-operative, one-world future. This too, sounds logical in theory. It is similar to Massimo Introvigne's perception of an individualistic phase in New Age that should be called Next Age (see below). However, as Introvigne points out, individualism has not killed New Age, simply transformed it. Melton's final reason in 1988 for predicting the death of New Age was the attack from both conservative Evangelical Christians and the sceptical community. But Melton himself acknowledges that neither has had a measurable effect in deterring the growth of New Age, mainly because New Agers tend not to read anti-New Age material.

So confident was Melton in his predictions that in a paper given in 1994 (published as Melton 1998b) he pronounced the death of New Age, claiming that it was difficult to locate anyone who professes allegiance to the New Age vision. He suggested that the Christian critique of New Age which appeared in the late 1980s was too late – most New Agers had begun to abandon the position which the Christian literature attacked (Melton 1998b: 139). He argued that the leaders of New Age had 'lost their faith in the central millennial element of the New Age' of 'social justice, peace and harmony' (ibid.: 140). As he had in 1988, Melton again argued that New Age lives on not in visions of social change, but as tools for personal transformation and evolution. 'The personal transformation, they [leaders of New Age] argued, was really the heart of the movement all along' (ibid.:141).

While New Age has died, suggests Melton, 'the community of people affected by its vision and transformed by its teachings remain' (ibid.: 141). It is hard to see in what sense such a remnant is not still a movement, especially when Melton points out that some of the movement's structures persist, for example in large annual conventions and the international network of publishers and bookstores. Two types of groups have perdured, Melton claims: the older groups which were in existence prior to New Age and co-operated with it, such as the Church of Religious Science and the Association for Research and Enlightenment; while groups founded during New Age 'have survived in so far as they have been able to adapt to the post-New Age condition' (ibid.: 143), for example, Ramtha's School of Enlightenment (Melton 1998a).

Strangely, Melton's final sentence in this lecture concludes, 'The dissenting opinions symbolised by the New Age movement are now strongly entrenched in Western society, and in the near future we can expect to see it offering a more direct challenge to more familiar modes of thinking and acting' (Melton 1998b: 148). If, as was suggested in

Chapter 6, 'mainstream assimilation may be defined as the success point of a NSRM,' then Melton's pronouncement of the death of New Age is not as final as it first seems.

However, my fieldwork has not confirmed Melton's hypothesis. New Age is still very much alive – as shown by the examples cited throughout this book – and has been the subject of a number of academic research projects, books and television documentaries in recent years. Indeed, it would be surprising if such a wide-ranging and all-encompassing phenomenon as New Age could disappear completely in such a short space of time. As Melton begins to hint in some passages, it is more plausible that New Age has modified to some extent, and that in patches it has changed significantly.

This is the thesis of Introvigne, who in a seminar in Turin in 1998 (Introvigne 1998, 1999) which formed the basis of his introduction to the second edition of his work on *New Age & Next Age* (Introvigne [1994] 2000), argued that New Age has passed and we are now on to Next Age. According to Introvigne (1999), the term Next Age was first applied in Italy in the early 1990s to a new type of New Age music, and came of age in 1998 when the annual New Age Fair in Milan renamed itself 'New Age and Next Age Fair'. 'Next Age can be described as the passing of New Age from the third to the first person singular,' (Introvigne 1998, my translation[1])

Introvigne suggests that Next Age is neither a movement nor a network, but rather a client cult as outlined in Stark and Bainbridge (1979) (see Chapter 6), or an 'archipelago' of isolated groups which have some things in common but are not in continuous communication (Introvigne 1998). At the centre of each archipelago, Introvigne finds a 'leader' such as Deepak Chopra. Other exemplars of Next Age cited by Introvigne include M. Scott Peck's *The Road Less Travelled* (1978), Paulo Coelho's *The Alchemist* (1988) and James Redfield's *The Celestine Prophecy* (1994).

Next Age for Introvigne is a new phase of New Age 'when prophecy fails' (Festinger et al. 1956). That is to say, when the utopian Golden Age that 'classic' New Age foresaw did not come to pass, as a result of this failure New Agers turned into themselves and concentrated on personal transformation rather than societal transformation. Introvigne refers to Wouter Hanegraaff's conception of an earlier New Age *sensu stricto*, in which utopianism was crucial, and a later New Age *sensu lato*, in which it was not so central. Although Introvigne does not follow this through, in a sense what he is doing is taking Hanegraaff's definitions one stage further: Next Age is New Age *sensu latiori*[2] ('New Age in an (even) wider sense'), in which utopianism has receded altogether, eclipsed by the privatisation of spirituality.

It must be remembered that Introvigne is writing from an Italian perspective. Even he admits that Next Age is a term which is not current in Anglophone circles (Introvigne 1999). However, it may be that the trends he and others have noticed are paralleled in the Anglophone world and that scholars outside of Italy should also take up the term Next Age, or a similar term such as my extension of Hanegraaff's terminology, in order to recognise these developments in New Age.

Sutcliffe (2002) made a similar observation, that New Age is a mere emblem invoked within alternative spirituality. The tone of Steven Sutcliffe's doctoral thesis (1998) is set in his first, lengthy footnote. 'New Age' is said to be 'merely a popular codeword or emblem that lacks substance and necessary referents'; Sutcliffe denies that there is 'a particular empirical phenomenon with constituent members and groups, practices, and ideology, the whole amounting to an identifiable "movement"' and questions 'whether "New Age" can be anything more than an ambiguous, contested, and ultimately misleading category with which to treat ... phenomena for which "New Age" functions as a catch-phrase or code term' (Sutcliffe 1998: 1). Sutcliffe summarises his thesis as follows:

> I will argue that we need to separate out the codeword or emblem 'New Age' from an eponymous sociological 'movement'. The evidence suggests that the emblem is most typically used as an optional, even rogue, term by 'seekers', those individuals finely tuned to the modern plurality of choice in religion, lifestyle and worldview. Seekers learn and associate via networks which extend both synchronically and diachronically across the century. (ibid.: 25)

In other words, there has never been a 'New Age movement': this is merely a popular construct that misleads by conflating 'movement' in the loose aesthetic–cultural sense of the 'Romantic movement' or the 'Existentialist movement' – with which New Age shares some limited functional similarities – with the more concrete dimensions of new religious or social movements. New Age is better understood as a potent emic emblem, usage of which can be documented from the 1930s onwards within networks, and amongst seekers, of alternative religiosity, according to Sutcliffe. 'The emblem becomes something of a rogue term, or 'wild' card, in popular and middlebrow cultures. In the 1990s New Age can mean more-or-less what you want it to mean' (ibid.: 25–6).

This approach was continued by Matthew Wood (1999), who suggested that New Age does not exist except as a collection of similar phenomena, and that the term 'New Age' should be replaced by 'non-formative spirituality' (see Chapter 9). Wood and Sutcliffe are the most radical scholars of New Age in that, to reduce their thesis to its crud-est expression, they argue New Age has never existed except as a con-struct of scholars. However, the evidence presented in this book is that New Age certainly did exist for some time between the 1960s and the 1990s, and most probably continues today, if perhaps in modified form as suggested by Introvigne.

A less radical approach to the extreme revisionism of Wood and Sutcliffe is the suggestion of new terms to describe what everyone has heretofore known as 'New Age'. Wood himself suggested the term 'nonformative spirituality' and Sutcliffe 'alternative spirituality'. Heelas (2000) has suggested the term 'expressive spirituality'; Shimazono (1999) 'New Spirituality Movements and Culture' and Possamaï (1998) 'perennism'. Likewise, in my own study of New Age Christians (Kemp 2003a), I coined the neologism 'Christaquarians', partly in order to avoid use of the term 'New Age'. Less controver-sially, Corrywright (2001), as we have seen in Chapter 9, prefers the term 'New Age spiritualities', and van Hove (1999) suggests 'spiritual market'.

Such scholarly attempts at alternative terms are analogous to the marketing techniques of booksellers and workshop leaders in the late 1980s, who dropped the label 'New Age' in favour of 'Mind Body Spirit', 'Holistic' or some other such term. No alternative term to 'New Age' has yet achieved popular or scholarly currency. Perhaps this is apt. New Age is averse to tightly-defined systems, and is inher-ently pluralistic in its approach to truth – whether that be historical, philosophical, anthropological, sociological, psychological, or even semantic.

Introvigne suggests (2000: 14–16) four possible exits to what he calls the 'crisis' in New Age. In addition to Next Age, which we have dis-cussed above, these are: a return to the mainstream Churches; desper-ation, as evidenced by the suicides of Heaven's Gate in March 1997; and the organisation of individual groups with structure, hierarchy and community such as Damanhur in Italy.

But there are other possibilities. Heelas and Seel (forthcoming) illustrate with statistical data from a study in Kendal, England, two scenarios:

> The first – the 'die out and not be replaced', 'self-limiting', 'ageing cohort' or 'pessimistic' scenario – is driven by the fact that an *ageing* cohort of spiritual practitioners, drawn from baby boomers who came of age during the 1960s and

1970s has played, and very much continues to play, the key role in sustaining, 'carrying' and developing New Age spiritualities of life . . .

As for the (less obvious) 'die out and will be replaced', 'self-perpetuating', 'cultural transmission' or 'optimistic' scenario . . . the basic argument is that spiritual practitioners will be replenished by virtue of the fact that New Age spiritualities of life have come to be widely transmitted within the culture. Accordingly, even if the '60s' experience is an important factor in explaining the involvement of current spiritual practitioners, people will become involved in the future (if not now) without having had this experience. (ibid.)

Alternatively, New Age may crystallise into a more cohesive and broadly based movement. From a sociological perspective, New Age may in the future develop into a sect and finally into a church. This process of consolidation could begin with the institutionalisation of a number of New Age networks, as in Ramtha's School of Enlightenment, which coalesced out of the audience and clients of J. Z. Knight (see Chapter 6). The next step could be the confederation of a number of these institutionalised New Age networks. Melton (1998a) suggests that such institutionalisation takes Knight, whom he agrees (ibid.: xiv) was once 'integral' to New Age, beyond the pale of New Age. Yet if we understand New Age as a new social movement, or more specifically as a new socio-religious movement (see Chapter 6), such a model can accommodate patches of institutionalisation without necessitating a new model or label.

A further scenario for the future of New Age is that it will not consolidate to any great extent, but will instead be absorbed into mainstream culture, as suggested in Melton (1988) (see above). Indeed, this has already happened to a large degree, as is apparent from the increasing cultural acceptability of New Age practices and traditions. For example, in the mid-1990s, the Chinese art of arrangement and position, Feng Shui, was a popular interest for a broad section of the population. Alternative healing has become available on many private health insurance policies and on the National Health Service in the United Kingdom. A number of New Age-oriented businesses, such as Holland & Barrett in the UK and Ben & Jerry's in the USA, have been phenomenally successful. To take another example, organically grown food, once the preserve of esoteric members of the Anthroposophically inclined Soil Association, is now a multi-million pound industry in the UK that is fully regulated.[3]

Future research will inevitably in the course of time confirm or negate these various hypotheses on the development of New Age. The most pressing need in New Age studies at the moment is for a consensus definition to emerge, even if this is a fuzzy concept along family resemblance lines, for example. It is hoped that this guide to New Age has brought together extant descriptions and explanations of New Age in a way that will facilitate such convergence.

Once the field is properly demarcated, more focused research can be undertaken and crucially, different studies will be able to be compared and contrasted. In the past, it has not been entirely clear whether scholars employing the New Age motif are all studying the same phenomena. Importantly, future research should include studies with a statistical element that can be calibrated against existing studies. Chapter 7 of this book gathers together a number of statistical survey tools, in the hope that they will be used more consistently and further refined.

A final reason for the survival of New Age as a concept may seem flippant but may also unfortunately be realistic. This is that, through the writings of all the scholars, critics and practitioners mentioned in (and a further myriad that have been omitted from) this book – including those Christians who campaign against its incursion and those scholars who theorise it out of existence – New Age has achieved the critical mass of consciousness that its early practitioners hoped for.

– Notes –

1. 'Il Next Age può essere descritto come il passagio del New Age dalla terza alla prima persona singolare.' I am grateful to Nicole Purin for checking this translation.
2. Hanegraaff had also earlier (1994: 31) suggested a third sense of New Age: 'New Age in oneigenlijke zin' – 'New Age in an incorrect sense', which represents the misguided tendency to use the New Age label to describe any new religious movement. Hanegraaff does not utilise this third sense any longer (personal communication, 20 February 2003).
3. The UK Register of Organic Food Standards (UKROFS) was established in 1987 to provide standards for organic produce and to monitor the work of organic certification bodies such as Soil Association Certification Limited (and others), and is maintained by the UK Government's Department for Environment, Food and Rural Affairs, implementing European Council Regulation (EEC) 2092/91 of 24 June 1991 on organic production of agricultural products and indications referring thereto on agricultural products and foodstuffs. See Kemp (2003b) for a more detailed presentation of this argument.

Bibliography

Adler, Margot (1986), *Drawing Down the Moon: Witches, Druids, Goddess-Worshippers, and Other Pagans in America Today*, Boston: Beacon Press.

Akhtar, Miriam and Steve Humphries (1999), *Far Out: the Dawning of New Age Britain*, Bristol: Sansom & Company.

Albanese, Catherine L. (1990), *Nature Religion in America from the Algonkian Indians to the New Age*, Chicago: University of Chicago Press.

Aldred, Lisa (2000), 'Plastic Shamans and Astroturf Sun Dances', *American Indian Quarterly*, 3.24: 329f.

Alexander, Kay (1992), 'Roots of the New Age', in James R. Lewis and J. Gordon Melton (eds), *Perspectives on the New Age*, Albany: State University of New York Press, pp. 30–47.

Amaral, Leila (1999), 'Sincretismo em Movimento – o Estilo Nova Era de Lidar com o Sagrado', in María Julia Carozzi (ed.), *A Nova Era no Mercosul*, Petrópolis, Brazil: Editora Vozes, pp. 47–79.

Amaral, Leila (2000), *Carnaval da Alma: Comunidade, Essência e Sincretismo na Nova Era*, Petrópolis, Brazil: Editora Vozes.

American Psychiatric Association (1994), *Diagnostic and Statistical Manual of Mental Disorders*, 4th edn, Washington, DC: American Psychiatric Association.

Anonymous (1985), *A Course in Miracles*, Harmondsworth: Arkana.

Attfield, Robin (1978), *God and the Secular*, Cardiff: University College Cardiff Press.

Bainbridge, William Sims (1997), *The Sociology of Religious Movements*, New York: Routledge.

Balch, Robert W. and David Taylor (1978), 'Seekers and Saucers: the Role of the Cultic Milieu in Joining a UFO Cult', in James T. Richardson (ed.), *Conversion Careers: In and Out of the New Religions*, London: Sage, pp. 43–64.

Barker, Eileen (1992), *New Religious Movements: A Practical Introduction*, London: HMSO.

Basil, Robert (ed.), (1988), *Not Necessarily the New Age: Critical Essays*, Buffalo, NY: Prometheus Books.

Becker, Howard (1932), *Systematic Sociology*, New York: John Wiley & Sons.

Bednarowski, Mary Farrell (1989), *New Religions and the Theological Imagination in America*, Bloomington: Indiana University Press.

Bednarowski, Mary Farrell (1991), 'Literature of the New Age: A Review of Representative Sources', *Religious Studies Review*, 17.3: 209–16.

Bednarowski, Mary Farrell (1992), 'The New Age Movement and Feminist Spirituality: Overlapping Conversations at the End of the Century', in James R. Lewis and J. Gordon Melton (eds), *Perspectives on the New Age*, Albany: State University of New York Press, pp. 167–78.

Beesing, Maria, Robert J. Nogosek and Patrick H. O'Leary (1984), *The Enneagram: a Journey of Self Discovery*, Denville, NJ: Dimension Books.

Berman, Morris (1981), *The Re-Enchantment of the World*, Ithaca, NY: Cornell University Press.

Best, Steven and Douglas Kellner (1991), *Postmodern Theory: Critical Interrogations*, Basingstoke: Macmillan.

Beth, Rae (1990), *Hedge Witch: A Guide to Solitary Witchcraft*, London: Hale.

Blavatsky, Helena Petrovna (1877), *Isis Unveiled*, 2 vols, New York: Stokes.

Blavatsky, Helena Petrovna (1888), *The Secret Doctrine*, 2 vols, London: Theosophical Publishing Co.

Bloom, William (1986), *Devas, Fairies and Angels: a Modern Approach*, Glastonbury: Gothic Image.

Bloom, William (1987), *Meditation in a Changing World*, Glastonbury: Gothic Image.

Bloom, William (1990), *Sacred Times: a New Approach to Festivals*, Forres: Findhorn Press.

Bloom, William (1995), *The Christ Sparks: the Inner Dynamics of Group Consciousness*, Forres: Findhorn Press.

Bloom, William (1996), *Meditation in a Changing World*, revised edn, Glastonbury: Gothic Image.

Bloom, William (1998), *Working with Angels, Fairies and Nature Spirits*, London: Piatkus.

Bloom, William (ed.) (1991), *The New Age: an Anthology of Essential Writings*, London: Rider.

Bloom, William (ed.) (2001), *The Penguin Book of New Age and Holistic Writing*, Harmondsworth: Penguin.

Bochinger, Christoph (1995), *»New Age« und Moderne Religion: Religionswissenschaftliche Analysen*, revised edn Gütersloh: Chr Kaiser.

Bordewich, Fergus M. (1988), 'Colorado's Thriving Cults', *New York Times*, 1 May 1988, section 6, p. 37.

Bowman, Marion (1993), 'Reinventing the Celts', *Religion*, 23 147–56.

Bowman, Marion (1995), 'The Noble Savage and the Global Village: Cultural Evolution in New Age and Neo-Pagan Thought', *Journal of Contemporary Religion*, 10.3: 139–50.

Bowman, Marion (1999), 'Healing in the Spiritual Marketplace: Consumers, Courses and Credentialism', *Social Compass*, 46.2: 181–90.

Braden, Charles S. ([1963] 1966), *Spirits in Rebellion: the Rise and Development of New Thought*, Dallas: Southern Methodist University Press.

Bremner, Charles (1990), 'Saddam joins Halloween Demon Kings', *The Times*, 31 October 1990.

Brown, Susan Love (1992), 'Baby boomers, American character, and the New Age: A Synthesis', in James R. Lewis and J. Gordon Melton (eds), *Perspectives on the New Age*, Albany: State University of New York Press, pp. 87–96.

Brown-Keister, Katherine (1982), *'Legitimation Strategies of an Alternative Health Occupation: The Lay Holistic Health Practitioner in the Bay Area*, Ph.D. thesis, Columbia University.

Bruce, Steve (2000), 'The New Age and Secularisation', in Steven Sutcliffe and Marion Bowman (eds), *Beyond New Age: Exploring Alternative Spirituality*, Edinburgh: Edinburgh University Press, pp. 220–36.

Bruce, Steve (2002), *God is Dead: Secularization in the West*, Oxford: Blackwell.

Burke, T. Patrick (1984), 'Must the description of a religion be acceptable to a believer?', *Religious Studies*, 20: 631–6.

Campbell, Colin (1972), 'The Cult, the Cultic Milieu and Secularization', in Michael Hill (ed.) *A Sociological Yearbook of Religion in Britain 5*, London: SCM Press, pp. 119–36.

Campion, Nicholas (1994), *The Great Year: Astrology, Millenarianism and History in the Western Tradition*, Harmondsworth: Arkana.

Capra, Fritjof (1982), *The Turning Point: Science, Society, and the Rising Culture*, New York: Bantam.

Carozzi, María Julia (1996), 'Las Disciplinas de la "New Age" en Buenos Aires', *Lecturas Sociales y Económicas* 5.2: 24–32.

Carozzi, María Julia (1999), 'Nova Era: A Autonomia como Religião', tr. Mario Gallicchio, in María Julia Carozzi (ed.), *A Nova Era no Mercosul*, Petrópolis, Brazil: Editora Vozes.

Carozzi, María Julia (ed.), (1999), *A Nova Era no Mercosul*, Petrópolis, Brazil: Editora Vozes.

Carson, Rachel (1962), *Silent Spring*, Boston: Houghton Mifflin.

Castro, Stephen (1996), *Hypocrisy and Dissent within the Findhorn Foundation: towards a Sociology of a New Age Community*, Forres: New Media Books.

Chadwick, Peter (1992), *Borderline: a Psychological Study of Paranoia and Delusional Thinking*, London: Routledge.

Chadwick, Peter (1997), *Schizophrenia: the Positive Perspective – In Search of Dignity for Schizophrenic People*, London: Routledge.

Chandler, Russell (1989), *Understanding the New Age*, Milton Keynes: Word (UK).

Chardin, Pierre Teilhard de (1955), *The Phenomenon of Man*, London: Fontana.

Chardin, Pierre Teilhard de (1957), *Le Milieu Divin*, London: Fontana.

Clarke, Michael (1982), *The Politics of Pop Festivals*, London: Junction Books.

Clarke, Peter B. (ed.) (forthcoming), *The Encyclopedia of New Religious Movements*, London: Routledge.

Coelho, Paulo (1988), *L'Alchimiste*, tr. Jean Orecchioni, Paris: J'ai lu.

Collin, Rodney (1954), *The Theory of Celestial Influence: Man, the Universe and Cosmic Mystery*, London: Vincent Stuart.

Congregation for the Doctrine of the Faith (1998), 'Notification concerning the writings of Father Anthony de Mello, SJ', Vatican City.

Cooper, Diana (2001), *A Little Light on Ascension*, Findhorn: Findhorn Press.

Corrywright, Dominic (2000), 'Praxis Prior to Doctrine: New Models of Relationship in Contemporary Spirituality', in Ursula King (ed.), *Spirituality and Society in the New Millennium*, Brighton: Sussex Academic Press, pp. 192–205.

Corrywright, Dominic (2001), *Theoretical and Empirical Investigations into New Age Spiritualities with Special Reference to the South West of England*, Ph.D. thesis, University of Bristol.

Corrywright, Dominic (2003), *Theoretical and Empirical Investigations into New Age Spiritualities*, Bern: Peter Lang.

Cumbey, Constance (1983), *The Hidden Dangers of the Rainbow*, revised edn, Lafayette, LA: Huntington House.

D'Andrea, Anthony (1997), *O Self Perfeito e a Nova Era: Individualism e Reflexividade em Religiosidades Pos-Tradicionais*, 2nd version, Masters degree thesis, Rio de Janeiro.

Dart, John (1987), '"New Age" Ideas and Theological Vacuum; Can Churches Resist Pull of Paranormal?', *Los Angeles Times*, 14 February 1987, part 2, p. 4.

deChant, Dell (forthcoming), 'New Thought and the New Age', in James R. Lewis (ed.), *Encyclopedic Sourcebook of New Age Religions*, Amherst, NY: Prometheus Books.

della Porta, Donatella and Mario Diani (1999), *Social Movements: an Introduction*, Oxford: Blackwell.

Deloria, Phillip J. (1998), *Playing Indian*, New Haven, CT: Yale University Press.

DeMarinis, Valerie (1998), 'Religious Ritual-Hunger and the Quest for Religious Ritual-Sustenance: A Psycho-Cultural Investigation of New Age Participants in California', in Eileen Barker and Margit Warburg (eds), *New Religions and New Religiosity*, Aarhus: Aarhus University Press, pp. 108–32.

Dery, Mark (1996), *Escape Velocity: Cyberculture at the End of the Century*, London: Hodder & Stoughton.

Descartes, René (1968), *Discourse on Method and The Meditations*, tr. F. E. Sutcliffe, Harmondsworth: Penguin.

Diani, Mario (1995), *Green Networks: a Structural Analysis of the Italian Environmental Movement*, Edinburgh: Edinburgh University Press.

Diem, Andrea Grace and James R. Lewis (1992), 'Imagining India: The Influence of Hinduism on the New Age Movement', in James R. Lewis and J. Gordon Melton (eds), *Perspectives on the New Age*, Albany: State University of New York Press, pp. 48–58.

Doktór, Tadeusz (1999), 'The "New Age" Worldview of Polish Students', *Social Compass* 46.2: 217–24.

Donahue, Michael J. (1993), 'Prevalence and Correlates of New Age Beliefs in Six Protestant Denominations', *Journal for the Scientific Study of Religion*, 32.2: 177–84.

Donato, Marla (1987), 'Welcome to the New Age: In the Universal Search for Truth, the Path Leads to the Higher Self – and, Sometimes, Bigger Bucks', *Chicago Tribune*, 4 November 1987, Style section, p. 13.

Drane, John (2001), *The McDonaldization of the Church: Consumer Culture and the Church's Future*, Macon, GA: Smyth & Helwys.

Draper, Mustafa (forthcoming), 'Sufism in Glastonbury: Alternative Spiritualities, Alternative Adaptations,' in D. Westerlund (ed.), *Living Sufism in Europe and North America*, London: Curzon.

Drury, Nevill (1989), *The Elements of Human Potential*, Longmead: Element Books.

Dubrow-Eichel, Steve K. and Linda Dubrow-Eichel (1988), 'Trouble in Paradise: Some Observations on Psychotherapy with New Agers', Cultic Studies Journal, 5.2: 177–91.

The Ecologist (1972), *Blueprint for Survival*, Harmondsworth: Penguin.

Ellwood, Robert (1992), 'How New is the New Age?', in James R. Lewis and J. Gordon Melton (eds), *Perspectives on the New Age*, Albany: State University of New York Press, pp. 59–67.

English, June Anne (1985), 'A Place for Healing: an Ethnography of Holistic Health Practitioners in Southern California', Ph.D. thesis, University of California, Santa Barbara.

English-Lueck, June Anne (1990), *Health in the New Age: a Study in California Holistic Practices*, Albuquerque: University of New Mexico.

Ezzy, Douglas, (2003), 'New Age Witchcraft? Popular Spell Books and the Reenchantment of Everyday life', *Culture and Religion*, 4.1: 47–66.

Faber, Michael D. (1993), *Modern Witchcraft and Psychoanalysis*, Rutherford, NJ: Farleigh Dickinson University Press.

Faber, Michael D. (1996), *New Age Thinking: a Psychoanalytic Critique*, Ottawa: University of Ottawa Press.

Faith and Order Committee (1994), 'The New Age Movement: Report to Conference 1994', Peterborough: Methodist Publishing House.

Farias, Miguel and Mansur Lalljee (2003), 'Who am I? Self-concepts and motivational goals in New Agers, Catholics and atheists/agnostics', paper presented at ASANAS conference 2003, Open University, Milton Keynes, 30 May–1 June.

Farrer, Frances (2002), *Sir George Trevelyan and the Spiritual Renaissance of Our Time*, Edinburgh: Floris.

Ferguson, Marilyn, ([1980] 1989), *The Aquarian Conspiracy: Personal and Social Transformation in the 1980's*, London: Paladin.

Ferreux, Marie-Jeanne (2000), *Le New-Age: Ritualités et Mythologies Contemporaines*, Paris: L'Harmattan.

Festinger, Leon, Henry W. Riecken and Stanley Schachter (1956), *When Prophecy Fails*, New York: Harper & Row.

Filoramo, Giovanni (1992), *A History of Gnosticism*, tr. Anthony Alcock, Oxford: Blackwell.

Forman, Robert K. C. (1991), *Meister Eckhart: Mystic as Theologian*, Longmead: Element Books.

Frazer, J. G. (1890), *The Golden Bough: a Study in Comparative Religion*, London: Macmillan.

Freeman, Anthony (1993), *God in Us: a Case for Christian Humanism*, London: SCM Press.

Frisk, Liselotte (2001), 'Globalization or Westernization? New Age as a Contemporary Transnational Culture', in Mikael Rothstein (ed.), *New Age Religion and Globalization*, Aarhus: Aarhus University Press, pp. 31–41.

Gallagher, Eugene V. (1994), 'A religion without converts? Becoming a Neo-Pagan', *Journal of the American Academy of Religion*, LXII.3: 851–67.

Gardner, Martin (1988), *The New Age: Notes of a Fringe Watcher*, Buffalo, NY: Prometheus Books.

Gardner, Martin (1996), *Weird Water & Fuzzy Logic: More Notes of a Fringe Watcher*, Buffalo, NY: Prometheus Books.

Gartrell-Mills, Claire F. (1991), *Christian Science: an American Religion in Britain*, D. Phil. thesis, Oxford University.

Gerlach, Luther P. (1971), 'Movements of Revolutionary Change', *American Behavorial Scientist*, 14.6: 812–36.

Gerlach, Luther P. and Virginia H. Hine (1968), 'Five Factors Crucial to the Growth and Spread of a Modern Religious Movement', *Journal for the Scientific Study of Religion*, 7.1: 23–40.

Gilhus, Ingvild Sælid (2001), 'The Gnostic Myth and the Goddess Myth: Two Contemporary Responses to Questions about Human Identity', in Mikael Rothstein (ed.), *New Age Religion and Globalization*, Aarhus: Aarhus University Press, pp. 113–32.

Glock, Charles Y. and Rodney Stark (1965), *Religion and Society in Tension*, Chicago: Rand McNally.

Goffman, Erving (1974), *Frame Analysis*, Cambridge, MA: Harvard University Press.

Goldstein, Eric (1996), 'Away from the Gurus, Back to the Rabbis', *Jerusalem Post*, 21 July 1996.

Goodrick-Clarke, Nicholas (1992), *The Occult Roots of Nazism*, London: I. B. Tauris.

Gordon, Henry (1988), *Channeling into the New Age: The 'Teachings' of Shirley MacLaine and Other Such Gurus*, Buffalo, NY: Prometheus Books.

Granqvist, Pehr and Berit Hagekull (2001), 'Seeking Security in the New Age: On Attachment and Emotional Compensation', *Journal for the Scientific Study of Religion*, 40.3: 527–45.

Green, Jonathon (1999), *All Dressed Up: The Sixties and the Counterculture*, London: Pimlico.

Green, Martin (1986), *Mountain of Truth: The Counterculture Begins – Ascona, 1900–1920*, Hanover, NH and London: University Press of New England.

Green, Martin (1992), *Prophets for the New Age: The Politics of Hope from the Eighteenth through the Twenty-First Centuries*, New York: Charles Scribner's Sons.

Greer, Germaine (1970), *The Female Eunuch*, London: MacGibbon & Kee.

Greer, Paul (1994), *The Spiritual Dynamics of the New Age Movement*, Ph.D. thesis, Stirling University.

Greer, Paul (1995), 'The Aquarian Confusion: Conflicting Theologies of the New Age', *Journal of Contemporary Religion*, 10.2: 151–68.

Griffiths, Paul J. ([1993] 1994), 'Indian Buddhist Meditation', in Takeuchi Yoshinori (ed.), *Buddhist Spirituality: Indian, Southeast Asian, Tibetan, Early Chinese*, London: SCM Press.

Groothuis, Douglas R. (1986), *Unmasking the New Age*, Leicester: InterVarsity Press.

Groothuis, Douglas R. (1988), *Confronting the New Age*, Leicester: InterVarsity Press.

Groothuis, Douglas R. (1990), *Revealing the New Age Jesus*, Leicester: InterVarsity Press.

Guest, Mathew (2002), *Negotiating Community: an Ethnographic Study of an Evangelical Church*, Ph.D. thesis, Lancaster University.

Guilane-Nachez (1999), *Sources, Mythes et Pratiques du New Age de ses Origines à Nos Jours*, Lille: Septentrion.

Guirdham, Arthur (1970), *The Cathars and Reincarnation: the Record of a past life in 13th-Century France*, London: Neville Spearman.

Gurdjieff, George Ivanovitch (1950), *Beelzebub's Tales to His Grandson – an Objectively Impartial Criticism of the Life of Man*, London: Routledge & Kegan Paul.

Gurdjieff, George Ivanovitch (1963), *Meetings with Remarkable Men*, tr. A. R. Orage, London: Routledge & Kegan Paul.

Gurdjieff, George Ivanovitch (1975), *Life Is Real Only Then, When 'I Am'*, New York: Dutton.

Hackett, Rosalind I. J. (1992), 'New Age Trends in Nigeria: Ancestral and/or Alien Religion?' in James R. Lewis and J. Gordon Melton (eds), *Perspectives on the New Age*, Albany: State University of New York Press, pp. 215–31.

Halevi, Yossi Klein (2001), 'Inner Peace', *New Republic*, 30 April 2001, pp. 20f.

Hamilton, Malcolm (2000), 'An Analysis of the Festival for Mind-Body-Spirit, London', in Steven Sutcliffe and Marion Bowman (eds), *Beyond New Age: Exploring Alternative Spirituality*, Edinburgh: Edinburgh University Press, pp. 188–200.

Hammer, Olav, (2001a), 'Same message from everywhere: the sources of modern revelation', in Mikael Rothstein (ed.), *New Age Religion and Globalization*, Aarhus: Aarhus University Press, pp. 42–57.

Hammer, Olav (2001b), *Claiming Knowledge: Strategies of Epistemology from Theosophy to the New Age*, Leiden: Brill.

Hammer, Olav, (forthcoming), 'Contradictions of the New Age', in James R. Lewis (ed.), *Encyclopedic Sourcebook of New Age Religions*, Amherst, NY: Prometheus Books.

Hanegraaff, Wouter J. (1994), 'Nieuwe Religieuze Bewegingen', *Religieuze Bewegingen in Nederland*, 29: 1–49.

Hanegraaff, Wouter J. (1996), *New Age Religion and Western Culture*, Leiden: Brill.

Hanegraaff, Wouter J. (1998), 'The New Age Movement and the Esoteric Tradition', in Broek, Roelof van den and Wouter J. Hanegraaff (eds), *Gnosis and Hermeticism from Antiquity to Modern Times*, Albany: State University of New York Press pp. 359–82.

Hanegraaff, Wouter J. (1999), 'New Age Spiritualities as Secular Religion: A Historian's Perspective', *Social Compass*, 46.2: 145–60.

Hanegraaff, Wouter J. (2001), 'Prospects for the Globalization of New Age: Spiritual Imperialism Versus Cultural Diversity', in Mikael Rothstein (ed.), *New Age Religion and Globalization*, Aarhus: Aarhus University Press, pp. 15–30.

Hanegraaff, Wouter J. (2002), 'New Age Religion', in Linda Woodhead, Paul Fletcher, Hiroko Kawanami and David Smith (eds), *Religions in the Modern World: Traditions and Transformations*, London: Routledge.

Harpur, Tom (1990), 'New Age Thought Deserves Long Look', *Toronto Star*, 14 January 1990, p. A9.

Hay, Louise L. (1984), *You Can Heal Your Life*, London: Eden Grove.

Heelas, Paul (1982), 'Californian Self Religions and Socializing the Subjective', in Eileen Barker, (ed.), *New Religious Movements: a Perspective for Understanding Society*, New York: Edwin Mellen, pp. 69–85.

Heelas, Paul (1993), 'The New Age in Cultural Context: The Premodern, the Modern and the Postmodern', *Religion*, 23: 103–16.

Heelas, Paul (1996a), *The New Age Movement: the Celebration of the Self and the Sacralization of Modernity*, Oxford: Blackwell.

Heelas, Paul (1996b), 'De-traditionalisation of Religion and Self: The New Age and Postmodernity', in Kieran Flanagan and Peter C. Jupp (eds), *Postmodernity, Sociology and Religion*, London: Macmillan, pp 64–82.

Heelas, Paul (1998), 'Introduction: On Differentiation and Dedifferentiation', in Paul Heelas (ed.), *Religion, Modernity and Postmodernity*, Oxford: Blackwell, pp. 1–18.

Heelas, Paul (2000), 'Expressive Spirituality and Humanistic Expressivism: Sources of Significance beyond Church and Chapel', in Steven Sutcliffe and Marion Bowman (eds), *Beyond New Age: Exploring Alternative Spirituality*, Edinburgh: Edinburgh University Press, pp. 237–54.

Heelas, Paul and Leila Amaral (1994), 'Research Report: Notes on the 'Nova Era': Rio de Janeiro and Environs', *Religion*, 24: 173–80.

Heelas, Paul and Benjamin Seel (forthcoming), 'An Ageing New Age?' in Grace Davie, Linda Woodhead and Paul Heelas (eds), *Predicting Religion: Christian, Secular and Alternative Futures*, Aldershot: Ashgate.

Hess, David J. (1993), *Science in the New Age: the Paranormal, Its Defenders and Debunkers, and American Culture*, Madison: University of Wisconsin Press.

Hetherington, Kevin (1993), *The Geography of the Other: Lifestyle, Performance and Identity*, Ph.D. thesis, Lancaster University.

Hetherington, Kevin (2000), *New Age Travellers: Vanloads of Uproarious Humanity*, London: Cassell.

Hexham, Irving (1972), *Some Aspects of the Contemporary Search for an Alternative Society*, M.A. thesis, Bristol University.

Hexham, Irving (1992), 'The Evangelical Response to the New Age', in James R. Lewis and J. Gordon Melton (eds), *Perspectives on the New Age*, Albany: State University of New York Press, pp. 152–64.

Hexham, Irving (1999), 'The New Age is Over', *Christianity Today*, 13 December 1999 http://www.christianitytoday.com/ct/1999/150/22.0.html

Hill, Michael (1987), 'The cult of humanity and the secret religion of the educated classes', *New Zealand Sociology*, 2.2: 112–27.

Hill, Michael (1993), 'The New Age – A Sociological Assessment', *Australian Religious Studies Review*, 6.2: 6–12.

Hirst, Désirée (1964), *Hidden Riches: Traditional Symbolism from the Renaissance to Blake*, London: Eyre.

Houtman, Dick and Peter Mascini (2002), 'Why do Churches Become Empty, while New Age grows? Secularization and Religious Change in the Netherlands', *Journal for the Scientific Study of Religion*, 41.3: 455–73.

Hunt, Dave and T. A. McMahon (1985), *The Seduction of Christianity*, Eugene, OR: Harvest House.

Hunt, Dave and T. A. McMahon (1988), *The New Spirituality*, Eugene, OR: Harvest House.

Hutton, Ronald (1991), *Pagan Religions of the Ancient British Isles*, Oxford: Blackwell.

Huxley, Aldous (1954), *The Doors of Perception*, London: Chatto & Windus.

Introvigne, Massimo (1994), *Storia del New Age 1962–1992*, Piacenza: Cristianita.

Introvigne, Massimo (1998), 'La Crisi del New Age e la Nascita di un Nuovo Fenomeno: Il Next Age', Turin: CESNUR. http://www.cesnur.org/testi/Next_A.htm

Introvigne, Massimo (1999), 'After the New Age: is there a Next Age?', Turin: CESNUR. http://www.cesnur.org/testi/NextAge_Renner.htm.

Introvigne, Massimo (2000), *New Age & Next Age*, Cassale Monferrato: Piemme. First edition published as Introvigne (1994).

Introvigne, Massimo (2001), 'After the New Age: Is There a Next Age?', in Mikael Rothstein (ed.), *New Age Religion and Globalization*, Aarhus: Aarhus University Press, pp. 58–72.

Irish Theological Commission (1994), *A New Age of the Spirit? A Catholic Response to the New Age Phenomenon*, Dublin: Veritas.

Ivakhiv, Adrian J. (2001), *Claiming Sacred Ground: Pilgrims and Politics at Glastonbury and Sedona*, Bloomington: Indiana University Press.

Ivakhiv, Adrian J. (2003), 'Nature and Self in New Age Pilgrimage', *Culture and Religion*, 4.1: 93–118.

Johnston, Hank, Enrique Laraña and Joseph R. Gusfield (1994), 'Identities, Grievances and New Social Movements', in Enrique Laraña, Hank Johnston and Joseph R. Gusfield (eds), *New Social Movements: from Ideology to Identity*, Philadelphia: Temple University Press, pp. 3–35.

Jones, Constance A. (forthcoming), 'Students in Ramtha's School of Enlightenment: A Profile from Demographic Survey, Narrative, and Interview', in James R. Lewis (ed.), *Encyclopedic Sourcebook of New Age Religions*, Amherst, NY: Prometheus Books.

Jorgensen, D. L. (1982), 'The Esoteric Community: An Ethnographic Investigation of the Cultic Milieu', *Urban Life*, 10.4: 383–407.

Jorgensen, D. L. (1983), 'Psychic Fairs: A Basis for Solidarity and Networks among Occultists', *California Sociologist*, 6.1: 57–75.

Jorgensen, D. L. and L. Jorgensen (1982), 'Social Meanings of the Occult', *Sociological Quarterly*, 23: 373–89.

Jung, Carl Gustav (1962), *Memories, Dreams, Reflections*, New York: Vintage/Random House.

Kalman, Matthew and John Murray (1995), 'New-Age Nazism', *New Statesman & Society*, 23 June, 1995, pp. 18f.

Kelly, Aidan A. (1992), 'An Update on Neopagan Witchcraft in America', in James R. Lewis and J. Gordon Melton (eds), *Perspectives on the New Age*, Albany: State University of New York Press, pp. 136–51.

Kemp, Daren (2000), 'A Platonic Delusion: The Identification of Psychosis and Mysticism', *Mental Health, Religion and Culture*, 3.2: 157–72.

Kemp, Daren (2001), 'Christaquarianism: A New Socio-Religious Movement of Postmodern Society?', *Implicit Religion*, 4.1: 27–40.

Kemp, Daren (2003a), *The Christaquarians? A Sociology of Christians in the New Age*, London: Kempress.

Kemp, Daren (2003b), 'NA Law: A Legal Studies Approach to New Age', *Culture and Religion*, 4.1: 141–58.

Kemp, Daren (2003c), 'Non-English Language Studies of New Age', paper presented at the ASANAS Conference, Open University, 30 May–1 June, 2003.

Kemp, Daren (forthcoming), 'The Christaquarians? a sociology of Christians in the New Age', in James R. Lewis (ed.), *Encyclopedic Sourcebook of New Age Religions*, Amherst, NY: Prometheus Books.

Kent, Stephen (1993), 'Radical Rhetoric and Mystical Religion in America's Late Vietnam War Era', *Religion*, 23: 45–60.

Klimo, Jon (1998), *Channeling: Investigations on Receiving Information from Paranormal Sources*, revised edn, Berkeley, CA: North Atlantic Books.

Kranenborg, Reende, (1998), 'The Presentation of the Essenes in Western Esotericism', *Journal of Contemporary Religion*, 13.2: 245–56.

Kranenborg, Reender (2001), 'New Age and Neopaganism: Two Different Traditions?', paper presented at the INFORM/CESNUR conference, London, 19–22 April 2001. http://www.cesnur.org/2001/london2001/kranenborg.htm

Kristensen, W. Brede (1954), *Religionshistorisk*, Oslo: Nie Wiem.

Kubiak, Anna E. (1999), 'Le Nouvel Age, Conspiration Postmoderne', *Social Compass*, 46.2: 135–43.

Kuhn, Thomas S. (1962), *The Structure of Scientific Revolutions*, Chicago: University of Chicago Press.

Lacroix, Michel (1995), *La Spiritualité Totalitaire: Le New Age et les Sectes*, Paris: Plon.

Lasch, Christopher (1979), *The Culture of Narcissism*, New York and London: W. W. Norton & Co.

Lasch, Christopher (1987), 'Soul of a New Age', *Omni*, 10.1: 78–85, 180.

Lemesurier, Peter (1990), *The Great Pyramid Decoded*, Longmead: Element Books.

Levin, Bernard (1994), *A World Elsewhere*, London: Jonathan Cape.

Lewis, I. M. (1971), *Ecstatic Religion: An Anthropological Study of Spirit Possession and Shamanism*, Harmondsworth: Penguin.

Lewis, James R. (2003), *The Astrology Book: the Encyclopedia of Heavenly Influences*, Detroit: Visible Ink Press.

Lewis, James R. (ed.) (1995), *The Gods Have Landed: New Religions from Other Worlds*, Albany: State University of New York Press.

Lewis, James R. (ed.) (forthcoming a), *Encyclopedic Sourcebook of New Age Religions*, Amherst, NY: Prometheus Books.

Lewis, James R. (ed.) (forthcoming b), *Encyclopedic Sourcebook of UFO Religions*, Amherst, NY: Prometheus Books.

Lewis, James R. and J. Gordon Melton (eds) (1992), *Perspectives on the New Age*, Albany: State University of New York Press.

Lindsey, Robert (1987), 'California Journal', *New York Times*, section A, p. 12.

Lucas, Ernest (1996), *Science and the New Age Challenge*, Leicester: Apollos.

Lucas, Philip (1992), 'The New Age Movement and the Pentecostal/ Charismatic Revival: Distinct yet Parallel Phases of a Fourth Great Awakening?', in James R. Lewis and J. Gordon Melton (eds), *Perspectives on the New Age*, Albany: State University of New York Press, pp. 189–212.

Luhrmann, T. M. (1989), *Persuasions of the Witch's Craft*, London: Picador.

Lynch, Frederick R. (1977), 'Toward a Theory of Conversion and Commitment to the Occult', *American Behavioral Scientist* 20.6: 887–908.

Lyon, David (1993), 'A Bit of a Circus: Notes on Postmodemity and New Age', *Religion*, 23: 117–26.

Lyon, David (1994), *Postmodernity*, Buckingham: Open University Press.

Lyon, David (2000), *Jesus in Disneyland: Religion in Postmodern Times*, Malden, MA: Polity.

McCormick, John (1989), *The Global Environmental Movement: Reclaiming Paradise*, London: Belhaven Press.

MacLaine, Shirley (1983), *Out on a Limb*, New York: Bantam.

MacLaine, Shirley (1985), *Dancing in the Light*, New York: Bantam.

MacLaine, Shirley, (1987a), 'MacLaine's Guide to the New Age', *Los Angeles Times*, 19 August 1987, Part 5, p. 1.

MacLaine, Shirley (1987b), *It's All in the Playing*, New York: Bantam.

MacLaine, Shirley (1989), *Going Within: a Guide for Inner Transformation*, New York: Bantam.

Marrs, Texe (1987), *Dark Secrets of the New Age*, Westchester, IL: Crossway Books.

Martin, Walter (1989), *The New Age Cult*, Minneapolis: Bethany House.

Marty, Martin (1970), 'The Occult Establishment', *Social Research*, 37.2: 212–30.

Matrisciana, Caryl (1985), *Gods of the New Age*, London: Marshall Pickering.

Meadows, Donella H., Dennis L. Meadows, Jorgen Randers and William W. Behrens III (1972), *The Limits to Growth*, New York: New American Library.

Melton, J. Gordon, (1988), 'A History of the New Age Movement', in Robert Basil (ed.), *Not Necessarily the New Age: Critical Essays*, Buffalo, NY: Prometheus Books, pp. 35–53.

Melton, J. Gordon (1998a), *Finding Enlightenment: Ramtha's School of Ancient Wisdom*, Hillsboro, OR: Beyond Words.

Melton, J. Gordon (1998b), 'The Future of the New Age Movement', in Eileen Barker and Margit Warburg (eds), *New Religions and New Religiosity*, Aarhus: Aarhus University Press, pp. 133–49.

Melton, J. Gordon (2001), 'Reiki: The International Spread of a New Age Healing Movement', in Mikael Rothstein (ed.), *New Age Religion and Globalization*, Aarhus: Aarhus University Press, pp. 73–93.

Melton, J. Gordon, Jerome Clark and Aidan A. Kelly (1991), *New Age Almanac*, Detroit: Visible Ink Press.

Melucci, Alberto (1989), *Nomads of the Present: Social Movements and Individual Needs in Contemporary Society*, eds John Keane and Paul Mier, London: Hutchinson Radius.

Merkur, Dan (1993), *Gnosis: an Esoteric Tradition of Mystical Visions and Unions*, Albany: State University of New York Press.

Mikaelsson, Lisbeth (2001), '*Homo Accumulans* and the Spiritualization of Money', in Mikael Rothstein (ed.), *New Age Religion and Globalization*, Aarhus: Aarhus University Press, pp. 94–112.

Miller, D. Patrick (1998), *The Complete Story of The Course*, Berkeley, CA: Fearless Books.

Mission Theological Advisory Group (1996), *The Search for Faith and the Witness of the church*, London: Church House.

Mitchell, J. C. (1973), 'Networks, Norms and Institutions', in J. Boissevain and J. C. Mitchell (eds), *Network Analysis: Studies in Human Interaction*, The Hague: Mouton.

Moore, James (1991), *Gurdjieff: The Anatomy of a Myth*, Shaftesbury: Element Books.

Morgan, Peggy (1996), 'The Authority of Believers in the Study of Religions', *Diskus*, 4.1: 1–10.

Mullins, Mark R. (1992), 'Japan's New Age and Neo-New Religions: Sociological Interpretations', in James R. Lewis and J. Gordon Melton (eds), *Perspectives on the New Age*, Albany: State University of New York Press, pp, 215–31.

National Statistics (2003), *Census 2001*, Crown copyright. http://www.statistics.gov.uk/census2001/default.asp

Needham, R. (1975), 'Polythetic Classification: Convergence and Consequences', *Man* (New Series), 10: 349–69.

Nelson, Geoffrey K. (1969a), 'The spiritualist movement and the need for a Redefinition of Cult', *Journal for the Scientific Study of Religion*, 8.1: 152–60.

Nelson, Geoffrey K. (1969b), *Spiritualism and Society*, London: Routledge & Kegan Paul.

Niebuhr, H. R. (1929), *The Social Sources of Denominationalism*, New York: Henry Holt & Co.

Noll, Richard (1997), *The Aryan Christ: The Secret Life of Carl Gustav Jung*, London: Macmillan.

Oosthuizen, Gerhardus C. (1992), 'The "Newness" of the New Age in South Africa and Reactions to it', in James R. Lewis and J. Gordon Melton (eds), *Perspectives on the New Age*, Albany: State University of New York Press, pp. 247–70.

Otterloo, Anneke H. van (1999), 'Selfspirituality and the Body: New Age Centres in the Netherlands since the 1960s', *Social Compass* 46.2: 191–202.

Ouspensky P. D. (1987), *In Search of the Miraculous: Fragments of an Unknown Teaching*, Harmondsworth: Arkana.

Palmer, Helen (1995), *The Enneagram: Understanding Yourself and the Others in Your Life*, New York: HarperCollins.

Partridge, Christopher H. (1999), 'Truth, Authority and Epistemological Individualism in New Age Thought', *Journal of Contemporary Religion*, 14.1: 77–95.

Pazola, Ron (1994), 'Sacred Ground: What Native Americans Believe', *US Catholic*, February 1994, pp. 16f.

Pearson, Joanne (1998), 'Assumed Affinities: Wicca and the New Age', in Joanne Pearson, Richard H. Roberts and Geoffrey Samuel (eds), *Nature Religion Today: Paganism in the Modern World*, Edinburgh: Edinburgh University Press.

Pearson, Joanne (2000), 'Religion and the Return of Magic: Wicca as Esoteric Spirituality', Ph.D. thesis, Lancaster University.

Pearson, Joanne, Richard H. Roberts and Geoffrey Samuel (eds) (1998), Nature Religion Today: Paganism in the Modern World, Edinburgh: Edinburgh University Press.

Peck, M. Scott (1978), The Road Less Travelled, London: Simon & Schuster.

Phelan, Janet (1992), 'Up All Night: Pagan Rituals', Los Angeles Times, 4 October 1992, part E, p. 8.

Poggi, Isotta (1992), 'Alternative Spirituality in Italy', James R. Lewis and J. Gordon Melton eds, Perspectives on the New Age, Albany: State University of New York Press pp. 271–86.

Pollock, Kelly T. (forthcoming), 'The Success of A Course in Miracles in the World of Material Culture', in James R. Lewis (ed.), Encyclopedic Sourcebook of New Age Religions, Amherst, NY: Prometheus Books.

Pontifical Council for Culture and Pontifical Council for Interreligious Dialogue (2003), 'Jesus Christ: the bearer of the water of life – a Christian reflection on the "New Age". http://www.vatican.va/roman_curia/pontifical_councils/interelg/documents/rc_pc_interelg_doc_20030203_new-age_en.html

Porquet, Jean-Luc (1994), La France des Mutants: Voyage au Cœur du Nouvel Age, Paris: Flammarion.

Possamaï, Adam (1998), In Search of New Age Spirituality: towards a Sociology of Perennism, Ph.D. thesis, La Trobe University.

Possamaï, Adam (2001), 'Not the New Age: Perennism and Spiritual Knowledges', Australian Religion Studies Review, 14.1: 82–96.

Possamaï, Adam (2002), 'Cultural consumption of history and popular culture in alternative spiritualities', Journal of Consumer Culture, 2.2: 197–218.

Possamaï, Adam (2003), 'Alternative Spiritualities and the Cultural Logic of Late Capitalism', Culture and Religion, 4.1: 31–46.

Possamaï, Adam (forthcoming), 'Diversity in alternative spiritualities: keeping New Age at bay', in James R. Lewis (ed.), Encyclopedic Sourcebook of New Age Religions, Amherst, NY: Prometheus Books.

Prince, Ruth (1992), An Anthropology of the 'New Age' with Special Reference to Glastonbury, Somerset, M.Phil. thesis, St Andrews University.

Prince, Ruth and David Riches (2000), The New Age in Glastonbury: the Construction of religious movements, New York and Oxford: Berghahn Books.

Raine, Kathleen (1968), Blake and Tradition, London: Routledge & Kegan Paul.

Raschke, Carl (1980), The Interruption of Eternity: Modern Gnosticism and the Origins of the New Religious Consciousness, Chicago: Nelson-Hall.

Redfield, James ([1993] 1994), The Celestine Prophecy, London: Bantam.

Reed, David (1990), 'How to Have a Holiday Romance with Your Self; The Cult of Mind, Body and Spirit now Organises its own Holidays', Independent, 17 November 1990, p. 46.

Richardson, James T. and Massimo Introvigne (2001), '"Brainwashing" Theories in European Parliamentary and Administrative Reports on "Cults" and "Sects"', *Journal for the Scientific Study of Religion*, 40.2: 143–68.

Riches, David (2003), 'Counter-cultural Egalitarianism: a comparative analysis of New Age and other 'alternative' communities', *Culture and Religion*, 4.1: 119–40.

Riordan, Suzanne (1992), 'Channeling: A New Revelation?', in James R. Lewis and J. Gordon Melton (eds), *Perspectives on the New Age*, Albany, NY: State University of New York Press, pp. 105–26.

Riso, Don Richard (1987), *Personality Types: Using the Enneagram for Self Discovery*, Boston: Houghton Mifflin.

Roberts, Susan Fries (1989), *Consciousness Shifts to Psychic Perception: the Strange World of New Age Services and their Providers*, Ph.D. thesis.

Roof, Wade Clark, Bruce Greer, Mary Johnson and Andrea Leibson (1993), *A Generation of Seekers: The Spiritual Journeys of the Baby Boom Generation*, San Francisco: Harper San Francisco.

Rose, Stuart (1996), *Transforming the World: An Examination of the Roles Played by Spirituality and Healing in the New Age Movement: 'The Aquarian Conspirators Revisited'*, Ph.D. thesis, Lancaster University.

Rosen, Jay (1988), 'Optimism and Dread: T.V. and the New Age', in Robert Basil (ed.), *Not Necessarily the New Age: Critical Essays*, Buffalo, NY: Prometheus Books.

Roszak, Theodore (1969), *The Making of a Counter Culture*, Garden City, NY: Doubleday.

Rothstein, Mikael (2001), 'The Myth of the UFO in Global Perspective: a Cognitive Approach', in Mikael Rothstein (ed.), *New Age Religion and Globalization*, Aarhus: Aarhus University Press.

Rothstein, Mikael (ed.), (2001), *New Age Religion and Globalization*, Aarhus: Aarhus University Press.

Rupert, Glenn A. (1992), 'Employing the New Age: training seminars', in James R. Lewis and J. Gordon Melton (eds), *Perspectives on the New Age*, Albany: State University of New York Press, pp. 127–35.

Russell, Peter (1982), *The Awakening Earth: the Global Brain*, Harmondsworth: Arkana.

St John, Graham (2000), *Alternative Cultural Heterotopia: ConFest as Australia's Marginal Centre*, Ph.D. thesis, La Trobe University.

Salamon, Karen (2001), '"Going Global from the Inside Out": Spiritual Globalism in the Workplace', in Mikael Rothstein (ed.), 2001, *New Age Religion and Globalization*, Aarhus: Aarhus University Press, pp. 150–72.

Saliba, John A. (1999), *Christian Responses to the New Age Movement: a Critical Assessment*, London: Geoffrey Chapman.

Saunders, Kate (1989), 'All you Need is Self-Love: New Age values', *The Times*, 29 October 1989.

Schumaker, John F. (1992), *Religion and Mental Health*, Oxford: Oxford University Press.

Scott, Alan (1995), *Ideology and the New Social Movements*, London: Routledge.

Scott, Gini Graham (1980), *Cult and Countercult: a Study of a Spiritual Growth Group and a Witchcraft Order*, Westport, CT: Greenwood Press.

Shea, Robert and Robert Anton Wilson ([1975] 1998), *The Illuminatus! Trilogy: The Eye in the Pyramid, The Golden Apple and Leviathan*, London: Raven Books.

Shimazono, Susumu, 1993, 'New Age and New Spiritual Movements: the role of spiritual intellectuals', *Syzygy*, 2.1–2: 9–22.

Shimazono, Susumu, 1999, '"New Age Movement" or "New Spirituality Movements and Culture"?', *Social Compass*, 46.2: 121–34.

Simes, Amy Caroline (1995), *Contemporary Paganism in the East Midlands*, Ph.D. thesis, Nottingham University.

Sipchen, Bob (1987), 'Expo Finds Right Channel to Usher in New Age', *Los Angeles Times*, 9 February 1981, part 5, p. 1.

Sjöö, Monica (1992), *New Age and Armageddon: the Goddess or the Gurus? Towards a Feminist Vision of the Future*, London: The Women's Press.

Sjöö, Monica and Barbara Mor (1987), *The Great Cosmic Mother: Rediscovering the Religion of the Earth*, San Francisco: Harper & Row.

Smith, Adrian B. (1990), *God and the Aquarian Age*, Great Wakering: McCrimmons.

Smith, Lynn (1986), 'The New, Chic Metaphysical Fad of Channeling', *Los Angeles Times*, 5 December 1986, part 5, p. 1.

Snow, David A. and Robert D. Benford (1992), 'Master Frames and Cycles of Protest', in A. Morris and C. Mueller (eds), 1999, *Frontiers in Social Movement Theory*, New Haven: Yale University Press, pp. 133–55.

Snow, David A., Burke E. Rochford, Steven Worden and Robert Benford (1986), 'Frame Alignment Processes, Micromobilization, and Movement Participation', *American Sociological Review*, 51: 464–81.

Snow, David A., Louis A. Zurcher and Sheldon Ekland-Olson (1980), 'Social Networks and Social Movements: A Microstructural Approach to Differential Recruitment', *American Sociological Review*, 45: 787–801.

Southwold, Martin (1978), 'Buddhism and the Definition of Religion', *Man* (new series), 13.3: 362–79.

Spangler, David (1993), 'The New Age: The Movement Toward the Divine', in Duncan S. Ferguson (ed.), *New Age Spirituality: an Assessment*, Louisville, KY: Westminster John Knox Press, pp. 79–105.

Spezzano, Chuck (1991), *Awaken the Gods: Aphorisms to Remember on the Way Home*, London: Wellspring Publications.

Spink, Peter (1991), *A Christian in the New Age*, London: Darton, Longman and Todd.

Stark, Rodney and William Sims Bainbridge (1979), 'Of Churches, Sects, and Cults', *Journal for the Scientific Study of Religion*, 18: 117–33.

Steyn, Chrissie (1994), *Worldviews in Transition: An Investigation of the New Age Movement in South Africa*, Pretoria: University of South Africa.

Steyn, H. Christina (2003), 'Where New Age and African Religion Meet: the case of Credo Mutwa in South Africa', *Culture and Religion* 4.1: 67–92.

Stoyanov, Yuri (2000), *The Other God*, New Haven: Yale Nota Bene.

Sutcliffe, Steven (1995a), 'The authority of the Self in New Age Religiosity: The Example of the Findhorn Community', *Diskus*, 3.2: 23–42.

Sutcliffe, Steven (1995b), 'Some Notes on a Sociology of New Age and Related Countercultural Religiosity in Scotland', *Journal of Contemporary Religion*, 10.2: 181–4.

Sutcliffe, Steven (1997), 'Seekers, Networks, and "New Age"', *Scottish Journal of Religious Studies*, 18.2: 97–114.

Sutcliffe, Steven (1998), '*New Age' in Britain: an Ethnographical and Historical Exploration*, Ph.D. thesis, Open University.

Sutcliffe, Steven (2002), *Children of the New Age: a History of Spiritual Practices*, London: Routledge.

Sutcliffe, Steven (2003), 'Category Formation and the History of "New Age"', *Culture and Religion*, 4.1: 5–30.

Sutcliffe, Steven and Marion Bowman (eds) (2000), *Beyond New Age: Exploring Alternative Spirituality*, Edinburgh: Edinburgh University Press.

Tarrow, Sidney (1998), *Power in Movement: Social Movements and Contentious Politics*, 2nd edn, Cambridge: Cambridge University Press.

Tart, Charles (ed.) (1990), *Altered States of Consciousness*, 3rd edn, London: HarperCollins.

Tart, Charles (ed.) (1992), *Transpersonal Psychologies*, 3rd edn, London: HarperCollins.

Terrin, Aldo Natale (1992), *New Age: La Religiosità del Postmoderno*, Bologna: Edizioni Dehoniane Bologna.

Thompson, E. P. (1993), *Witness against the Beast*, Cambridge: Cambridge University Press.

Trevelyan, George (1977), *A Vision of the Aquarian Age*, London: Coventure.

Trevelyan, George (1983), 'The Emergence of a New Humanity: the Challenge of the 1980s', lecture at Mind-Body-Spirit Festival http://www.sirgeorge trevelyan.org.uk/tht-newhumanity.html

Turner, R. and L. Killian (1972), *Collective Behavior*, Englewood Cliffs, NJ: Prentice-Hall.

Underhill, Evelyn (1911), *Mysticism: the Nature and Development of Spiritual Consciousness*, London: Methuen & Co.

van Hove, Hildegard (1999), 'L'émergence d'un "marché spirituel"', *Social Compass*, 46.2: 161–72.

Vernette, Jean (1990), *Le Nouvel Age: à L'Aube de L'Être du Verseau*, Paris: Tequi.

Versluis, Arthur (1999), *Wisdom's Children: A Christian Esoteric Tradition*, Albany: State University of New York Press.

Vitz, Paul C. (1994), *Psychology as Religion: The Cult of Self-Worship*, 2nd edn, Carlisle: Paternoster Press.

Vitz, Paul C. and Deidre Modesti (1993), 'Social and Psychological Origins of New Age Spirituality', *Psychology and Christianity*, 12: 47–57.

Walker, Alex (ed.) (1994), *The Kingdom Within: A Guide to the Spiritual Work of the Findhorn Community*, Findhorn: Findhorn Press.

Wallis, Roy, (1975), 'Scientology: Therapeutic Cult to Religious Sect', *Sociology*, 9: 89–100.

Walsch, Neale Donald (1995), *Conversations with God: Book 1*, London: Hodder & Stoughton.

Walter, Tony (1993), 'Death in the New Age', *Religion*, 23: 127–45.

Walter, Tony and Helen Waterhouse (1999), 'A Very Private Belief: Reincarnation in Contemporary England', *Sociology of Religion*, 60.2: 187–97.

Wapnick, Kenneth (1989), *Love Does Not Condemn: The Word, the Flesh, and the Devil According to Platonism, Christianity, Gnosticism, and A Course in Miracles*, Roscoe, NY: Foundation for Inner Peace.

Wapnick, Kenneth (1999a), deposition at New York in *Penguin Books USA v New Christian Church of Full Endeavor, Ltd*, 96 Civ 4126 (RSW), 3 March 1999.

Wapnick, Kenneth (1999b), *Absence from Felicity: The Story of Helen Schucman and Her Scribing of A Course in Miracles*, Roscoe, NY: FACIM.

Wapnick, Kenneth and W. Norris Clarke (1995), *A Course in Miracles and Christianity: a Dialogue*, Roscoe, NY: Foundation for Inner Peace.

Washington, Peter (1993), *Madame Blavatsky's Baboon: a History of the Mystics, Mediums, and Misfits Who Brought Spiritualism to America*, London: Secker & Warburg.

Webb, James (1976), *The Occult Establishment*, La Salle, IL: Open Court.

Webb, Karen (1996), *Thorsons Principles of The Enneagram*, New York: Harper.

Weidner Maluf, Sônia (1996), *Les Enfants du Verseau au Pays des Terreiros: les Cultures Thérapeutiques et Spirituelles Alternatives au Sud du Brésil*, Lille: Septentrion.

Wellbeloved, Sophia (2002), *Gurdjieff, Astrology and Beelzebub's Tales: an Analysis of G. I. Gurdjieff's Beelzebub's Tales to his Grandson in Terms of Astrological Correspondences*, New Paltz, NY: Solar Bound.

Wellbeloved, Sophia (2003), *Gurdjieff: the Key Concepts*, London: Routledge.

White, Jim (1993), 'The Legend According to Arthur's Missus', *Independent*, 15 January 1993, p. 13.

White, Lynn (1967), 'The Historical Roots of our Ecological Crisis', *Science*, 10 March 1967, 1203–7.

Wilber, Ken (1991), *Grace and Grit: Spirituality and Healing in the Life and Death of Treya Killam Wilber*, Boston and London: Shambala.

Williams, Michael Allen (1996), *Rethinking 'Gnosticism': An Argument for Dismantling a Dubious Category*, Princeton: Princeton University Press.

Williamson, Marianne (1992), *A Return to Love: Reflections on the Principles of A Course in Miracles*, London: Thorsons.

Wilson, Bryan R. (1970), *Religious* Sects: *a Sociological Study*, London: Weidenfeld and Nicolson.

Wittgenstein, Ludwig, (1953), *Philosophical Investigations*, tr. G. E. M. Anscombe, Oxford: Blackwell.

Wood, Matthew, (1999), *Spirit Possession in a Contemporary British Religious Network: a Critique of New Age Movement Studies through the Sociology of Power*, Ph.D. thesis, Nottingham University.

Wood, Matthew (2003), 'Capital possession: a comparative approach to 'New Age' and control of the means of possession', *Culture and Religion*, 4.1: 159–82.

Yates, Frances A. (1964), *Giordano Bruno and the Hermetic Tradition*, Chicago and London: Chicago University Press.

Yinger, J. Milton (1970), *The Scientific Study of Religion*, London: Macmillan.

Yinger, J. Milton (1982), *Countercultures: the Promise and Peril of a World Turned Upside Down*, New York: Free Press.

York, Michael (1995), *The Emerging Network: A Sociology of the New Age and Neo-Pagan Movements*, Lanham, MD: Rowman & Littlefield.

York, Michael (1999), 'Le Supermarché Religieux: Ancrages Locaux du Nouvel Age au Sein du Réseau Mondial', *Social Compass*, 46.2: 173–9.

Zablocki, Benjamin (1998), 'The Blacklisting of a Concept: the Strange History of the Brainwashing Conjecture in the Sociology of Religion', *Nova Religio*, 1.1.

Zoccatelli, Pierluigi (1998), *Il New Age*, Turin: Editrice Elle Di Ci.

Index

Maslow, Abraham, 107, 112, 131
massage, 114
Mathers, Samuel Liddell MacGregor, 40
Matrisciana, Caryl, 131
media, 130–3, 157
meditation, 26, 77–9, 165–6, 170
medium, 57, 126
Melton, J. Gordon, 5, 38, 100–1, 138, 146, 148, 164, 177–9
Melucci, Alberto, 93, 105
mental health, 111, 124–7
meridian line, 30
Merkur, Dan, 45
meronymy, 7
Merton, Thomas, 137
Mesmer, Franz Anton, 41
Messina, 50
metaphysics, 53–4
Methodist Faith and Order Committee, 136
Mikaelsson, Lisbeth, 146
millenarianism, 154, 173
Miller, D. Patrick, 23, 28
Mind-Body-Spirit Festival see Festival of Mind-Body-Spirit
Miracle Café, 24
Miracle Distribution Center, 23
Miracle Worker, 24
modernisation, 98
monism, 53
Montgomery, Ruth, 138
Moore, James, 40
Moral Re-Armament see MRA
Morya, Master, 39
movement, 89, 95, 152
MRA, 35
Muggleton, Ludowick, 42
Murphy, Michael, 108
Mystik, die, 87, 160

Nachenmoser, Adam, 62
Nag Hammadi, 46
NAOS, 84–5
NAS, 164, 170
National Federation for Spiritual Healers see NFSH
Native American, 72, 98, 140
nature religion, 149
Nature Religion Today conference, 141

Nazism, 134, 143
NDE, 59
near-death experience see NDE
Nelson, Geoffrey, 37
Neognosticism, 88
Neoplatonism, 42, 60
Netherlands, 9
Neuro Linguistic Programming see NLP
New Age
culture, 154
movement, 180
New Age Orientation Scale see NAOS
New Age sensu latiori, 179–80
New Age sensu lato, 154, 159, 179–80
New Age sensu stricto, 154, 159, 179–80
New Age spiritualities see NAS
as new period of history, 60–3
religion, 145–6, 159
spirituality, 154
as term, 170
New Group of World Servers, 40
new middle class, 114
New Physics, 56
New Religious Movement see NRM
New Social Movement see NSM
New Socio-Religious Movement see NSRM
New Spirituality Movements and Culture see spirituality
New Thought, 35, 38–39, 56, 76, 147
New Yorker, 142
Next Age, 146, 178, 179
NFSH, 68, 74–6, 77
Niebuhr, H. Richard, 87
NLP, 103
NRM, 24, 82, 87, 88–90, 96–7, 123
NSM, 92, 96–7, 104, 123
NSRM, 25, 82, 96–7, 104, 179
Nuer, 49

occultism, 135, 146, 159, 168
Oimelc, 48
Omega Order, The, 133, 137, 142
Omega Point, 60
Ó'Murchú, Fr Diarmuid, 61, 137
Osmond, Humphry, 33
other-worldiness, 14
Ouspensky, P. D., 40
Oxford Group see MRA

Daren Kemp maintains a website at www.Christaquarian.net for the study of New Age Christianity, with links to other sites concentrating on non-Christian New Age, including the website of the Alternative Spiritualities and New Age Studies conference, www.asanas.org.uk.

Dr Kemp also maintains the ScholarsOfNewAge (SONA) email discussion list for serious scholars of New Age, including (but not limited to) sociologists, anthropologists, theologians, philosophers, historians and psychologists. Membership is moderated, and prospective members are requested to send details of their institutional affiliation and publications in the field to Daren.Kemp@Christaquarian.net.